What if...
BOOK OF **Alternative History**

What if...

BOOK OF Alternative History

Revisit Major Milestones That Shaped World History
and Discover the Outcome If They Had Happened Differently

CONTRIBUTORS
Jeff Greenfield, Catherine Curzon, Elizabeth Norton, and Nicola Tallis

FOX CHAPEL
PUBLISHING

©2023 by Future Publishing Limited

Articles in this issue are translated or reproduced from *What if...Book of Alternate History* and are the copyright of or licensed to Future Publishing Limited, a Future plc group company, UK 2022.

Used under license. All rights reserved. This version published by Fox Chapel Publishing Company, Inc., 903 Square Street, Mount Joy, PA 17552.

ISBN 978-1-4971-0376-4

Library of Congress Cataloging-in-Publication Data

To learn more about the other great books from Fox Chapel Publishing, or to find a retailer near you, call toll-free 800-457-9112 or visit us at *www.FoxChapelPublishing.com*.

We are always looking for talented authors. To submit an idea, please send a brief inquiry to acquisitions@foxchapelpublishing.com.

Printed in Malaysia
First printing

Welcome to

What if...

BOOK OF Alternative History

History is a fascinating topic, but one aspect that really fires the imagination is asking, "What if things had gone differently?" So-called 'alternative history' has long speculated along these lines, with the Romans wondering if they could have defeated Alexander the Great as early as 27 BCE, medieval writers wishing the Crusades had been more successful, and the Victorians terrifying themselves with Napoleon's global conquest. In *What if . . . Book of Alternative History*, experts consider what might have happened if key moments in time had gone differently, including the Nazis winning World War II, Abraham Lincoln surviving his assassination, the Allies losing the Battle of the Atlantic, China discovering America first, and much more. Each one is complemented by astonishing artwork, photography, and timelines so you can see the flashpoints where truth and fantasy diverge. We also celebrate the greatest stories inspired by alternative history, including *The Man in the High Castle*, *The Plot Against America*, *SS-GB*, and *11.22.63*.

Contents

42

94

150
The best alt-history fiction

66

138

144

140

134

38

16

Royalty & Leaders

Find out how altered the world would be if the most powerful people had made different decisions

24

26

22

What if...
Attila the Hun survived his wedding night?

NOTABLE NAMES:
- King Attila
- Ildico

IMPORTANT DATES:
March 453

What Really Happened...

From 434–453, King Attila was a brutal warrior and the ruler of a group of nomadic people called the Huns who lived in Central Asia and Eastern Europe during the 4th through the 6th century. To the Roman Empire, Attila the Hun was one of their most feared enemies.

Attila had many wives, but it was after he married the beautiful Germanic Ildico that he was found dead the very next morning. The circumstances surrounding his death remain a mystery, but what is known is that after a long night of celebrating, he eventually went to bed and fell asleep on his back. When guards heard the hysterical bride and entered the room the next morning, Attila was found dead covered in blood, but without any physical wounds. It was speculated he either died from alcohol poisoning or from choking on his own blood, as he was prone to nosebleeds. Some even theorize it was Ildico who was given orders to assassinate him by the Byzantine Emperor, but what actually happened will always be a mystery.

How important was Attila the Hun in the history of the Hunnic Empire? Some say he was the only thing that held the whole creaky structure of the Hunnic Empire together in the middle of the 5th century. But my view is a little bit different.

I think the Huns inherited quite a sophisticated political model — even before Attila came to the throne, it was already in place — so he was the last powerful king of a united Hunnic states, who inherited political powers from his predecessor. He was more of a cautious leader, not that aggressive despite the literature that portrays him as a megalomaniac seeking world conquest.

In fact, if you look carefully at what he does, he is very cautious in battle. Instead of seeking to conquer the Roman Empire and create a huge territory like the Mongols, for example, he tried to levy tribute from the Eastern and Western Romans. He was a very traditional Hunnic king, in my opinion. His invasions were designed not to conquer the Roman Empire, but to subject the Romans to the payment of tribute in order to build an inner Asian tributary empire.

Was Attila's rule different to his predecessors? The Huns had two kings, who ruled over the two halves of the empire. The Eastern King was normally superior to the Western king. But Attila staged a coup and overthrew his brother in the East, and the power equation was reversed. That caused all kinds of problems later, and it was part of the reason the Hunnic state imploded after Attila died, because the East refused to accept subordination to the West, and it started a civil war.

What was his plan leading up to his death? He wanted to force the Romans, the Eastern and Western half, to pay tribute to him. What the Huns would do was conquer outright states close to them, so the Germanic tribes were directly ruled by the Huns. But once you go beyond the territory the Huns regarded as quintessential to their empire, then you come to more distant regions where the levying of tribute was enough. The Romans fell into that category.

In 447 CE, Attila invaded the Eastern Roman Empire and annexed a huge chunk of the Balkans. But then immediately afterwards, he negotiated to give it back because he wasn't interested in territory. What he was interested in was getting a steady flow of tributes, which would enhance his prestige among the Hunnic elite. The objective wasn't to bleed the Romans dry — it was to gain prestige. This was necessary because Attila was a usurper [he had killed his brother to become the sole ruler of the Huns].

Was he trying to conquer Europe? Priscus, one of the primary sources on Attila's reign, says his objective was nothing less than the conquest of half of the Roman Empire. Of course the Romans would have felt it like that — they wouldn't have thought an invasion of that magnitude could be anything but an outright conquest. But what's curious is that when the Huns invaded, they would sack cities, try to extract tribute from them,

The Romans feared that Attila would not rest until he had conquered Europe

" What he was interested in was getting a steady flow of tributes, which would enhance his prestige among the Hunnic elite"

and then just withdraw again after a major battle or great siege.

I would say Attila's motivation was to force the Romans into a tributary system as he understood it. In fact, at the time of his death, he was planning another invasion of the Eastern Roman Empire because the incumbent Roman emperor of the East, Marcian, had refused to pay the tribute that his predecessor had promised.

What do we know about Attila's death around 453 CE? Well this comes solely from Priscus. Attila had many wives and he took another one [named Ildico]. After cavorting during his wedding night and drinking too much, he burst a vein and choked on his own blood. In the morning when the Hunnic nobles realized something was wrong, they rushed in and found the new wife weeping and the king dead, drowned in his

own blood. This is the image that Priscus wanted to create — that of a bloodthirsty tyrant who got his just desserts by divine judgement.

Whether he really died that way or not, who knows. He was actually at an advanced age, probably in his 50s at the time, the normal age of death at the time, so there's no reason to suspect that he was poisoned. Right there after he died, there was a huge civil war because his sons couldn't agree what would go to whom. There was a huge civil war between the Eastern and Western half [of the Hunnic Empire] and then, of course, the state imploded as a consequence. The Eastern half survived but the Western side completely fragmented.

If Attila hadn't died that night, what do you think would have happened? My guess would be that he would have invaded the Eastern Roman Empire. They did not have a sizeable army with which to attack

INTERVIEW WITH... DR. HYUN JIM KIM

A senior lecturer in Classics at the University of Melbourne, Dr. Hyun Jim Kim is an expert on all things Attila. He is the author of *The Huns, Rome, and the Birth of Europe* and other books examining the Hunnic Empire and Asia's role in the fall of Rome.

the Huns, so it's unlikely they could have defended the Balkans from another Hunnic incursion. But Attila wouldn't have been able to take Constantinople because he had no navy — a prerequisite to take that impregnable fortress — so he probably would have rampaged through the Balkans yet again and the Eastern Romans would have ended up paying some kind of tribute to pay him off as usual.

Would this have meant the Roman Empire would have fallen earlier that 476 CE? The Western Roman Empire would never have disintegrated in the way it did after his death. That's a bit of a perplexing statement but the reason that it collapsed in 476 CE is because there was a whole bunch of Germanic tribes and Hunnic troops that were originally under the rule of the Huns that left the Hunnic state and marched into Italy. They were the ones who put an end to Roman imperium in the West.

If Attila had not died, and had been able to control those tribes, then of course the Western Romans would have paid a bit of tribute, but their rule in Italy would have remained intact. We might have actually seen a continuation of the Western Roman Empire for a lot longer than what actually happened in history.

How would Europe have been different after that? We would never have had a Frankish Europe. When the Hunnic Empire imploded and the Western Roman Empire followed suit, there was an incredible power vacuum in Western Europe. This allowed the Franks to unify what is essentially Western Europe and that evolves into the Holy Roman Empire.

If neither the Western Roman nor Hunnic Empires dissolved, then we would have had a state called Hunnia somewhere in Europe and the Franks would have been confined to Belgium and the Netherlands. France would be in Belgium rather than what is now France.

Would Attila have tried to conquer the Roman Empire? No, I seriously doubt that. First of all, the Hunnic Empire was already massive. It had extended to such a degree that it was difficult to control under

Attila planned to attack the Eastern Roman Empire to force them to pay tributes again

Attila perçoit un tribut devant les murs de Byzance.

"He could have conquered Europe, but I don't think he would have"

a single ruler. That's what Attila effectively attempted — he created a dictatorship and tried to run things by himself and that caused all kinds of problems. He was executing Hunnic princes left and right and oppressed Hunnic princes were fleeing to the Eastern Roman Empire. That was one of the main reasons Attila went to war with the Eastern Romans — because Constantinople was harboring fugitive Hunnic princes.

I think that he might have replaced an emperor or two if he had lived longer, or possibly enthroned somebody who was more to his liking and paid regular tribute. That is shown by the fact that he even just gives or is willing to give back territories conquered in the Roman Empire. He has no interest in ruling them.

How would it be different?

Real timeline

Attila Comes to Power
Following the death of Rugila, Attila and his brother Bleda become rulers of the Huns in the West and East respectively. **434 CE**

Betrayal of Brother
Attila likely murders Bleda and becomes the single ruler of the Huns, shifting their center of power west. **445 CE**

A New Target
Attila begins plotting a new attack on the Eastern Roman Empire to force them to pay tribute to him. **452 CE**

Death of Attila
After marrying an East German woman, Ildico, Attila dies on his wedding night, possibly after choking on a severe nosebleed. **453 CE**

The Huns Divided
The empire is split between Attila's three sons but civil war soon breaks out. **454 CE**

Real timeline

Alternate timeline

Attila Rides On
Attila marries Ildico but their wedding night passes without incident. The next day, he rides for Eastern Rome. **453 CE**

Balkans Defeated
Attila easily defeats the Eastern Roman Empire, sacking the Balkans. But he leaves immediately, after receiving tributes. **454 CE**

Did he have that much power, to dictate who became emperor? Possibly. He had an army no nation could withstand, so in terms of military strength the Huns were stronger than either the Western or Eastern Romans at the time. Militarily, he could have imposed a rule to his liking on the Romans if he wanted to push that far — but, as I said earlier, he was a very cautious man, so he was unwilling to engage too deeply in prolonged overseas campaigns. He was always fearing some kind of rebellion at home, so he couldn't vacate his territories too often. These campaigns against the Romans were more a display of strength — not only to the Romans, but also to his Hunnic subjects.

Could he have conquered Europe if he had wanted to? He could have. But then he would have destroyed his own state in the process. The conquest actually happens, the Hunnic troops from Hunnic territory later conquer Italy and create the first barbaric kingdom of Italy, so that could have happened. But if I was Attila, would I risk the disintegration of my empire, just to add more territory that was difficult to govern? I don't think so. The answer would be yes, he could have conquered Europe, but I don't think he would have.

How long would the Hunnic Empire have lasted? The Hunnic Empire in Europe collapsed about 80 years [after Attila's death]. If he had been able to secure successions in an orderly fashion, then it probably would have lingered on for another century or so and we would have seen a vastly different Europe geopolitically than now. In essence, you get pretty similar borders, except that maybe instead of a Germany confined to what it is now, you might have had a larger Germany that includes Austria, the Czech Republic, Hungary, and bits of Poland.

How would Attila's legacy have been different? If he had lived longer and established a long-lasting dynasty that produced a line of kings, then I think we'd probably be talking about Attila in the same way we talk about

Clovis, the king of the Franks. We often talk about Attila as an alien king who invaded from Asia, but that's not true. He was the fourth generation of the first Huns who entered Europe. He was basically European, and Hunnic remains show that the Huns were completely European in appearance, so he was basically a European ruler who could speak multiple languages. If his descendants became Germanic kings of Germany, he would be considered as just another European ruler. That's how he would be regarded — not as someone who was about to destroy European civilization.

Attila razed the Western Roman city of Aquileia to the ground in 452 CE

I think the literature on Attila tends to dramatize the Battle of the Catalaunian Plains, the big conflict between Aetius and Attila, a clash of East and West. Europe was apparently saved because the Huns were stopped there. That's not true, because the composition of the armies in the battle were practically the same. It didn't really matter who won in terms of the trajectory of European civilization.

Even if Attila had conquered all of Western Europe — if he had bothered to do so — the empire would inevitably have become Christian and the culture of the aristocracy would have been Germanic. You're looking at the same kind of Europe even with Attila fighting on, and he would be remembered as another Germanic king.

Sacking of Rome
Rome is sacked by Vandals, signaling the beginning of the end for the Roman Empire. **455 CE**

White Huns
The White Huns, or Hephthalites, lead raids into India, continuing the legacy of the Huns. **470 CE**

Fall of Rome
The Roman emperor Romulus is overthrown by the Germanic leader Odoacer. The Roman Empire is finished. **476 CE**

Rise of the Franks
Clovis, king of the Franks, sweeps through Europe, leading eventually to the formation of the Holy Roman Empire. **486 CE**

Barbarians Tamed
Germanic tribes and Hunnic troops remain under the rule of the Huns, rather than marching into Italy. **466 CE**

The Huns Collapse
The Hunnic Empire collapses, leaving barbarian and Germanic tribes in its place to head for Europe. **469 CE**

Franks Weakened
Clovis, king of the Franks, does not unify Western Europe as there is no power vacuum to fill any more. **486 CE**

France Sidelined
The Franks are confined to Belgium and the Netherlands as the Hunnic Empire continues to dominate Europe. **500 CE**

Huns United
Attila manages to keep the Hunnic Empire together with the center of power remaining in the west in Hungary. **460 CE**

Roman Empire Continues
The Roman Empire lives on as Attila does not conquer Europe — but ensures a regular supply of tribute flows after his death. **476 CE**

Attila's Successors
With a clear line of succession laid out, Attila's sons continue his reign and keep the Huns united. **480 CE**

Welcome to Hunnia
The Huns create a state known as Hunnia in Europe, as their empire lives on for more than a century. **490 CE**

Greater Germany
Attila leaves behind a Germany that includes modern-day Austria, the Czech Republic, Hungary, and parts of Poland. **510 CE**

What if...
Richard II kept his throne?

ENGLAND, 1386-1810

What Really Happened...

At the time of his coronation in 1377, Richard II was only 10 years old. Unfortunately, his reign was fraught with many troubling times. He was quite autocratic as king, focused more on art and culture rather than military matters, and he later became erratic, vengeful, and cruel.

His final demise came from exiling his cousin, Henry Bolingbroke. Six months later, Henry's father, John of Gaunt—Richard II's uncle, early advisor, and Duke of Lancaster—died. Instead of allowing Henry a pardon to attend the funeral, the king cut off his inheritance and exiled him for life. In retaliation, Henry formed alliances and grew an army to help him regain his inheritance and remove Richard from the throne.

Richard willingly gave up his throne on September 30, 1399, was formally deposed on October 1, and by October 13, 1399, Henry Bolingbroke was crowned king as Henry IV. He agreed to let Richard live, but on February 14, 1400, Richard was found dead in jail from starvation—possibly self-inflicted.

On September 29, 1399, the 32-year-old King Richard II was deposed by—or abdicated in favor of—his cousin Henry Bolingbroke, who became Henry IV, the first Lancastrian king. It represented a breach in the Plantagenet line of descent, which ultimately led to further ructions throughout the 15th century. However, it could have been very different if Richard II had survived the attempt on his throne.

Returning from Ireland, Richard finds that his cousin Henry made a failed bid for the crown, with his power-grab seeing him arrested and executed on landing at Ravenspur by Henry Percy. Percy is then made a duke for his loyal service.

The king is made even more wary of the wider nobility as a result of this attempted betrayal, and relies increasingly on his tight inner circle who are rewarded but required to pander to the king's sense of personal majesty and divine authority. Richard's second marriage to Isabella, daughter of King Charles VI, preserves the peace

How would it be different?

The Peasants Revolt
A young Richard II proves himself by suppressing the crisis, personally meeting with the rebels to hear their grievances. **1381**

Richard II Abdicates
Richard II surrenders to Henry at Flint Castle, asking that his life be spared if he abdicates the throne.
August 19, 1399

A New King
Bypassing the heir presumptive, Edward de Mortimer, Henry Bolingbroke is crowned Henry IV. He makes his address in English, a first since 1066.
October 13, 1399

Real timeline

1386

The Second Lancaster
The future Henry IV and his first wife Mary de Bohun give birth to their son Henry at Monmouth Castle in Wales.
1386

Bolingbroke Comes Ashore
After being disinherited by Richard, Henry, the son of John of Gaunt, lands in England with a small force.
June 1399

Real timeline

Alternate timeline

Execution of Henry Bolingbroke
Henry's attempt to take the crown under the guise of claiming his late father's duchy of Lancaster fails and he is executed. **July 20, 1399**

The King Returns
Richard returns to London from Ireland, rewarding those loyal to him but with his suspicion of the wider nobility heightened.
August 25, 1399

with France throughout Charles's bouts of mental illness.

The lack of foreign wars allows Richard to focus on tightening his grip on England, Wales, and Ireland. As a counterbalance to the nobility he remains suspicious of, the wage laws implemented after the Black Death that led to the Peasants' Revolt are repealed and a merchant class flourishes under his kingship. Monarchy grips England and, with no need for taxation for war and a thriving economy, there is no reason to summon Parliament, while the increase in wealth and at lower levels of society keep the population happy.

After a 55-year reign peppered with success, Richard dies in 1432. He is succeeded by his eldest son, the 20-year-old Richard III, who is supported ably by his 17-year-old brother Edward, named for Richard's father. Charles VII succeeds his father in France in 1422 and the peace allows France, never cowed by a defeat at Agincourt, to focus its attention on Italy. After almost ten years of war, Charles VII asks his young cousin King Richard III for aid but the new king finds that he is unable to raise a feudal levy after decades of weakening of the nobility, and is only able to send mercenaries.

An early Renaissance flourishes under Richard II's patronage of art and architecture. England leads European cultural development with its merchants traveling the breadth of the continent. However, Richard III's inability to raise an effective army later marks England as a soft target. The Holy Roman Empire sees a chance for expansion and England must summon the first Parliament in decades. Taxation for army maintenance is voted through but Parliament is denied the wider constitutional role it desires, leaving England secure throughout the 15th century but open to internal revolution.

After his attempt to usurp the crown fails, Henry Bolingbroke makes his peace with God before his death

MATT LEWIS

Matt Lewis is an author and historian specializing in Medieval history, particularly the Wars of the Roses, Richard III, and the early Tudor period. He has written a biography of Edward IV and Richard III's father. Matt's latest book is a biography, *Henry III: Son of Magna Carta*, and he has also written two historical fiction novels, *Loyalty* and *Honor*.

Starved to Death
Richard II is thought to have starved to death in the Tower of London, although the details of his death are still debated.
c. February 14, 1400

The Gold Dragon
Owain Glyndŵr revolts against Henry's rule. His rebellion ultimately failed but he is still known as the father of Welsh nationalism.
1400-1415

Constant Rebellions
Henry, beset by near constant rebellions, defeats Harry 'Hotspur' at the Battle of Shrewsbury and keeps his crown. **1403**

Very Precious Cargo
Pirates capture the future James I of Scotland on his way to France. Henry keeps him prisoner for his entire reign. **1406**

Henry IV Dies
Henry IV dies not on crusade like he believed but in the Jerusalem chamber in Westminster. His son inherits a strong royal position. **1413**

Prince Richard Born
Richard II and his second wife Queen Isabella celebrate the birth of the king's first child and long-awaited heir, Prince Richard.
March 15, 1412

Richard II Dies
After 55 years as king, Richard II dies at the age of 65, mourned by his two sons Richard and Edward.
February 14, 1432

Parliament is Summoned
Parliament had not been summoned since 1397, with no need to vote taxation to the wealthy crown. England's Parliament never acquires a constitutional role.
February-March 1436

English Revolution
England succumbs to the European trend of revolution as the people revolt against the absolutist monarchy that was never challenged by parliament.
1760

Repealing of Labor Laws
To balance the threat of the nobility, Richard repeals laws created after the Black Death to restrict wage increases and free movement of workers.
June 1402

England: Renaissance Powerhouse
With a full treasury, no foreign wars, and a thriving merchant class, Richard II's England becomes the home of the early Renaissance. **1420-1430**

Aid to France
Charles VII of France asks his English cousin for aid against Italy but Richard III finds himself unable to raise an army.
April 1434

The King Fights Back
After the revolution ousted his father, George IV attempts to reinstate the monarchy but is unable to win support due to his contemptible nature. **1810s**

What if...
Richard III lived?

ENGLAND, 1485-1517

NOTABLE NAMES:
- Richard III of England
- Henry Tudor, Henry VII of England

IMPORTANT DATES:
August 22, 1485

What Really Happened...

Richard III was King of England for a very short time, from June 26, 1483, until his death on August 22, 1485, which marked the beginning of the Tudor Age (1485–1603). His death also marked the end of the War of the Roses, which were civil wars between the Houses of Lancaster and York that began in 1455.

While Richard III wasn't king for long, he had many rivals, one of whom was Henry Tudor. Henry conspired to seize the throne, and on August 22, 1485, Richard III confronted Henry at the battle of Bosworth. While it was a close fight and Richard III fought well and bravely, he was eventually unhorsed and cut down. In the aftermath, Henry declared himself king by right of conquest and his coronation took place on October 30, 1485.

King Richard III lost the Battle of Bosworth on August 22, 1485, and with his death, 331 years of Plantagenet rule ended and the Tudor dynasty was born. For more than a century the Tudors went on to reshape England. Richard III remains a man who divides opinion, often bitterly. So how different might England have been if the Yorkist king's cavalry charge had succeeded and Henry Tudor had died that day?

With the last threat to his throne extinguished, Richard returns to his plans. Embassies step up negotiations to marry the widowed king to Joanna of Portugal, sister to King John II, and his niece Elizabeth of York to John's cousin, Manuel. The deeply religious Joanna had turned down the king of France but pressure

from her brother encourages her to agree to marry Richard. In 1487, Joanna arrives in England with her cousin for a double wedding. The Lancastrian blood of the Portuguese royal family is joined to Richard's Yorkist line, uniting the red and white roses.

King Richard continues the work of his first parliament, taking his vengeance on the nobility who failed to support him at Bosworth while promoting the causes of the common and merchant classes. Many of the great families of England are lost, with only a small number of Richard's supporters rewarded, but trade flourishes as the general population feel more enfranchised. With the birth of a son named Richard, in 1489, the king's dynastic confidence grows. As plans

How would it be different?

Real timeline

1485

Crossing the Channel
Henry Tudor sails from France with up to 5,000 men and lands on the English shore unopposed.
August 7, 1485

The Battle Begins
The Yorkist army under Richard III faces off against the outnumbered Lancastrians led by Henry Tudor, the Earl of Richmond.
August 22, 1485

Death of Richard
After a failed cavalry charge, Richard III becomes the last English king to meet his death on the battlefield.
August 22, 1485

Henry is Crowned
Henry Tudor is crowned Henry VII of England in Westminster Abbey. He rewards those who fought for him at Bosworth.
October 30, 1485

Wedding Bells
Henry VII honors his pledge to marry Elizabeth of York, uniting the red and white roses. They were third cousins.
January 18, 1486

Real timeline

Alternate timeline

The Battle of Bosworth
Henry Tudor is killed by a cavalry charge led by King Richard III. The final threat to the Yorkist crown is extinguished. **August 22, 1485**

King Richard's Second Parliament Sits
Laws promoting trade and justice are again published in English and a weakened nobility cannot oppose the measures.
January-March 1486

for a war against France progress, his efforts are frustrated by a lack of nobles to provide feudal levies for mercenaries as Scotland uses the Auld Alliance to create trouble on the northern borders.

Exploration features highly in England's outlook as English ships are requested to help in his voyages along the African coast. When Columbus returns from his voyage to discover America in 1493, the Treaty of Tordesillas splits new discoveries between Spain, Portugal, and England. Trade blossoms further in England with new routes opening up, no fractious nobility to threaten internal security, and a rising middle class. The English fleet focuses west, seeking to exploit the opportunities of the New World.

In 1495, King John dies without a legitimate heir and is succeeded by Manuel with Elizabeth as his queen. The couple have several children and make strong matches across Europe. Richard's inflexibility causes friction between England, Portugal, and Spain as the vast wealth of the New World sows seeds of discord. The rest of his life is spent trying to protect the flow of treasure from the west from increasing French piracy.

Richard III dies in 1509, succeeded by his son Richard IV. As the Reformation sweeps across Europe, the influence of Richard IV's parents keeps England Catholic in alliance with Portugal and Spain. Protestant nations support French efforts and the alliance turns France away from Rome, leaving the center of Europe Protestant, encircled by Catholic nations, leading to years of conflict.

Richard's reign might have seen England take a leading role in the exploration of the New World

---

A Pretender Appears
Perkin Warbeck, a young Fleming, claims to be a "Prince in the tower." His rebellion fails and he is executed.
1490

A King is Born
Henry VII's second son, also called Henry, is born. He will go on to become Henry VIII, one of England's most famous monarchs.
June 28, 1491

Henry VII Passes On
Henry VII dies of tuberculosis at Richmond Palace and is buried at Westminster Abbey. His son Henry succeeds him.
April 21, 1509

A New Queen
Henry VIII shocks the Christian world by annulling his marriage to Catherine of Aragon and marrying his latest fancy, Anne Boleyn.
June 1, 1533

Acts of Supremacy
Henry VIII, and all subsequent monarchs, become head of the Church of England. This is the beginning of the English Reformation.
November 3, 1534

A Royal Wedding
Princess Joanna of Portugal arrives to marry Richard III. Her cousin Manuel accompanies her to marry Richard's niece, Elizabeth of York.
May 1487

Joint Settlement Establishing in West Africa
England joins Portuguese voyages of exploration and a settlement at São Tomé and Principe provides a platform for colonization of Africa.
1491-93

Death of King John II
John II, known as the Perfect Prince, dies. Richard tries to negotiate the crown for his son, but Manuel's primogeniture claim wins.
October 25, 1495

Pacific Ocean Reached
England beats the Spanish to the Pacific Ocean and dominates North and Central American colonization, increasing the nation's wealth.
1512

Birth of Prince Richard
Queen Joanna gives birth to a son named Richard. The Yorkist king's dynastic security grows, increasing his authority at home.
February 1489

Columbus Returns Home
The Treaty of Tordesillas splits new territories three ways, between Spain, Portugal, and its increasingly important naval partner, England. **March 4, 1493**

Richard III Dies
At the age of 57, Richard III dies at Windsor and is buried in the mausoleum his brother established there. Richard IV is crowned. **April 21, 1509**

The Reformation Fails
The influence of Richard IV's mother and ties with Portugal and Spain keep England Catholic. The Reformation succeeds in France. **1517**

© KEVIN McGOVERN

What if...

Henry VIII and Catherine of Aragon had a son?

LONDON, JANUARY 1, 1511

NOTABLE NAMES:
- King Henry VIII
- Catherine of Aragon
- Queen Mary I
- Queen Elizabeth I
- King Edward VI

What Really Happened...

The second son of Henry VII, King Henry VIII became the King of England after his older brother and heir to the throne, Arthur, died when he was only 15 years old. Arthur had been betrothed to marry Catherine of Aragon since he was two, and in 1501, they were married. After Arthur's passing, Henry VIII took the throne and was set to marry his brother's widow.

Henry VIII and Catherine had three sons and three daughters, but sadly, all but one of the children died in infancy. Their sole surviving child was a girl, (future Queen Mary I). In his desperation for a male heir, a happy marriage, and political allies, Henry VIII went on to marry several women. Out of his six marriages, two ended in annulment, two in death, and two in beheadings for adultery and treason. However, he did have another daughter, future Queen Elizabeth I, and eventually a son—the future King Edward VI. Henry VIII died at age 55, and after succeeding him at age nine, Edward VI also passed away only a few years later at age 15.

INTERVIEW WITH... DR. STEVEN GUNN

Doctor Steven Gunn is an associate professor of modern history at the University of Oxford. His research speciality, spawning a number of acclaimed and respected journal articles and book contributions, is 15th- and 16th-century English, Dutch, and European history. Among his published works as an author are *Early Tudor Government, 1485-1558* (Basingstoke, 1995) and *Charles Brandon: Henry VII's Closest Friend* (Amberley Publishing), which was highly anticipated among scholars of British history.

What would have happened if Henry VIII had a son with Catherine of Aragon? Well, first of all, let us not forget that the couple did have a son—on January 1, 1511, Catherine gave birth to Prince Henry, but he died suddenly, only living for 52 days. So what we do know is that there was enormous public rejoicing and people would have been pleased if the king's son had lived and grown to take the throne.

When the later Edward VI was born, people were also extremely happy, but by that time Henry had been trying for many years to have a son. However, the people of England liked the stability that came from a male on the throne so there would have been jubilation if Prince Henry, for instance, had lived and grown up to be king.

The second thing is that Henry VIII wouldn't have needed to keep getting married to other people. That would have been dependent on Catherine's health, of course, and once you change history it is uncertain what else might be different. For instance, would Catherine have died in 1536, only weeks after turning 50 and having been banished, or would she have had a longer and healthier life?

Also, naturally, the third thing that would have changed is the effect on the Catholic Church in England, because Henry's immediate cause to break with Rome would not have been there anymore. He wouldn't have had to divorce Catherine because she couldn't give him a male heir.

Could we have seen more than just one son? Yes, I think this is very likely. Henry's elder brother had died young and I don't think he would have been satisfied with just one. So you could have had a larger royal lineage.

How about international relations? This is one of the most interesting questions to think about. I suspect we would have seen closer relations with the House of Habsburg. I think Henry VIII being married to Catherine strengthened their natural alliance against France. The Habsburgs were the natural rival to France for control of the low countries and Italy, and Catherine's nephew, Charles V, remained allied to the Habsburgs and waged war against France. Charles V was a Habsburg, his father was a Habsburg, and his mother was from the Trastámara family, or house of Aragon, just like Catherine. There was a geopolitical logic behind an alliance between the English and the Habsburgs and you do have to wonder if a new prince, with Habsburg blood in his veins, would have been even more bound to that. A son of Henry and Catherine wouldn't have had that same bloodline, but he would have shared Trastámara blood with Charles V, leader of the Habsburgs.

Could Henry have had other reasons to divorce Catherine if the logic that she could not produce a male heir to the throne was no longer there? Well, yes, he might have wanted more sons, as we mentioned, but then he did not accept his daughter with Catherine, Princess Mary, as legitimate. The argument was that he and Catherine had never had a marriage that should

England may have remained a staunchly Catholic country if Henry had no reason to break with Rome, leading to Christ the Redeemer calling London his home, not Rio

Not a real photo, has been altered.

If Catherine had given Henry a son, it is unlikely he would have wanted a divorce

"He might well have taken even more power over the Church of England"

have been given legal recognition, so Mary couldn't have been a legitimate daughter. So had Henry tried to divorce Catherine after she had given him a son on the same principle, then it would have made the child illegitimate. As a result, he wouldn't have done that. When Henry broke with Rome he felt that he should have power over the English Church. He felt he was like King David or King Solomon—so when the opportunity was there to give up his power over the English Church, he really didn't want to. He wanted to keep that authority. So who knows how things would have turned out? Henry certainly didn't like Protestant doctrine. He might well have taken even more power over the Church of England and perhaps even taxed it harder.

Would having a son have saved this marriage? Or do you suspect it was always doomed? He was very fond of Catherine when he first married her and I think that relationship would have carried on if they had been

able to produce a son and, especially, if they had many male children. If you compare Henry with Francis I of France, for instance, he is not a sexual libertine. He did not have a lot of mistresses. So he would probably have stayed married. Remember that his father had remained happily married to his mother, and that was an example of a good royal marriage.

A big part of Henry's problem is that he had a conscience and he wanted to be married to the people he fell in love with. It is possible that if he had fallen out of love with Catherine, and fallen in love with someone else, he might have wanted to abandon her in the end. But, again, his main argument for divorcing her was that they had not had a son and that was proof their marriage was wrong and should never have been. He genuinely convinced himself that was true. That was what was behind the divorce campaign. Everyone eventually agreed the paperwork was messed up and he wanted the pope to agree that no religious authority should have married them in the first place.

Of course, Henry VIII went on to marry Anne Boleyn. Does she still have a big role in history if Catherine is the mother of a son and remains queen? It's very hard to know what would have happened there. It is difficult to figure out that relationship and how it would have transpired with Catherine bearing him a son. Would he still have fallen in love with Anne? That is impossible to say. Certainly, we might not have heard of Anne Boleyn on the same scale—she might be barely remembered.

Can we see a son as having a different legacy and attitude than Mary I who was, of course, authoritarian in imposing her theocratic beliefs? I think we have to assume he would have been brought up to be as much like Henry as Henry could have made him. Young Edward VI was the same—he even stood the same way as his father when he was having his portrait painted. So Henry's son would have been well-educated, in the way that Prince Arthur, Henry's older brother,

How would it be different?

Real timeline

1491

Birth of Henry VIII
The future, and controversial, king of the land was the second monarch of the Tudor dynasty. His father, King Henry VII, had seized the throne in the wake of the notorious Wars of the Roses. **June 28, 1491**

Real timeline

Death of Arthur, Prince of Wales
Aged just 15, the Prince of Wales dies. He had married Catherine of Aragon a year earlier. His death haunts his brother, Henry VIII, who is later worried that one royal son might not be enough. **April 2, 1502**

Alternate timeline

Death of Arthur, Prince of Wales
Despite being just 14, Arthur dies from a mysterious disease. Prior to his passing he was rumored to be considering a marriage to Catherine of Aragon, who soon becomes linked with his brother. **January 2, 1501**

Henry VIII Takes the Throne
After national mourning over the death of Henry VII, there is jubilation across England as his son takes his place as the new ruler of the land. **April 21, 1509**

Henry VIII Marries Catherine
Prior to taking the throne, Henry VIII reveals his romance with Catherine of Aragon. The two take their vows prior to the passing of his father, Henry VII. **December 21, 1508**

Henry VIII Marries Catherine
Seven years after the death of her first husband, 23-year-old Catherine is married to Henry VIII. She swears that she was a virgin until her second marriage took place. **June 11, 1509**

Catherine and Henry's First Daughter
Perhaps an ominous indication of what is to come. A royal child is announced to the people of England and Wales but, unfortunately, what would have been Henry and Catherine's first daughter together is stillborn. **January 31, 1510**

Their First Son
Catherine has her second child, this time a son, just as a new year dawns. The couple are delighted as Henry, Duke of Cornwall, is officially named. Yet, 52 days later, the baby passes mysteriously. **January 1, 1511**

Henry VIII Takes the Throne
The new king also lets the people of the land know that his first intention is for his wife to birth a new prince. Still haunted by his brother's early demise, Henry VIII plans for many successors. **April 21, 1509**

had been. He would have brought in expert English schoolteachers and continental academics. How much of Mary's personality comes from the fact that for most of her adult life she had been put through the ringer by Henry is also up for discussion. Here was a woman who had been told she was illegitimate and told she might not even be in royal path of succession. At one point she even contemplated escaping to the continent. So I think a lot of her style was from the hard time she had. So without that, who knows how she would have turned out?

Do you think Catherine could have had greater influence on things such as women's rights? How much do you think her treatment by Henry VIII has inspired her sympathetic legacy? I think she would have gone on to be seen as a successful queen. She was a strong character, politically, when she got the chance. Henry was abroad and she was in charge when the Scots invaded in 1513 and they were defeated at the Battle of Flodden. She didn't lead the armies but she did preside over domestic politics at the time. In a sense, though, part of doing her duties as queen would have been having a lot of sons. That was just the way it was back then.

Do you think this scenario might have affected the industrial revolution in some way? No, I really do not see that connection at all. I suppose, and this is a huge stretch, that there are two ways you could argue that. The first is that the vague Protestant ethic in capitalism would not have surfaced. But even then I'm not so sure that happens if Henry doesn't break with Rome. England was a major manufacturing country, and all of that was already there before the break with Rome. Second, there is the dissolution of the monasteries, which created a new land market and led to agrarian capitalism—but you also saw that in countries such as the Netherlands long before Protestantism. So I don't really see how this would have affected the industrial revolution.

Anne Boleyn may never have been featured in the history books had Henry had a son

Before his break with the Catholic Church, Henry VIII had a good relationship with Pope Leo X

Third Time Lucky?
Henry VIII leaves to battle France. No one will ever know whether or not her husband's absence led to Catherine's health decreasing, and a premature labor that resulted in another dead baby boy. **June 30, 1513**

Successful Birth of Mary I
After another failed pregnancy, the only child who successfully comes from the marriage of Henry VIII and Catherine of Aragon arrives. Mary I would later be claimed by her father to be illegitimate. **February 18, 1516**

An Unintentional Reformation
Henry convinces himself that his marriage vows must be annulled. The church refuses to grant a divorce leading to the English Reformation. Henry appoints an archbishop, Thomas Cranmer, who acts in his interests. **Marriage annulled by Cranmer on May 23, 1533**

Banishment of Catherine of Aragon
Henry VIII marries Anne Boleyn, who will later be executed on his orders, and Catherine is sent to live a secluded life in a single room in Kimbolton Castle. She never relinquishes her claim to the title of queen. **Dies: January 7, 1536**

Birth of Henry, Duke of Cornwall
Catherine has her second child, Henry, Duke of Cornwall, just as 1511 arrives. News from the palace confirms the child healthy and the happy father reportedly could not be more in love with his wife. **January 1, 1511**

Taxation of the Catholic Church
With a fiscally disastrous reign as monarch, the king opts to tax the church and its land. There are some grumbles, but the measure proves a financial success and supports a costly war. **July 10, 1516**

Execution of Protestants
Henry VIII, encouraged especially by his daughter Mary, steps up the execution of anyone identified to sympathize with Protestant doctrine. No admirer of Luther, the king makes a decree for execution without trial of any converts. **Decree made March 16, 1531**

Catherine and Henry's First Daughter
The first child of the new monarchs is a daughter, Mary. So far so good for the royal couple, although a son is foremost in Henry's mind. **January 31, 1510**

A Second Son
Deciding to delay his trip to France in order to oversee what is rumored to be a tough pregnancy for his wife, Henry VIII remains at Catherine's side as a further male heir is birthed: Edward VI. **June 30, 1513**

All-Out War Against France
The king once again makes a claim as ruler of French lands. Supported by the House of Habsburg, the result is bloody war. Nevertheless, Britain captures and sustains the city of Boulogne for nearly a century. **January 2-October 8, 1530**

Rough Wooing With rumors of the blasphemous Scots starting to find a 'reformation' of their own, Henry VIII calculates an invasion. It is another costly war, but Catholic doctrine is reaffirmed north of the border. Reformation? What Reformation? **February 22-May 29, 1532**

What if . . .

Lady Jane Grey wasn't deposed?

ENGLAND, 1547-1589

NOTABLE NAMES:
- King Edward VI
- Lady Jane Grey
- John Dudley
- Queen Mary I

IMPORTANT DATES:
July 10, 1553
February 12, 1554

What Really Happened...

Cousin to King Edward VI and great-granddaughter of King Henry VII, Lady Jane Grey ascended the throne after her father-in-law, John Dudley, persuaded a dying King Edward VI that Jane should rule over Edward's half-sister, Mary. Jane was a Protestant and Mary was a Catholic, and while the Royal Council supported Jane, the public supported Mary.

On July 10, 1553, at 15 years old, Lady Jane Grey became the queen of England, but for only nine days before she was deposed by her cousin, who became Queen Mary I. After her father-in-law was accused of high treason and executed in August 1553, both Jane and her husband were also found guilty of treason and sentenced to death that November. Because Jane was so young, Mary spared her, but soon after, a revolt broke out and Mary decided to execute all her opponents, including Lady Jane Grey, on February 12, 1554.

When Lady Jane Grey was deposed after a 13-day reign, her cousin ascended in her place as Mary I. Just months later, on February 12, 1554, Jane was executed. But what if the tables had been turned, and it was Mary who faced the executioner's axe?

Edward VI is dead: in his final will he left the throne to his cousin, Lady Jane Grey, thereby disinheriting both of his half-sisters, Mary and Elizabeth. On July 10, 1553, Jane is taken to the Tower of London, where she

is proclaimed queen. The common people, who are loyal to Mary, greet the news with hostility. Meanwhile, Mary flees to East Anglia in the hope of gathering support, and is hotly pursued by Jane's father-in-law, the Duke of Northumberland. Within days he has captured her and returns to London in triumph, bringing his royal prisoner with him. That still leaves Elizabeth, who is placed under house arrest while Mary is incarcerated

in the Tower, to await her fate. Shortly after, Elizabeth dies of smallpox.

Meanwhile, plans are made for Jane's coronation, and on July 29 she is crowned in a magnificent ceremony in Westminster Abbey. Jane's family bask in her glory, and she takes up residence at the royal palace of Whitehall in order to begin her reign. The Duke of Northumberland had assumed that he would be the main power force in the land, but Jane quickly asserts her authority and makes it

How would it be different?

Lady Jane Marries
Lady Jane Grey marries Lord Guildford Dudley, the son of the Duke of Northumberland, one of the most powerful men in the country.
May 25, 1553

Mary Enters London
At the head of a force almost 20,000 strong, Mary marches into London amid great celebration and deposes Lady Jane Grey.
July 19, 1553

It's Treason, Then
Both Lady Jane Grey and her husband are tried for high treason and unsurprisingly found guilty on all counts.
November 13, 1553

Real timeline

1547

Real timeline

A Protestant King
Edward VI, the first English king to be raised as a Protestant, takes the throne after his father's death.
1547

Mary's Right
Mary sends a letter to the privy council asserting her 'right and title' to be queen. The message is rebuffed and Mary marches on London.
July 1553

Alternate timeline

Edward VI Dies
Edward dies at Greenwich Palace. In his final will, "My Devise for the Succession," the king leaves his throne to Lady Jane Grey.
July 6, 1553

Jane Pronounced Queen
A proclamation announcing her succession is read. Meanwhile, Mary flees to East Anglia to rally support for her claim to the throne. **July 10, 1553**

clear that she intends to rule. Nevertheless, it is with his support that she immediately reaffirms all of the radical religious policies that had been implemented by King Edward, for she is determined to make England a thoroughly Protestant nation and stamp out Catholicism. Within a short space of time, Catholics are being burned at the stake for refusing to convert.

The problem of Mary still remains, and escape attempts are already being planned on her behalf. While she is alive she is a permanent risk to Jane's security, but if she dies Jane risks the declaration of war from Mary's powerful cousin, the Holy Roman Emperor Charles V. However, Jane's hand is forced when a plot to overthrow her and install Mary in her place is uncovered. Aware of their familial relationship but under pressure from her advisers, particularly Northumberland, Jane reluctantly issues orders for her cousin's execution. She makes a last ditch attempt in order to persuade Mary to abandon her Catholic faith and convert to Protestantism, but Mary is horrified and refuses to renounce her beliefs.

On February 12, 1554, Mary is executed within the confines of the Tower. Her death causes shock and fury both in England and abroad, and the Emperor Charles V immediately declares war. With Mary's death, all thoughts of England returning to the folds of the Catholic Church are dashed: under Queen Jane, the country becomes thoroughly Protestant, but in a state of war against the most powerful nation in Europe. Despite allying with France, it is clear that the threat of war is imminent and the outcome is unpredictable.

A year after Jane's succession, the threat of war fades, and she is now the undisputed queen of England. Her claim is strengthened by the fact that she is now pregnant. She gives birth to a son, named Edward: the Protestant succession of England and Jane's legacy now appears secure.

Refusing to abandon her beliefs, Mary would have awaited execution in the Tower of London if Lady Jane Grey had not been deposed

NICOLA TALLIS

Nicola Tallis is an author and historian whose three books, *Crown Of Blood*, *Elizabeth's Rival*, and *Uncrowned Queen*, are all available on nicolatallis.com. She specializes in the Tudor period and has worked as a researcher, lecturer, and curator.

● **The Headman's Block**
Although given time to convert, Lady Jane Grey stoically refused and showing great courage, is executed.
February 12, 1554

● **Making Martyrs**
The first execution of Protestants under Mary begins. In all, 283 would lose their lives because of their faith.
February 1555

● **Succession Acceptance**
Mary, having suffered two phantom pregnancies, reluctantly accepts that her half-sister Elizabeth, a Protestant, is her rightful heir.
May 1558

● **Bloody Mary Dies**
Ill health finally caught up with Mary and she passed away at St. James Palace. Reginald Pole also died the same day.
November 17, 1558

● **Coronation of Elizabeth**
Once queen, Elizabeth sets about creating the Protestant Church of England. She would also sponsor voyages to the New World.
January 15, 1559

● **Queen Jane's Coronation**
Jane becomes the first queen regnant of England. Her coronation banquet—a huge celebration—is hosted in Westminster Hall.
July 29, 1553

● **War with Spain**
Mary's execution sends shockwaves around Europe. A furious Charles V immediately declares war on England, who enlist France as an ally.
February 1554

● **A Prince is Born**
Queen Jane gives birth to her first child by Guildford Dudley, Duke of Clarence. Prince Edward is now the heir to the throne.
September 1555

● **Queen Jane Dies**
Queen Jane dies. Throughout the course of her reign she has given birth to five children, and is succeeded by her son, Edward VII.
February 12, 1589

● **Mary is Captured**
The Duke of Northumberland surrounds Mary's stronghold, Framlingham Castle, forcing her to surrender. She is captured and taken to London.
July 19, 1553

● **Mary is Executed**
Mary is beheaded at the Tower of London. She meets her end with strength and dignity, and defiantly defends her Catholic faith.
February 12, 1554

● **First Catholic Burnings**
All Catholics who refused to convert to Protestantism face death and the first three Catholics are burned at Smithfield.
April 1554

● **Saint Jane**
Instead of becoming a martyr, Queen Jane becomes a beacon of Protestantism and is celebrated for centuries to come. **1600s**

© IAN HINLEY

What if . . .
Queen Elizabeth I got married?

ENGLAND, 1559-1624

NOTABLE NAMES:
- Queen Elizabeth I
- Robert Dudley

IMPORTANT DATES:
January 15, 1559
March 24, 1603

What Really Happened…

Queen Elizabeth I was the daughter of King Henry VIII and Anne Boleyn. Her half-siblings, King Edward VI and Queen Mary I, ruled England before Edward's early death and Mary's death in 1558. After Mary's passing, Elizabeth ascended the throne and was crowned queen on January 15, 1559. She was tasked with the challenge of not only winning the support of both her Catholic and Protestant citizens, but also people who didn't think a woman could rule a country by herself.

Queen Elizabeth I had many suitors, but she would never marry. There are many theories as to why; one being the way her father mistreated his many wives, and another being abuse suffered at the hands of Thomas Seymour. However, while she never wed, she was in love with Robert Dudley. Unfortunately for her, he was married, and even after his wife died in 1560, Elizabeth didn't find it appropriate to marry him. They remained close until his death in 1588, and Queen Elizabeth I went on to rule without a husband or an heir until she died on March 24, 1603, marking the end of the Tudor dynasty.

Elizabeth's sister and previous Tudor monarch, Mary, had been married to King Phillip II of Spain until her death in 1558. There was a possibility that Elizabeth would marry her half-sister's widower, but neither were particularly interested in the match and Phillip would have only proposed for the good of Catholicism. Elizabeth also realized Phillip had been an unpopular Spanish king with the people of England during his marriage to Mary. Another candidate for the queen's hand was Eric of Sweden, but her advisers believed there would be few benefits from an alliance with the House of Vasa. Elizabeth also insisted on never marrying someone she hadn't seen before, so Archdukes Charles and Ferdinand of Austria were out of the frame, as was John Frederic, Duke of Saxony. None of them would risk the public ridicule of journeying to England to face being rejected. As for potential English suitors, Sir William of Pickering and the Earl of Arundel were never considered seriously, while Robert Dudley, thought to be Elizabeth's true love, was out of contention due to rumors that he had murdered his wife. The best choice of husband for Elizabeth I would have been

How would it be different?

Real timeline

1559

The Virgin Queen
Elizabeth I, daughter of Henry VIII, ascends to the throne. She would be the last monarch of the Tudor dynasty.
Janaury 15, 1559

Foreign Suitors
As Elizabeth shops around for a husband, foreign suitors vie for her attention but her heart belongs to her childhood friend, Robert Dudley.
1559

Refuses to Marry
Elizabeth berates parliament for trying to force marriage on her. The queen dictates her own terms regarding matrimony.
1566

The New World
Francis Drake becomes the first man to navigate the globe. A few years later Virginia is settled and named in honor of the 'Virgin Queen'.
September 26, 1580

The Spanish Armada
Despite overwhelming odds, good fortune and a surprise attack using fire ships sees England see off a Spanish invasion fleet.
1588

Real timeline

Alternate timeline

Royal Wedding
A grand wedding is held. With a new Anglo-French alliance, there is no war with Spain and no national armada.
1581

Move to Marriage
Francis, Duke of Alencon, asks for Elizabeth's hand for a second time and sends a trusty servant over on his behalf.
1578

Francis, Duke of Alencon. An alliance with France would have supported the English cause against the Spanish, and Alencon had met with Elizabeth on two prior occasions, even sending his servant Jean de Simier to woo the queen on his behalf in January 1579.

If, in an alternate timeline, Elizabeth and Alencon did end up getting married, the English and French dynasties would have joined as one. The marriage would have shocked Spain, which would delay its attacks on England, and no armada would ever be raised. Alencon would postpone campaigns in the Netherlands for the occasion and the French influence on England would have increased. This wouldn't be welcomed by everyone, and the country might begin to tear itself apart socially. The tension would simmer for decades, but Elizabeth would eventually give birth to a son, Henry. Being older than her husband, she would die, leaving Alencon to rule France and their son to rule England as king. This would probably not be a popular move with vast swathes of the population, as Protestantism would be well established and the idea of a Catholic French king could be met with much disdain. Uprisings would begin all over the nation and a civil war could even break out in England between Catholic and Protestant factions. James VI and the Scots would join with the Protestant cause while Ireland might benefit from a lack of Tudor campaigns in the Emerald Isle. The bloody war would mean the Stuart dynasty could never claim the English crown as the Catholic forces, bolstered by the French, would eventually come out on top. In this alternate timeline, there would be no union of the crowns, but the opportunity for Scottish armies to move south once again would be possible, and they would seek to install James's son Charles as a puppet king. The conquest of the New World would then become a joint Anglo-French venture as the two powers might try to focus their efforts on nullifying the growing Spanish Empire.

ELIZABETH NORTON

Elizabeth Norton is a historian specializing in the queens of England and the Tudor period. Her most recent book, *The Lives Of Tudor Women*, is available on elizabethnorton.co.uk, along with her 14 other books, including biographies of four of Henry VIII's wives.

Not a real photo.

Timeline

Support for France
Elizabeth sends aid to the new Protestant French king Henry IV. The expeditions are a disaster and further support is pulled.
1589

Union of Crowns
When Elizabeth dies, James VI, the son of Mary, Queen of Scots, takes the throne and unites the Scottish and English crowns.
March 24, 1603

Gunpowder Treason Plot
A disgruntled group of English Catholics plan to assassinate the king by blowing up the Houses of Parliament, but are unsuccessful.
November 5, 1605

James I Dies
King James I dies and is widely mourned by his subjects because of the peace and prosperity he brought during his reign.
March 27, 1625

A Royal Execution
Charles I, having been defeated in the Wars of the Three Kingdoms, is executed. His death sends shockwaves across Europe.
January 30, 1649

Uncertain Royal Future
Alencon succeeds to the French throne. Elizabeth divides her time between France and England and the population becomes uneasy over her heir. **1589**

Path to War
The English public don't take kindly to a French king and there is unrest. A civil war breaks out in the country. **1615**

Catholic Victory
The Anglo-French army manage to hold power after a costly conflict. England is rebuilt but dissent is still felt in some quarters. **1622**

England's New Reputation
A Catholic England experiences much improved relations with both France and Italy, and the alliance makes Spain its number one rival. **1623**

Royal Baby
Fast-forward a few years and Elizabeth gives birth to a son. The child's dual nationality brings England and France closer together. **1582**

Death of Elizabeth
The Queen's death sees Francis's son installed as the regent of England surrounded by advisers. Francis stays on the French throne. **1603**

Bloodshed in the Capital
The Catholics have support from France while the Protestants have Scottish aid. The war centers on London with fierce fighting outside Westminster Abbey. **1616**

Future of Friendship
The Anglo-French monarchy endures with successful expeditions to the New World. There is no union of the crowns and relations with Spain remain frosty. **1624**

© JAY WONG

What if...

Charles I won the English Civil War?

ENGLAND, 1642-1649

NOTABLE NAMES:
• King Charles I

IMPORTANT DATES:
January 30, 1649

What Really Happened...

King Charles I ascended the throne in 1625, and after he married a Catholic princess, Henriette Maria of France, there was worry he would introduce Catholicism back into the Church of England. After the war in Scotland, tensions were high and in August 1942, civil war broke out between Royalist forces (the Cavaliers) of northern and western England, and the Parliamentarians (Roundheads) of southern and eastern England.

From 1642–1646, the First English Civil War swept the country, resulting in a Royalist defeat, but King Charles I refused to give up. As peace treaties were being negotiated, uprisings across England transpired in the spring and summer of 1648, initiating the Second English Civil War. When it was realized there would never be peace as long as King Charles I ruled, he was put on trial for treason, found guilty, and was executed on January 30, 1649.

What would have happened if Charles I had won the Civil War?

Christopher Langley: A serious policy of purging national and local councils of those who were clearly disaffected with the royalist cause. Those who had changed sides would be tolerated in exchange for an oath declaring their allegiance—similar to the oaths administered by his son [Charles II] after 1660. Charles would have had to change his religious policy. A broad-based system would continue with bishops at its head, but perhaps local disciplinary structures may have been tweaked to allow local management. Extremists on either side (Presbyterian, Catholic, or radical) would have been excluded. **John Morrill:** It depends on whether it was won by a knock-out blow, such as complete victory at Edgehill or Turnham Green and a royal occupation of London, or as a result of a 'winning draw'—in which case, a negotiated settlement in which Charles agreed to honor the concessions he had made in 1640 and 1641 but not the new demands of 1642 and later.

Which battles would Charles have had to win to regain control in the war?

Langley: This is a difficult question as much depended upon political machinations after battles. I am inclined to mention that a decisive victory at Edgehill may have allowed for a more dramatic march toward the capital—the loss of any real royalist presence in the southeast severely hindered the war effort. A real royalist victory at the first Battle of Edgehill may have inclined some in Parliament to soften their stance and provide Charles with an important bargaining chip. Alternatively, Marston Moor in 1644 was critical as it had serious consequences for any royalist desire to connect supporters in Scotland, Ireland, and the north of England.

What would have happened to Oliver Cromwell, the Roundhead Army and the Parliamentary supporters?

Langley: With the possibility of routing the New Model Army [the force raised by the Parliamentarians], the royalist negotiating position would have been much stronger. While Charles may have wanted the New Model disbanding, he would have had to deal with the arrears in pay accrued since its formation. If Charles would have carried the day early on in the conflict, Cromwell may have been imprisoned, but his position would not have been so prominent. After Marston Moor in 1644, Cromwell's star really rose. Cromwell's destiny would have been dependent on his own response. However, if he continued to oppose Charles and refused to accept his authority, he would have been executed for treason.

Would Charles now have complete power over the English Parliament?

Morrill: In the unlikely event of Charles winning an all-out victory, he would have attempted to resume Personal Rule [the period from 1629 to 1640 when he didn't call Parliament]. With no foreign threat and the economy bouncing back from the wartime recession, he could probably have managed on the funds available but being Charles there would likely have been provocations. The genie of Puritanism was out of the bottle and it is almost impossible to see him behaving as sensibly as his son did in managing that problem.

"If Cromwell continued to oppose Charles and refused to accept his authority, he would have been executed for treason"

INTERVIEWS WITH...
DR. CHRISTOPHER LANGLEY

A historian of the social and religious aspects of Early Modern Britain and Ireland, Dr. Christopher Langley is a lecturer at Newman University. In 2015 he published his first book, *Worship, Civil War, and Community, 1638-1660*, which focuses on warfare and religion in the Civil War era. In 2020 he released his second book, *Cultures of Care: Domestic Welfare, Discipline, and the Church of Scotland*.

PROFESSOR JOHN MORRILL

John Morrill FBA is Life Fellow of Selwyn College Cambridge and Emeritus Professor of British and Irish History. He is a prolific author of more than 120 books and essays, mainly about the civil wars of the 17th century and about the aftermath of the Reformation.

Oliver Cromwell, the leader of the Parliamentary forces, would have been executed if he hadn't accepted the king's rule

Oliver Cromwell and Roundhead troops at the Battle of Marston Moor, which was a decisive victory for the New Model Army

"We might have got the 1921 partition [of Ireland] into Catholic South and Protestant North 300 years earlier"

Would England have regressed as a country without having a parliament?

Langley: Following the 1641 Triennial Act [requiring that Parliament meet for at least a 50-day session once every three years], Parliament would certainly have been recalled. The question of 'when' is more tricky. I am inclined toward thinking that Charles would have recalled a purged Parliament and pressured it to pass acts against treasonable figures. Of course, Charles would have had to deal with the 'ordinances' (rather than full-blown 'acts') that Parliament had passed in his absence. As many of these were associated with cash generation, one is inclined to feel that Charles would have kept some of them and rubber-stamped them as full acts. Following the fears of social unrest, the return to stability may have been greeted happily in some quarters. Parliament had already obtained concessions from Charles, so England would not have emerged from a Royalist victory as an absolutist state. Despite the 11 years when Charles ruled without a parliament, he had no designs on serious reform along the lines we see by 'absolutist' French kings later in the century.

What would have been the religious response?

Langley: Charles was committed to a broad Church of England with himself at the head, buttressed by a series of archbishops. In the event of any victory, Charles could not simply turn the clock back. If a decisive victory occurred before 1646 (when the Westminster Assembly abolished key parts of the Anglican Church) then less work would have had to be done. Pressure to reform the Church would have continued to exist and some Presbyterians at the Westminster Assembly were already pushing for a middle way.

Morrill: Charles believed he would answer to God for his actions as head of the Church. He also believed the Church of England was both Catholic and Reformed—that it was in direct descent from the apostolic church but had thrown off the corruptions introduced in worship and practice by bishops and patriarchs of Rome who had also claimed authority over all other patriarchs.

How would Ireland and Scotland have fared under Charles' continued kingship?

Langley: Charles governed Scotland like his father: in absentia. I cannot see Charles becoming any more 'hands on' with Scotland if he had been victorious in England. The idea of one religious policy for England, Scotland, and Ireland may have slowed down, but it was something to which Charles was committed. An English invasion of Scotland would have been avoided

How would it be different?

Real timeline

1628

Petition of Right
After numerous disagreements over tax, Parliament forces Charles I to sign a petition reducing non-parliamentary taxation and imprisonments without trial. **1628**

War with France Ends
Following a series of defeats, England ends its involvement with the Thirty Years' War and makes peace with France and Spain. The end of English involvement means Charles has less need to raise taxes, and thus less need for Parliament. **1629**

Personal Rule
After further disagreements in government sessions, Charles dissolves Parliament and rules personally for 11 years without calling Parliament even once. **1629**

Grand Remonstrance
As rebellions are quashed in Ireland, Parliament presents to Charles the Grand Remonstrance, a list of grievances. Parliament looks to take full control over the English Army. **October 1641**

Attempted Arrests
Charles, accompanied by 400 soldiers, attempts to arrest five members of the House of Commons on charges of treason. This attempt fails, as they are not present and the speaker of the house pledges his loyalty to Parliament. **October 1641**

The Civil War Begins
Civil war now seems inevitable and Charles flees to Nottingham from London. Both forces prepare for war and cities declare which side they are supporting. **August 1642**

Real timeline

Alternate timeline

as it would have opened divisions in the English—many English puritans still saw Scotland's Presbyterians as a beacon of hope and may have sided with them.

As for Ireland, the situation was different. Charles had significant pockets of support but more decisive action would have been needed. Victory in England would have allowed Charles to either change tactics or break off negotiations with the Catholic Confederation altogether. While Dublin and the Pale remained largely loyal, it is difficult to envisage Charles quelling Irish resistance without a land invasion.

Morrill: Charles could have left Scotland well alone. He had cut a deal with them in 1641 which we would nowadays call devolution max—self-determination and self-governance with him as puppet king. He could have tried to divide and rule, but it would have been low on his list of priorities as he tried to rebuild in England. Ireland as early as late-1642 was 85 percent under Irish-Catholic control and he might well have cut a deal with the Irish Confederation—a kind of devolution max—so as not to have to pour money into reconquering Ireland. We might even have got the 1921 partition into Catholic South and Protestant North 300 years earlier!

What would have England been like in 1651 after a royalist victory?

Langley: Some historians have described the Cromwellian 1650s as a 'police state.' Charles may have feared similar dissent from disaffected individuals and chosen to do something about the unregulated printed presses in London and tried to control their output. The presence of many troops created problems for the Cromwellian regime—I see no reason why an army would not have caused Charles a headache, too. In Scotland, demobilized troops would have gone back to fight in the final stages of the Thirty Years' War.

The religious experiments that took place in the 1650s under Cromwell would have been totally different under Charles. Charles would have attempted to settle England back to an Anglican middle-way—and there is plenty of evidence to suggest that moderate Anglicans dotted throughout 1650s England would have welcomed it. Religious dissent would have gone underground—like before the war—but would have perhaps led to problems in subsequent decades for Stuart rule.

How would it have affected the likelihood of future revolutions in other nations?

Morrill: The inspiration of the English Revolution for later revolutions is precisely that; the revolution of 1649 and the extraordinary outpouring of radical writing in the years 1646-59—Milton, Harrington, Algernon Sidney, Cromwell. If there was no 1649 revolution, none of those might have happened.

The balance of power

How was England split between support for Charles I and Cromwell's forces when the Civil War broke out in 1642?

Key to the map

- ▬ Royalist territory
- ▬ Parliament territory
- ● Towns controlled by Parliament
- ○ Towns controlled by Royalists
- ✗ Key battles

(Map labels: Marston Moor, Hull, Nottingham, Naseby, Edgehill, Pembroke, Gloucester, Oxford, London, Bristol, Lyme Regis, Poole, Plymouth)

- **Unsuccessful Siege of Hull**
  Royalist forces unsuccessfully besiege Kingston Upon Hull and fail to gain access to the city's armories. **July 1642**

- **The New Model Army**
  A speech by Cromwell to Parliament overrides the military high command and gives all power to this new military force. **February 1645**

- **Battle of Naseby**
  A decisive victory for the Parliamentarians sees Charles flee to Scotland. He is eventually sent back to London to face his enemy and the charges they bring against him. **June 1645**

- **Battle of Marston Moor**
  The royalists gain several small victories until Parliamentarian cavalry rout Charles' men at the Battle of Marston Moor in North Yorkshire. **July 1644**

- **Parliament Disbanded**
  With no organized force to oppose him, Charles strips Parliament of its power and purges any of his political rivals. Oliver Cromwell refuses to accept his king's victory and is executed. **January 1643**

- **Church Control**
  Charles tightens his grip on religious affairs by becoming the self-proclaimed head of the Church of England, with personally hand-picked bishops in support. **1645**

- **Charles Executed**
  Despite many Parliamentarians not wanting to put the king on trial, he is and is found guilty of a "traitorously and maliciously levied war against the present Parliament and the people therein represented." Charles does not recognize the legality of the trial and refuses to defend himself. The king is beheaded. **January 30, 1649**

- **Successful Siege of Hull**
  By bribing the city's governor, Kingston-Upon-Hull opens its gates to royalist forces and they fully equip their arsenal for the march south. **July 1642**

- **The March South**
  After victory at Edgehill, London is besieged by Charles. Cromwell's forces fall and the capital and Parliament come back under Caroline rule. **October 1642**

- **Loyal to the King**
  Cromwell's New Model Army is dismantled and a new royal army is created, loyal and answering only to a victorious King Charles. **1644**

- **War in Europe**
  Shying away from an invasion of Scotland or Ireland, Charles' head turns to Europe where he attempts to restart the Thirty Years' War. **1647**

- **Revolts**
  Uprisings are common throughout the country but with no organized revolution on the horizon, England remains firmly under monarchical rule once more. **1649**

What if...
Queen Victoria was assassinated?

LONDON, ENGLAND 1840

What Really Happened...

Weeks after she turned 18 on June 20, 1837, Queen Victoria ascended the throne of England and would continue to rule for 64 years, making her reign the second-longest in English royal history, after Queen Elizabeth II.

During her reign, there were several assassination attempts, with the first being on June 10, 1840, when she was 21 years old and 5 months pregnant. Two years later, on May 29, 1842, there was another attempt to kill the queen, but the gun failed to fire. Just a few weeks after that on July 3, 1842, while on her way to church, another man attempted to shoot Victoria, but again, his gun failed. More assassination attempts were made in 1849, 1850, 1872, and 1882, but all failed, and Queen Victoria continued on. Along with establishing the British Empire as the largest and most powerful it had ever been, Victoria also had nine children and 42 grandchildren. One of her great-great-grandchildren was Queen Elizabeth II.

INTERVIEW WITH... CATHERINE CURZON

Catherine Curzon is a royal historian specializing in the 18th century. Her work has featured in numerous publications and she has spoken at venues including the Royal Pavilion, Brighton, and Dr. Johnson's house. She is the author of Life in the Georgian Court and Kings of Georgian Britain.

What was the background to the assassination attempt on Queen Victoria? Victoria was 21 years old and pregnant with her first child when Edward Oxford made his attempt on her life on June 10, 1840. As was her habit, the queen and Prince Albert were riding in a carriage on Constitution Hill, and Oxford, who was just 18, took two pistols and waited for his chance. When the queen came within striking distance, Oxford fired. Luckily, he missed with both bullets. Victoria and Albert were unharmed, while Oxford was incarcerated in Bedlam and Broadmoor before starting a new life in Australia. Queen Victoria, meanwhile, went on to become a legendary figure among the monarchies of the world. Of course, if one of those bullets had found its mark, history would have been very different indeed.

What would Victoria's death have meant for Europe? It's not unfeasible that the face of modern Europe would have been changed forever. The violent termination of Victoria's line before she had any children would have had a massive impact on the continental royal families and one of the most significant must surely be that, had Victoria, princess royal, died in the womb when her mother was assassinated, the German Empire would have looked very different indeed. After all, as wife of Frederick III, she was mother to Wilhelm II, the emperor who steered his country into World War I.

Had she died, who would have succeeded her? The next in line to the throne was King George III's son, Ernest Augustus, king of Hanover. Ernest was massively unpopular in Britain and had been for decades, largely thanks to gossip that implicated him in murder, suicide, electioneering fraud, and several sex scandals, including numerous homosexual affairs with members of his household.

These rumors were unfounded and their root could be found in his political opinions. He voted against the Reform Act, opposed Catholic emancipation, and even attempted to install a government to replace Wellington's own when he learned that the Iron Duke intended to seek a reconciliation with Irish Catholics. A hardline Tory who sported a disfiguring facial scar, Ernest was a convenient bogeyman for the British public, and it was a mantle he never truly shed.

Was there any chance Parliament would have amended the line of succession to avoid Ernest Augustus? No. Regardless of his personal popularity, any move to pass over Ernest Augustus in favor of another would have been constitutionally virtually impossible, let alone hugely unwise at a time when the nation was reeling. If they had pressed ahead anyway, the most obvious candidate was Ernest Augustus' brother, Prince Adolphus, Duke of Cambridge. He'd shown no interest in becoming king of anywhere and held no ambitions to rule in Britain.

Despite the enduring public image of Victoria and Albert, there was absolutely no precedent that could have seen the late queen's young husband become king. Less than six months into his marriage, he held no claim to the British crown whatsoever and to appoint him, or even attempt to, would have been a massive

"If one of those bullets had found its mark, history would have been very different indeed"

misstep by Parliament at a time when they needed unity above all else.

With Ernest Augustus so unpopular in Britain, what would the impact of his succession have been? Ernest Augustus had ruled in Hanover since 1837, and he had made his mark immediately upon arriving in his new realm. He dissolved parliament, suspended the disputed Hanoverian constitution, and ordered that all holders of public office must swear an allegiance to the crown under threat of expulsion. Though his moves did bring a shifting and conflicted political system into line,

things would barely have been settled in 1840, when he would be called to Britain to take his place on the throne, renewing the personal union between Hanover and Britain under his rule.

Though it's easy to throw around talk of revolution in any alternate timeline, history suggests that in the case of Ernest Augustus taking the throne as king of Britain, we might have had rather more public saber-rattling than true action. In fact, the nation as a whole would likely have welcomed its new monarch, gripped by patriotism in light of the tragic assassination of its queen.

The young Queen Victoria, painted in 1842 by Winterhalter

With famine left to sweep through Ireland unchecked, in Britain the people would become restless once more. Now the rumors of scandal might return, with gossip linking Ernest Augustus to the assassination of Queen Victoria. With Oxford long since executed for treason, her assassin became known as the king's patsy, used to remove the obstacle of the young queen and rushed to the gallows to silence him.

In 1848, revolutions echo through Europe. At the first faint stirrings of discord in Britain, Ernest Augustus orders troops out onto the streets. Any agitators could expect to be met with swift punishment, and the fledgling British revolution is crushed before it even begins.

However, with Ernest Augustus no longer present in Hanover, he might have taken his eye off the ball just long enough for revolutionary fever to take hold of his continental kingdom. Ernest Augustus would turn to Prussia to stamp out the uprising in Hanover and see it was swiftly terminated. In Britain, however, this move would only make the king less popular as the man who opened the door to the Prussians.

Would Augustus have attempted reforms in Britain?
Ernest Augustus might have been an autocrat, but he wasn't a fool. He was well-aware that the people could be won by more peaceful methods. Rather than sweeping reform, he would attempt to stamp his influence on the country through its landscape and culture, a tried and tested approach. Just as he did in Hanover, he ploughs funding into the arts, as well as the transport infrastructure, laying the foundations for a rail network that eventually criss-crossed the country.

With the careful stewardship of Lord Bentinck, the king would continue his Hanoverian policy of allowing all social classes to hold ministerial office. In practice, however, this promising development might prove to be little more than lip service thanks to the machinations of the ultra-Tory government that provided the backbone of the king's support. Of course, Catholics would be barred from holding any office regardless of class or party.

Would he have retained popularity longer term?
With the new king as hardline as ever, the honeymoon period would not last. Ernest Augustus was likely to prove a dominating monarch, used to the absolutism of Hanover, and he had always held strong views on Ireland in particular. When the Irish potato famine struck, Ernest Augustus would have seen his opportunity to hit the country hard and personally intervened to prevent the repeal of the Corn Laws. In protest at this unprecedented intrusion into Parliamentary business, Robert Peel stands down as prime minister and Ernest Augustus looks to steady the ship, appointing hardliner Lord George Bentinck as the leader of a new ultra-Tory government.

How would it be different?

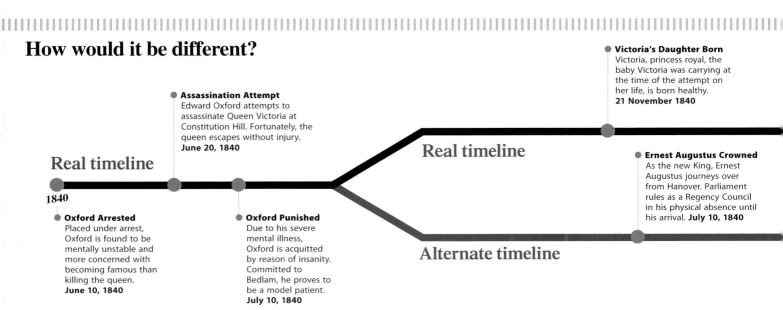

Victoria's Daughter Born
Victoria, princess royal, the baby Victoria was carrying at the time of the attempt on her life, is born healthy.
21 November 1840

Assassination Attempt
Edward Oxford attempts to assassinate Queen Victoria at Constitution Hill. Fortunately, the queen escapes without injury.
June 20, 1840

Real timeline

Real timeline

1840

Ernest Augustus Crowned
As the new King, Ernest Augustus journeys over from Hanover. Parliament rules as a Regency Council in his physical absence until his arrival. July 10, 1840

Oxford Arrested
Placed under arrest, Oxford is found to be mentally unstable and more concerned with becoming famous than killing the queen.
June 10, 1840

Oxford Punished
Due to his severe mental illness, Oxford is acquitted by reason of insanity. Committed to Bedlam, he proves to be a model patient.
July 10, 1840

Alternate timeline

When Ernest Augustus dies in 1851, what becomes of his territories? Ernest Augustus' two crowns would be inherited by his son, George V of Hanover and Britain. Like his father, George was a believer in absolutism. Aware that many considered him an unsuitable candidate for monarch since he was totally blind, George became determined to make himself known as a hard and uncompromising king and to make his mark on the land.

If his father ascended to the British throne thanks to Oxford's assassination of the queen, George V would have been 21 years old when he became heir. The young crown prince had neither bride nor heir, placing the long-term succession in doubt. With a quick marriage now a matter of urgency, the easiest candidate for the role would have been Princess Augusta of Cambridge. As daughter of Prince Adolphus, she was George's cousin, and they would be expected to set to work on producing an heir and a spare.

Far from a progressive monarch, in a changing Europe George would have been seen as a dinosaur, embodying a royal despotism that was swiftly becoming a thing of the past. From his home in England he might attempt to rule both his territories, but the reins of power would never be held firmly, and when the Austro-Prussian War broke out, it would prove a fateful conflict for King George V.

Would George V have brought Britain into the Austro-Prussian War, or would British influence have kept Hanover from becoming involved? Since George theoretically now rules Hanover and Britain, plunging into the war of 1866 would be easier said than done. The 1701 Act of Settlement included a provision stating, "This nation be not obliged to engage in any war for the defense of any dominions or territories which do not belong to the Crown of England, without the consent of Parliament."

George V, however, was a man who passionately believed in the absolutism of the monarch, and in Hanover it was a power he enjoyed. In Britain, he would find things to be considerably more difficult.

Reminded of Prussia's part in putting down the Hanoverian revolution of 1848, George would appeal for Britain to enter the conflict on their side. Parliament was unequivocal, however: Britain must remain neutral. With any efforts to dissolve Parliament and force British involvement in the war proving fruitless, George V would be faced with a difficult choice. Constitutionally, the personal union of Hanover and Britain was now causing serious headaches for all concerned. After all, how could a monarch be at war in one realm and neutral in another? The answer, of course, was that he could not.

Understandably, it's unlikely that George V would be willing to abdicate the powerful British throne in favor of the Hanoverian one, nor would he be willing to give Hanover, which his family had ruled for centuries, to Prussia. Instead, Hanover's best path would be to follow Britain into a declaration of neutrality. This would carry the implicit understanding that any belligerent who chose to bloody Hanover's nose might somewhere along the line invite problems with the superpower of Britain.

Though Prussia was victorious in the short, brutal war, Hanover would likely be left mostly unscathed apart from some small-scale conflicts between citizens who were loyal to one side or another. At the close of hostilities, George V would have learned an important lesson from Parliament and it's unlikely that he would attempt to force his will on his Parliament again.

What would have been the longer-term fate of Britain? The line of George V would naturally continue to his heir, George VI. Mindful of his father's own troubles as a duel head of state, the new king might be expected to learn from the problems his predecessor faced and immediately make enquiries about splitting the line of succession between the British and Hanoverian crowns. Ultimately, he would likely choose to abdicate his crown in Hanover—certainly the lesser of the two territories—in favor of his brother, thus keeping control of Britain and continuing the growth of its territories and allegiances. As the years passed, the successors of Ernest Augustus would settle into the role of constitutional monarchs, presiding over a British Empire that spanned the globe.

After years in Broadmoor, Edward Oxford began a new life in Australia

Ernest Augustus Dies
After 24 years as king of Hanover, the scandalous Ernest Augustus dies. He is succeeded by his son, George V.
November 18, 1851

George V Deposed
A triumphant Prussia annexes Hanover. To the end of his days, George V refuses to acknowledge his deposition.
September 20, 1866

Queen Victoria Dies
After a monumental six decades on the throne, the legendary Queen Victoria dies at the age of 81. **January 22, 1901**

Succession of Edward VII
Edward VII ascends to the throne. His personal dislike of his nephew, Wilhelm II, causes tension between the two nations.
January 22, 1901

Oxford Punished
Oxford is found guilty of treason. On the day of Ernest Augustus' arrival in England, he witnesses Oxford's execution by hanging. **July 10, 1840**

Austro-Prussian War
When war breaks out, Hanover allies with Austria against Prussia. Ultimately, Prussia claims the victory.
June 12-August 23, 1866

George V Dies
The last monarch of Hanover dies having never officially recognized the annexation of his realm by Prussia.
June 12, 1878

George V Dies
George VI's successor accepts the separation of government and crown in Britain and the conflict in ruling two such very different kingdoms.
June 12, 1878

George V Marries
George V and Princess Augusta of Cambridge are married. Their job is simple: secure the line of succession.
December 1, 1840

Lord Bentinck Appointed
Facing constant intervention from the anti-Irish king, Peel stands down. He is replaced by Lord George Bentinck.
December 1, 1846

Ernest Augustus Dies
The hardline Ernest Augustus dies. He is succeeded in Britain and Hanover by his son, George V.
November 18, 1851

Austro-Prussian War
George V cannot convince Britain to enter the war and, faced with possible abdication, elects instead to declare Hanover neutral too.
June 12-August 23, 1866

Line of Succession Split
George VI abdicates the throne of Hanover in favor of his brother and instates constitutional change, splitting the personal union forever.
January 1, 1879

What if...

Abraham Lincoln wasn't assassinated?

UNITED STATES, 1865

NOTABLE NAMES:
- President Abraham Lincoln
- Vice President Andrew Johnson
- John Wilkes Booth
- Major Henry Rathbone

IMPORTANT DATES:
April 14, 1865
April 15, 1865

What Really Happened...

Abraham Lincoln served as the 16th president of the United States from 1861 until his death on April 15, 1865. A moderate Republican who led the Union through the Civil War, Lincoln defended the nation as a constitutional union and vehemently opposed slavery and abolished it, among many other accomplishments.

On April 11, 1865, President Lincoln gave a speech advocating for Black voting rights. In the crowd was a man named John Wilkes Booth, who devised a plan to assassinate the president. A few days later, on April 14, 1865, President Lincoln attended a play called *Our American Cousin* at Ford's Theatre in Washington D.C. with his wife, Mary Todd Lincoln, Major Henry Rathbone, and Rathbone's fiancée, Clara Harris. During the performance, Booth approached Lincoln from behind, shot him, stabbed Major Henry Rathbone, escaped, and remained at large for 12 days before he was eventually killed.

From his head injury, Lincoln fell into a coma for eight hours and died on the morning of April 15, 1865. His vice president, Andrew Johnson, was sworn in as president later the same day.

What if Abraham Lincoln hadn't been assassinated? It's a question that many historians—and many writers—have pondered over since that fateful day in 1866. In short, had Lincoln survived his assassination (or if someone else had been shot in his place, such as the original intended target, Andrew Johnson) history would have certainly deviated. However, Lincoln's actions before and during the Civil War would have ultimately sealed his position as one of the most tenacious yet pragmatic politicians to have ever held office in the United States.

Had Lincoln lived, would there have been further attempts on his life? From the records we have, it appears that most of the former leaders of the Confederacy, including many of the members of the planter aristocracy, were appalled at Lincoln's assassination. This was not, as some Southern apologists used to argue, because of some sense of honor, still less from a moral squeamishness. The leaders saw Lincoln, who had so crushed them, as their best hope of holding off radical demands for further punishment of the South.

Incidentally, some of Lincoln's rivals did worry that he might seek a third term in office, contrary to what was then still the unbroken practice of US presidents. There were even rumors that he planned to serve as president for life. How these fears would have played out had he lived—or even whether he would have run again in 1868—there is no way to know [whether that would have happened].

What were Lincoln's reconstruction plans for the country after the Civil War had ended? Lincoln was somewhat cagey on his precise plan for reconstruction. He began publicly discussing how to reconstruct the South in 1863 and 1864, while the war was still going on. Many historians therefore take the view that Lincoln's plan should be taken with a grain of salt: he was quite likely dangling it as a carrot, to induce some or all of the states in rebellion to surrender. We don't know for sure what he would have done later.

This plan had three essential elements. The best known is probably the "ten percent" rule, holding that a state in rebellion could be readmitted once ten percent of its eligible voters foreswore the Confederacy and pledged allegiance to the Union. At that point, the state would be allowed to form a new government, create a constitution, and send representatives to Congress. Second, Lincoln promised to pardon all those who took part in the rebellion, apart from the high-ranking leaders. Third, he promised to protect private property other than slaves.

This last point was particularly clever. It's often forgotten that slaves were owned mainly by the planter aristocracy. The poor and working-class men who fought for the Confederacy were very unlikely to come from slaveholding families. Throughout the South, resentment of the slave-holding class was considerable. This resentment helped the northwestern corner of Virginia to secede from the state during the war (laying the foundation for the state of West Virginia), and might

New York Herald

SATURDAY, OCTOBER 17TH 1868

No.522

LINCOLN IN IMPEACHMENT THREAT!

President accused of overstepping constitutional authority during civil war and may be subjected to trial

"Lincoln did many things any modern president would be impeached for"

easily have led to secession (and return to the Union) of the western hills of North Carolina, where poor farms were plentiful and slaves were few.

Would Lincoln have been willing to compromise?
Lincoln was a wily politician—one of the best at the art of horse-trading. Had he lived, he likely would have reached a compromise with the radicals. He preferred, as he liked to say, an oath in which a man would pledge to do no wrong hereafter (as opposed to an oath insisting he had never done wrong), but he also made it clear that he could live with the stronger oath that Johnson preferred. The parties would surely have settled on some percentage between—perhaps 25—of the eligible voters.

What's harder to predict is what Lincoln would have done about the freedmen. He wound up in a position of largely supporting black suffrage—not at

all where he had begun—but he insisted that it not be made a condition of readmission to the Union. It isn't clear what sort of civil rights legislation he would have supported. However, even had he supported the bills that Congress adopted after his assassination, the chances are that the Supreme Court would have held them unconstitutional anyway, which is what happened.

Andrew Johnson was eventually impeached by Congress—had he lived, would Lincoln have faced a similar fate? Here I want to be crystal clear. Although I have written a novel imagining a world in which Lincoln lived and was impeached, I do not think it likely that he would have been impeached. He was, as you suggest, too savvy. I am not sure that, as in my novel, he would have used various intrigues to battle his opponents. But I think he would have found compromise on the big issues.

INTERVIEW WITH... PROFESSOR STEPHEN L. CARTER

Stephen L. Carter is a professor of law, a newspaper columnist, and a best-selling novelist. He currently teaches law at Stanford University's Yale School of Law. His fifth novel, *The Impeachment Of Abraham Lincoln*, follows an alternative reality where the iconic political figure must defend his seat of office and his legacy against a seemingly inescapable political trap.

The Civil War was fierce and bloody—as this painting of the Battle of Manassas depicts

John Wilkes Booth changed the course of history when he assassinated Lincoln

"During the war years [. . .] he became content with the idea that the freed slaves would stay in the US"

Moreover, I doubt his opponents would seriously have tried. Lincoln enjoyed enormous prestige in the Union, without regard to the disdain in which he was held by the leadership of his own party. Breaking down that public support would have been an enormous task, and one that I suspect the leaders of the radicals would have hesitated to undertake.

How would the journey toward civil rights for all US citizens been different under Lincoln's direction?
This is a question over which many historians have puzzled. Lincoln himself evolved during the course of the war. Originally he was against slavery, but thought the freed slaves should be returned to Africa. Originally

he took the view that perhaps some of the more intelligent black men should be allowed to vote, but that was all. Lincoln also took the view that the white man and the black man, whatever their legal rights, could never be truly equal. He was a product of the frontier in which he grew up, and his views for that time and place, were actually somewhat progressive.

During the war years, his views began to change. He became content with the idea that the freed slaves would stay in the United States. He seemed to embrace the cause of what was known as "universal Negro suffrage." As I mentioned above, I don't want to claim that had Lincoln lived, the great sweep of history would have been different. That attaches too much importance

How would it be different?

Real timeline

1861

Civil War Breaks Out
South Carolina, Mississippi, Florida, Alabama, Georgia, Louisiana, and Texas secede from the United States, forming the Confederate States of America and plunging the country into war. **April 12, 1861**

Lincoln is Inaugurated
Mere weeks before the main slave states would secede from the United States, Republican Party leader Abraham Lincoln is inaugurated as the 16th US president. He's also the first Republican to hold the highest seat of office. **March 4, 1861**

Emancipation Proclamation is Issued
As part of his crusade to abolish slavery in the United States, Lincoln issues a presidential proclamation that deems all the slaves in the ten rebellion states of the Confederacy to be free. **January 1, 1863**

Lincoln is Assassinated
Just six days after the Confederate States surrender to the Union, Lincoln attends Ford's Theater with his wife Mary Todd Lincoln, diplomat Henry Rathbone, and Rathbone's fiancé Clara Harris. John Wilkes Booth, a Confederate sympathizer, and his conspirators decide to kill Lincoln. After barging into Lincoln's box at the theater Booth shoots Lincoln in the head at point-blank range. **April 11, 1865**

Johnson Becomes President
Lincoln's vice president, Andrew Johnson, is named the 17th president of the United States. A Democrat who ran with Lincoln on the Union Ticket, Johnson begins his presidency with plans to quickly reintegrate the seceded states. **April 15, 1865**

Real timeline

Alternate timeline

An Assassin Thwarted
Confederate sympathizer John Wilkes Booth enters Ford's Theater in Washington, D.C., with the desire to kill President Lincoln, the symbol of the South's undoing. However, the plot is discovered and Booth is wounded. **April 11, 1865**

to a single individual. But would there have perhaps been more progress, more swiftly, at least in a few areas? I would like to think so.

What would the repercussions of such an impeachment have been for Lincoln? How would it have affected his political career and ultimately his place in history? Those who are martyred often fare better in history than those who are not. In Lincoln's day, it was common for members of the educated classes to claim that every president since Andrew Johnson (whom the elite didn't like anyway) had been mediocre. Lincoln plainly wasn't mediocre; the Civil War, the Emancipation Proclamation, and the 13th Amendment proved that.

I think his place in history would, or should, in any case have been secure. But it is the assassination, I think, that raised him to an exalted status that leaves him difficult to criticize. Would I still consider him, as I do, the greatest of the US presidents? I would like to think the answer is yes. But of course I have no sure way to tell.

Lincoln had to make some rather unpopular, perhaps even brutal, decisions to help facilitate the end of the Civil War. What would the repercussions have been for him following the end of the war? In prosecuting the war, Lincoln suspended the right of habeas corpus. He ignored court orders to release prisoners. He allowed his secretary of state and his military to imprison journalists. He had his secret service read every telegram sent in the United States. He used force to prevent the Maryland legislature from meeting to vote on secession. The list goes on. Lincoln did many things any modern president would be impeached for. But it's important to remember that the office itself was young in his day, and his understanding of his own powers arose at a time when the government was weak, and the need for action was strong. I'm not justifying the things he did; I'm just trying to place them in context.

Lincoln wasn't Booth's original target—he originally intended to assassinate Ulysses S. Grant and Andrew Johnson

---

● **Reconstruction Begins**
A plan detailed by Lincoln before his death, 'Reconstruction' is designed to reunify the states and heal a country ravaged by war. Under Johnson, the process is accelerated. **1865-1877**

● **Alaska is Purchased**
Alongside secretary of state William Seward, Andrew Johnson oversees the purchase of Alaska from Russia for $7.2 million. The newly acquired territory is renamed the District of Alaska. **March 30, 1867**

● **Secretary of War Suspended**
Johnson, increasingly unpopular with Congress, comes to blows with secretary of war Edwin Stanton. Johnson demands his resignation, Stanton refuses and Johnson suspends him. **August 12, 1867**

● **A Public Trial**
Booth is publicly tried for his crime. The court, made up mostly of Northerners, finds him guilty by unanimous vote. He's sentenced to hang. Lincoln, keen to strengthen the fragile relationship with the South, pardons him. **June 9, 1865**

● **Civil Rights Act is Enacted**
Despite Johnson's attempt to veto it, Congress passes the first federal law that defines that all US citizens are equal in the eyes of the law, including former slaves and members of the defeated Confederacy. **April 9, 1866**

● **Lincoln is Impeached**
A radical movement manages to organize an impeachment of the president based on the Reconstruction's lack of substance and his unwillingness to punish the rebel states. Lincoln is savvy enough to use the event to his advantage. **1868**

● **Congress Impeaches Johnson**
Johnson informs Congress of Stanton's suspension. Congress reinstates Stanton, who is then suspended again by Johnson. Congress impeaches Johnson for being in breach of the Tenure of Office Act. **February 24, 1868**

● **Civil Rights Act Passed**
Lincoln appeases the radical movement within the Republican Party by pushing through the 14th Amendment, ensuring the rights of every US citizen. **January 15, 1866**

● **Reconstruction Starts**
Congress pushes hard for a tangible start to Reconstruction, but Lincoln is unwilling to accelerate it, much to VP Johnson's chagrin. However, in late-1867, Lincoln commences the process. **September 1867**

● **The White Uprising**
The newly formed Ku Klux Klan attacks African-American families and agents of the Freedman Bureau. With the help of war hero Ulysses S. Grant, Lincoln sees the Klan dismantled. **August 1868**

● **A Country Reunited**
A shaken yet resolute Lincoln concedes that Reconstruction needs a swifter resolution. Eventually, the rebel states are reintegrated into the Union with enough sanctions to appease the North. **1870**

● **Lincoln Passes Away**
Having seen Reconstruction through to its end, Lincoln passes away a year after his beloved wife Mary. The country mourns the loss of their former president. **November 1882**

What if...
Communism failed?

BOLSHEVIK REVOLUTION RUSSIA, NOVEMBER 1917

What Really Happened...

Outlined by Karl Marx in the 1840s, communism is a political and economic ideology that calls for a classless society and equal distribution. Other the last century, it has seen a series of surges and declines, but today, only China, Cuba, Laos, Vietnam, and North Korea remain under communist rule.

Russia became the world's first communist government on November 7, 1917, as a result of Vladimir Lenin seizing power during the October Revolution. After being inspired by the Russian Revolution, on July 1, 1921, the Communist Party of China was formed under Mao Zedong. On January 21, 1924, Lenin died, and Joseph Stalin took control of the Soviet Union. Under his dictatorship, 1 million people were executed during the Great Purge.

Between 1940 and 1979, there was a global shift and communism was established by force in well over 35 countries worldwide, but collapsed in the late 80s and early 90s in many countries. On December 25, 1991, the Soviet Union was dissolved and the new Russian president, Boris Yeltsin, banned the Communist party.

INTERVIEW WITH... RICHARD PIPES

Richard Edgar Pipes was an expert in Russian history—particularly the Soviet Union. He was a Polish-American academic who, in 1976, headed up a team of analysts commissioned by the CIA to analyze the threat the Soviet Union posed to the US. He wrote extensively about Russia in the 20th century, including titles *Communism: A History* and *Russia Under The Bolshevik Regime*.

What if the Bolsheviks hadn't come to power in Russia? The Bolshevik uprising was a coup d'état, a power seizure. The masses were not involved in any way and, in fact, the general public did not know that anything was happening. If you read the newspapers from that time you find that the theaters were operating, there were concerts, and nobody knew what was happening. It was [just] a real power seizure. So I think if the Bolsheviks had not seized power in November 1917, the most likely scenario is that the military—the officers—would have overthrown the Provisional Government and probably established some type of military dictatorship for a while and eventually reinstated Tsar Nicholas II to the throne. I think that's probably the most likely scenario.

Could the Bolshevik uprising have been stopped? Well, I think if the Provisional Government that [the Bolsheviks] toppled had been more effective then, yes, it could have been. But the trouble was that the prime minister [Alexander Kerensky] was a weak leader and he didn't know how to cope with the Bolsheviks. So it's possible that if there had been a stronger leader then the Bolsheviks would have been stopped. But the leadership was weak and Russia had no experience in governing because they had so many years under an autocracy that they didn't develop an effective [government]. Kerensky, whom incidentally I knew personally, didn't know how to stand up to Lenin.

Was there ever a turning point when the course of events could have gone either way? The Provisional Government could have rallied the army [to stop the uprising]. In August 1917 there was a general [Lavr Kornilov]—a very effective and popular man—who tried to save the Provisional Government [by rallying the army].

But Kerensky disarmed the army [in fear of a coup from Kornilov] and armed the Bolsheviks [to defeat the army], so when the uprising began in November Kerensky had no one to help him. He really mismanaged the whole thing very badly. There were military people who realized the danger of Bolshevism and tried to stop it, and they wanted to help the Provisional Government, but [Kerensky] rejected their help and disarmed them. Kornilov sent troops to Petrograd, which was then the capital, and they were disarmed. And the Provisional Government armed his own opponents. So when November came the army just stood by and didn't help.

Would Russia still have become a communist nation without the Bolshevik uprising? Oh no, certainly not. The only support that the Bolsheviks had for communism at that time was that they wanted peace [from World War I]. The nation was quite tired of a war that wasn't getting anywhere, and the Bolsheviks were the only party that advocated peace. And that's what got them some support—not the communist [ideology]. Communism was never an [important] issue [for the Russian people].

What do you think Russia would have been like without communism? Russia probably would have developed into what it is today—a kind of semi-autocratic and semi-democratic government. According to public opinion polls, Russians do not like democracy. They identify democracy with crime, anarchy, and so on. And they like a strong hand—a strong ruler. So probably what you would have had is an autocratic regime with some civil rights and very likely private enterprise. They probably would have reinstated the monarchy in this semi-autocratic and semi-democratic regime. I think you would have had a parliament as you had before the war, before the revolution, which would have had limited powers although they would have had to approve the legislation, but the monarchy would have been very strong.

How would Russia's relationship with the West have differed without communism? I think [relations] would have been comparably better than they were under the communists. The Russian monarchy was on the whole friendly to the West, and learned a lot from it. It was not anti-Western [indeed, Tsar Nicholas II and King George V were cousins]. The anti-Western strategy and tactics were brought in by the communists because they wanted to communize the whole world, including the West.

Without a communist Russia would other nations like China still have followed suit? I don't think so, no. Russia provided a model and also provided support—so, for example, China wouldn't have become communist if Russia was not communist. Communism was essentially imported from Russia and I don't see that anywhere had anything like a [notable] communist party [before Russian influence].

Was communism important for Russia? Did it help the country develop in any way? It was a disaster in every respect. Tens of millions of people perished. It's true that they built up their industries, but the bulk of their industries were directed towards the military. And, as you can see today, after all these years of communism, Russia cannot export anything abroad except primary materials. You don't see any Russian consumer goods; all the consumer goods that we import here come from China, not from Russia. [Before the Bolshevik uprising] Russia was developing very rapidly towards an industrial country. In the 1890s Russia had an industrial role and was leading in the world, and I think Russia would have become an industrial country without the communists. The communists industrialized but just in a military way. Under the communists roughly 25 percent of the gross domestic product (GDP) went on military expenditure.

Would Russia still have had a civil war in 1918, and would they have entered World War II? There would have been no civil war, certainly, and I think if there was no communism there probably would have been no World War II either, because this [conflict] broke out only because communists in Germany helped Hitler come to power, and in August 1939 Russia gave him carte blanche to launch a war against Poland, France, and England. I can't guarantee [there would have

With the Bolshevik Revolution, Russia began its transformation from imperial autocracy to a communist state: the Soviet Union

"The military would have eventually reinstated Tsar Nicholas II to the throne"

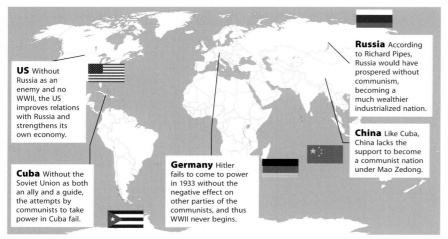

US Without Russia as an enemy and no WWII, the US improves relations with Russia and strengthens its own economy.

Russia According to Richard Pipes, Russia would have prospered without communism, becoming a much wealthier industrialized nation.

China Like Cuba, China lacks the support to become a communist nation under Mao Zedong.

Cuba Without the Soviet Union as both an ally and a guide, the attempts by communists to take power in Cuba fail.

Germany Hitler fails to come to power in 1933 without the negative effect on other parties of the communists, and thus WWII never begins.

"There would have been no civil war and I think if there was no communism, there probably would have been no World War II either"

been no war], but, you know, the Russians certainly helped Hitler come to power. If the communists [in Germany] in 1933 had aligned themselves with the social democrats they would have won the elections [rather than Hitler's Nazi party]. But Stalin ordered the communists in Germany not to collaborate with the social democrats, so they divided the opposition and Hitler won.

Without communism would Russia not have had figures like Stalin and Lenin? There would have been no such dictatorship [and so no such dictators]. Russia before the revolution was a semi-constitutional country, but there were no dictatorships. The laws were obeyed and parliament had a right to veto legislation, but there's no comparison between what happened before the revolution and what happened after.

If Russia hadn't been losing to Germany in WWI, would the Bolsheviks still have seized power? The Bolsheviks were [able to take power] not because people wanted communism but because they wanted an end to [WWI], and if [Russia] had won the war I think the communists would have had no chance. They brought in communism on an anti-war platform. Lenin was very careful not to propagate communism when he first came to power; he was just talking about peace, and when he made peace with the Germans a few months after seizing power it was very popular. But, you know, in the elections to the constituent assembly that were held in November 1917 when the Bolsheviks were already in power, the Bolsheviks only got one-quarter of the vote. They did not have widespread support around the country, and to the extent that they had support it was on the platform of peace, not of communism. The majority [of the public] were for socialism—for regular democratic socialist parties that were not [in favor of] dictatorship and abolition of private property and so on [like the Bolsheviks were]. The [socialists] had the majority in the constituency general elections.

So would you say that communism was forced upon Russia and the rest of the world? Lenin had a very clear goal, but he knew that he couldn't establish a communist Russia without spreading communism worldwide, so his idea was to spread communism first through Europe and then the rest of the world, and he knew that communism in Russia alone could not work. Mao Zedong in China emulated both Lenin and Stalin, then [communism started] in North Korea, Cuba, and so on, but it never became a worldwide phenomenon.

Would the Cold War with America still have broken out in the latter half of the 20th century? No, there would have been no Cold War. The Cold War was the result of the desire of the communists to spread communism worldwide—and particularly to defeat the US as their main rival. I mean, before the Bolshevik Revolution relations between Russia and America were

How would it be different?

Real timeline

1914

WWI Starts World War I begins—a war that caused great loss to Russia and one that was not supported by the general public. **July 28, 1914**

February Revolution The February Revolution begins (although it was in March in the Gregorian calendar), with the public calling for the abdication of Tsar Nicholas II. **March 8, 1917**

Provisional Government Formed The Tsar abdicates and the Provisional Government is formed to run the country in the monarchy's stead. **March 15, 1917**

Kerensky Appointed Alexander Kerensky (left) becomes the prime minister of the Provisional Government. **July 24, 1917**

October Revolution The October Revolution begins with the Bolsheviks, led by Lenin, deciding to seize power from the Provisional Government. **November 7, 1917**

Provisional Government is Overthrown Kerensky fails to stop the uprising and the Bolsheviks duly seize power by taking control of the Winter Palace. **November 8, 1917**

Uprising Halted The Provisional Government rallies the Russian army and stops the Bolshevik uprising in its tracks. **November 8, 1917**

quite friendly. I think without the revolution relations would have been as good as they had been at least from the 18th century.

So overall, would Russia back then have been a better country without communism in your opinion? I think that Russia was developing reasonably well before World War I. It had its problems—[for example] there were too many peasants and not enough land, but these problems could have been solved. When the Bolshevik party came to power they generally exacerbated all these problems rather than solving any of them.

And would Russia have been better off today if the Bolshevik uprising hadn't happened? Oh, it would have been much better off in my view—the mentality of the people would have been different. I think that Russians today are very confused about where they belong. They don't feel they belong to the West, but they don't belong to the East [either], so they're isolated.

Without that Bolshevik Revolution telling them for 70 years that they are a unique people and that they are the future I think they would have been much more able to accommodate themselves to the world at large.

Real timeline

Brest-Litovsk
The Bolsheviks sign the Treaty of Brest-Litovsk with Germany, bringing Russia's involvement in World War I to an end. **March 3, 1918**

Russian Civil War
The Russian Civil War between the Bolsheviks—now the Communist Party—and their enemies begins, raging for three bitter years. **June 1918**

Cuban Missile Crisis
The world comes close to a nuclear war as the communist Soviets and capitalist Americans clash in the Cuban Missile Crisis. **October 14-28, 1962**

World War II Ends
Nazi Germany surrenders to the Soviet Union following the suicide of Hitler as the Soviets successfully take Berlin. **May 9, 1945**

Communism Fails
Without a communist Soviet Russia as a benchmark, communism fails in other countries around the globe. **1970s**

Alternate timeline

Military Coup
The military rises up and overthrows Kerensky, reinstating Tsar Nicholas II to the throne and restoring Russia's monarchy. **December 1917**

Hitler is Stalled
Without anti-communist support, Hitler fails to seize power and the Nazis do not take control of Germany. **1933**

Russia Prospers
Without America as an enemy, Russia grows as a dominant industrial nation and, as a result, becomes one of the greatest world powers. **1960s**

What if…
JFK wasn't assassinated?

US, 1963

What Really Happened…

On November 22, 1963, John F. Kennedy, the 35th president of the United States was assassinated while riding in a convertible during a 10-mile motorcade through the streets of Dallas, Texas. His wife and first lady, Jacqueline Kennedy was riding in the car with him, along with Texas Governor, John Connally, and his wife.

At 12:30 p.m., a man named Lee Harvey Oswald fired three shots from the sixth floor of a building as the motorcade passed below, killing President Kennedy and injuring Governor Connally. At the age of 46, the president was pronounced dead 30 minutes later at a nearby hospital. By 2:39 p.m., Vice President Lyndon Johnson was sworn in as the 36th president.

**INTERVIEW WITH…
JEFF GREENFIELD**

Award-winning US television journalist Jeff Greenfield has worked for CNN, ABC News, and CBS as well as writing for *Time Magazine*, *The New York Times*, and *The Los Angeles Times* in a career spanning more than 30 years. He has also written or co-authored 13 books, including the best-seller *If Kennedy Lived: The First and Second Terms Of President John F Kennedy*.

What would have happened if JFK hadn't been assassinated in Dallas in 1963? It's entirely possible that if Kennedy had survived that his vice president, Lyndon Johnson, would have been forced out of public life. The day Kennedy was shot in Dallas there were two different investigations into Lyndon Johnson's finances. One on Capitol Hill by a Senate committee that had alleged he had taken kickbacks and the other by *Life Magazine*, which at the time was one of the most important publications in America. It asked how a man who had been on the public payroll all his life could accumulate so much money. Now, when Kennedy was killed, these came to an instant end because nobody was interested in further shocking an already-traumatized nation.

Had Kennedy survived, the impulse would have been accelerated to figure out what was up with this guy who after all, would have remained a heartbeat, as they say, away from the White House. So I think the first consequence was that Lyndon Johnson would have been forced out of public life by a scandal and there's a very good chance of that.

Would the Cold War and tensions with the Soviet Union have escalated in the same way if Kennedy had survived two terms? The thing I would stress is that a lot of people look at the way Kennedy ran for president, very hawkish, very militant and in his inaugural speech he said would pay any price, bear any burden. But they failed to recognize how much the Cuban Missile Crisis had affected him. It's pretty clear that he and Khrushchev [Former General Secretary of the Communist Party of the Soviet Union] had come close to presiding over a nuclear holocaust, it

dramatically changed the way he looked at the world. That's when he began looking for common ground with the Soviet Union: a test-ban treaty, possibly other steps to turn down the temperature of the Cold War.

How would the Vietnam War been affected? In terms of an international scandal, the big debate was of course the war in Vietnam. Here you're dealing in probabilities: when you do alternate history—at least when I do it—is get as close as possible to what the players said and thought at the time when you take history down a different path. The evidence is, during the fall of 1963, Kennedy had realized that Vietnam was a losing proposition. He had carelessly authorized—or didn't stop—a coup that had put new people in charge of South Vietnam. He saw this as a situation that violated a fundamental belief of his about committing large numbers of Americans to a land war in Asia. He had always said to people that he wanted to disengage but he couldn't do it until he was re-elected in 1964—the politics wouldn't let him. He would have been accused of being soft on communism. My best guess is that he would have played for time in 1964, tried to keep the status quo, and tried to keep any incidents from arising. I think that the Gulf of Tonkin incident [two separate confrontations involving North Vietnam and the United States around the Gulf of Tonkin] would never have happened. He would have been confronted in 1964 with a possible incident in the Gulf of Tonkin, but he certainly never would have asked congress for the blank check that Johnson sought.

My best guess is that he would not have moved the way Johnson did, very quickly and secretly, to increase the American commitment. I think we would have

"By the time he would have served a second term, no one knows how his health would have been"

been spared a war in Vietnam. And if we had been, the cultural clash in the US would have been very different in the late 1960s. We would have drugs, we would have had sex, we would have had long hair . . . we wouldn't have had a group of protestors who saw in Vietnam proof that the country was not thrown on the wrong course, but it was somehow malicious . . . to use George Bush's term, "a kind of general protest movement."

Do you think that he would have become more of an icon for that generation? Interestingly enough I think not—or less so. Because it was his death, his martyrdom, that made him such an icon. I think that wouldn't have been the case, because when you take someone violently off the scene at his peak, he becomes idolized. I think he would have [become more involved in] public service, domestic Peace Corps, stuff like that: I think that would have been accelerated, because that was something he was very passionate about. On the other hand, the other thing that was a danger when he went to Dallas was that his private life was being looked at very carefully by some members of the press. The idea that nobody knew, that it was a different era was true, but you had some very significant investigative reporters who were sniffing around Kennedy's private life. I think he and his brother Robert would have worked very hard to keep that secret. Maybe they would have succeeded—we forget how tough-minded he could be back then in terms of intimidating the press with threats of hack investigations and anti-trust. But I think enough would have leaked out to have an impact on his reputation. Not dying

If JFK had served a second term, the US might have become less involved in the Vietnam War

at 46 [years old] means the martyrdom and idolization wouldn't have happened.

JFK's relationship with Marilyn Monroe is legendary today. Do you think the US would have experienced something akin to the Clinton scandal? I tell you what would have been different: I asked some people whether Kennedy could have survived this scandal—they said "of course not." The cultural climate of the US in [the early-1960s] compared to the 1990s was just radically different. In 1964 we had a presidential candidate—Nelson Rockefeller—who lost a key presidential primary just as his wife gave birth to a baby and it reminded people that he had left his older wife for a younger woman. We had never had a divorced president in 1964 and there was no idea of, "oh well, it's private, everybody plays around a bit." I think it would have been far more shocking. The culture was only beginning to change by the mid-1960s. So that's why I think they would have had to work so hard to prevent the story from becoming public. It was just a different time completely.

How long do you think Jackie would have endured it? What Jackie might do is create a kind of informal separation, "I'm going to New York, I'm setting up my own life, we're not going to divorce or anything but I'm finding my own way." I have no way of knowing, but I do think she would have tried to make a life for herself. You forget that when Jackie was first lady, she was 31 years old—breathtakingly young. So you're talking about a woman now, not quite reaching her 40th year and she's stood by her husband. But she doesn't have to do that any more because he's not running for anything, so I do think she would have tried to find a life for herself, with or without Kennedy.

We also don't know what his health was like. Someone asked him: "Why are you running for president?" in 1960, "You're so young." He said: "I don't know what my health is going to be like in eight years." He suffered from all kinds of ailments: he had

How would it be different?

JFK Assassinated
While visiting Dallas, Texas, riding in an open-top car, Kennedy is shot three times: once in the head, once in the back, and once in the neck, dying from his wounds. **November 22, 1963**

Peace Corps Created
Executive Order 10924 establishes this volunteer US program to promote relations between America and the rest of the world. **March 1, 1961**

Real timeline

Real timeline

Alternate timeline

1952

JFK is Elected to the Senate
After eight years in the House of Representatives, Kennedy wins the 1952 election for a seat in the Senate. He marries Jacqueline Lee Bouvier the following year. **November 4, 1952**

Kennedy Becomes President
A well-organized campaign and support from Lyndon B. Johnson sees Kennedy defeat Republican candidate Richard Nixon in the presidential election, to become the 35th president of the United States of America. **November 8, 1960**

Start of the Cuban Missile Crisis
A CIA spy plane takes photographs of ballistic missile sites being built in Cuba by the Soviets. Kennedy reacts by creating a naval quarantine that inspects all Soviet ships arriving at Cuba. **October 14, 1962**

Concerns About Vietnam
In his assessment of the Vietnam situation, Kennedy says: "We don't have a prayer of staying in Vietnam [. . .] They are going to throw our asses out [. . .] but I can't give up that territory to the communists and get the American people to re-elect me." **April 1963**

The March on Washington for Jobs and Freedom in 1962 was an important moment for civil rights, but JFK's record on this issue wasn't as strong as his successor's would be

Addison's disease, he had horrible intestinal problems, he apparently had an untreated venereal disease, the combination of drugs he was taking for Addison's and his injury from the war made his back [ache], just agony. One historian praises him for his sheer raw courage going through a day, given what he had. But by the time he would have served a second term and in his early 50s, no one knows how his health would have been.

JFK pushed for the Civil Rights Act—his death was a kind of catalyst for the 1964 act. Would it have been legislated as quickly if it weren't for his assassination? Here I think Johnson's success would not have been equalled by Kennedy, for a couple of reasons: Johnson used him and his death as a very powerful emotional lever to get those laws through. Second: Johnson was a master of the Senate. He understood how it worked in a way that the Kennedys just didn't. As a southerner, a Texan, he was able to understand the inner workings of the Senate and, following 1964, he had a kind of legislative—or in your terms—parliamentary majority. He actually had the votes in Congress to get it through.

I also think Kennedy wasn't as passionate about Civil Rights. He came to it late and Johnson, even though he was a southerner, had a kind of gut feeling that he could actually do this. That speech Johnson gave, the 'we shall overcome' speech in 1965 is, I believe, an honest assessment of what he wanted. Johnson said to the Congress—I'm paraphrasing: "I always thought as a young man that if I ever had the power to right this wrong, I'd do. I'll let you know a secret: I've got that power and I intend to use it."

Kennedy was also much more a foreign-policy president. If Kennedy could have avoided the war in Vietnam at the cost of going easy on civil rights, he would have done it. We would have gotten there eventually, but more slowly than it would have happened under Johnson.

> "Johnson was a master of the Senate. He understood how it worked in a way that the Kennedys just didn't."

Warren Report Issued
A year after the Warren Commission, which investigates the assassination of JFK, is established, the report is returned to Lyndon Johnson: it concludes that Lee Harvey Oswald and Jack Ruby had acted alone. **September 24, 1964**

US Responds to Gulf of Tonkin Incident
The war in Vietnam escalates rapidly as President Johnson uses the authority given to him by Congress to send in ground troops, starting with 3,500 US marines who land in South Vietnam. **March 8, 1965**

Richard Nixon Elected President
Former Vice President Richard Nixon, who ran against JFK in the 1960 election, finally gets his shot at being president. His first term is popular: he negotiates treaties with the Russians, enforces civil rights, and he is re-elected in a landslide victory. **November 5, 1968**

The Civil Rights Act is Legislated
New president Lyndon Johnson uses Kennedy's death as a catalyst to push the Civil Rights Act of 1964 through Congress. The act outlaws discrimination against race, religion, gender, color, or nationality in schools, work, and public facilities. **July 2, 1964**

Race Riots Across the US
The promise of a Civil Rights Act to end discrimination in the US, which never materializes, proves too much for America's black and ethnic communities. Violent and nonviolent protests explode across the States. **1966**

Watergate Scandal
President Nixon's popularity takes a downswing early into his second term and, in an effort to fight his opponents, the Nixon administration tries to bug the Democrat headquarters, among other clandestine activities. They are caught and Nixon is forced to resign. **June 17, 1972**

Kennedy Re-Elected
Kennedy runs against Republican Barry Goldwater and wins his second term in the White House in a landslide victory. Charisma and a tough stance against the perceived threat of the Soviet Union wins him over two-thirds of the vote. **November 3, 1964**

JFK Holds Back from Vietnam
Reluctant to commit any kind of force to a "land war in Asia," the USS Maddox and three Vietnamese torpedo boats enter a standoff in the Gulf of Tonkin, but ultimately nothing happens. **March 8, 1965**

US-Soviet Tensions Ease
With JFK holding back from further involvement in Vietnam and avoiding war with the North Vietnamese completely, talks open between the two major players in the Cold War and tensions ease. **1967**

Jackie Kennedy Leaves John
After Kennedy's second term ends and Richard Nixon takes his place in the White House, the former first lady feels she has done her duty and informally separates from her unfaithful husband. **November 5, 1968**

Kennedy Dies
JFK is in poor health by the end of his second term. His ailments finally catch up with him and he dies ten years after leaving office. **1978**

© PRESS, SARA BIDDLE

What if...

Watergate wasn't uncovered?

USA, 1972-2016

NOTABLE NAMES:
- President Richard Nixon
- Bob Woodward
- Carl Bernstein
- Judge John J. Sirica

IMPORTANT DATES:
June 17, 1972
August 9, 1974

What Really Happened...

In 1972, the United States was in the middle of the Vietnam War, the people were deeply divided, and President Richard Nixon was running for reelection.

In May, members of Nixon's Committee for the Re-Election of the President broke into the Democratic National Committee's office in the Watergate complex and stole top-secret documents and bugged their phones. However, they realized the wiretaps weren't working properly, so on June 17, 1972, they broke in and tried again. They were caught in the act and arrested, and it was later discovered they were connected to the president, who denied any association. The public believed him and that November, he won reelection.

Two reporters, Bob Woodward and Carl Bernstein, Judge John J. Sirica, and others were growing more suspicious of Nixon and his efforts to cover up his mounting crimes, which by now included illegal espionage, abuse of presidential power, and obstruction of justice. Some conspirators began to crack, and Woodward and Bernstein received an anonymous tip from a whistleblower. All prosecutors needed was proof of the tapes Nixon was accused of secretly recording and possessing. Eventually, the cover-up unraveled, the tapes were made public, and Nixon officially resigned on August 9, 1974.

On August 8, 1974, Richard Nixon became the first US President to resign under threat of impeachment as a result of the Watergate scandal. It remains one of the most pivotal moments in the history of US politics. But what if he'd never been caught?

Nixon resigned less than two years after he was re-elected in a landslide victory in 1972. His first term had seen him act as a relatively liberal and progressive Republican. While this seemed like it might continue with the chance of health care reform, the fact he was

---

How would it be different?

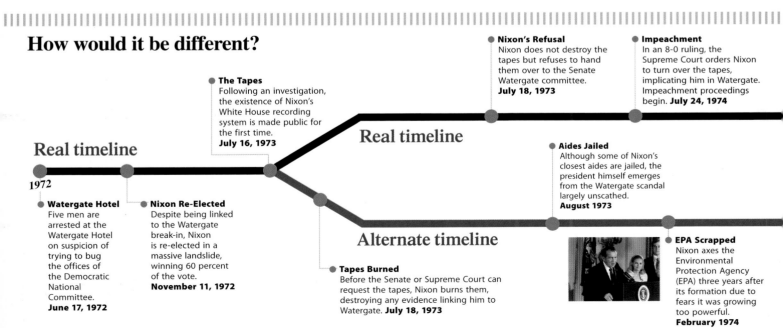

Real timeline

1972

The Tapes
Following an investigation, the existence of Nixon's White House recording system is made public for the first time. **July 16, 1973**

Nixon's Refusal
Nixon does not destroy the tapes but refuses to hand them over to the Senate Watergate committee. **July 18, 1973**

Impeachment
In an 8-0 ruling, the Supreme Court orders Nixon to turn over the tapes, implicating him in Watergate. Impeachment proceedings begin. **July 24, 1974**

Real timeline

Watergate Hotel
Five men are arrested at the Watergate Hotel on suspicion of trying to bug the offices of the Democratic National Committee. **June 17, 1972**

Nixon Re-Elected
Despite being linked to the Watergate break-in, Nixon is re-elected in a massive landslide, winning 60 percent of the vote. **November 11, 1972**

Aides Jailed
Although some of Nixon's closest aides are jailed, the president himself emerges from the Watergate scandal largely unscathed. **August 1973**

Alternate timeline

Tapes Burned
Before the Senate or Supreme Court can request the tapes, Nixon burns them, destroying any evidence linking him to Watergate. **July 18, 1973**

EPA Scrapped
Nixon axes the Environmental Protection Agency (EPA) three years after its formation due to fears it was growing too powerful. **February 1974**

considering scrapping the Environmental Protection Agency (EPA) lead some to think he might have swung more to the right.

"His intention to whittle down the EPA is often pointed to as a sign that he would have moved in a more conservative direction," Professor Kendrick Oliver from the University of Southampton told us. "[But] there is evidence prior to the election that he was talking with Ted Kennedy about a sort of bipartisan approach to healthcare."

Things may have turned out very differently with the Vietnam War, too. Nixon had inherited this conflict from his predecessor, Lyndon Johnson. While the Paris Peace Accord supposedly brought the conflict to an end in 1973, when US troops withdrew, the Soviet-backed North Vietnamese attacked, ultimately conquering the South in 1975. Had Nixon been in power things might have turned out very differently.

"There are some historians who think that Nixon expected it [the Paris Peace Accord] to fail and intended all along to come back in to Vietnam with a very strong display of air power," said Professor Oliver. "[But] what happens is the Nixon administration is weakened by Watergate to the point that it was never able to get the response to the North Vietnamese incursions in the South, which led eventually to the fall of [South] Vietnam."

Perhaps one of the more interesting things that would have been different, though, was the public's perception of Nixon. While he was never "beloved," notes Professor Oliver, there was a certain air of respect that was eroded by the tapes—made in the White House—linking him to Watergate.

"One of the most embarrassing things for Nixon was the language he used," said Professor Oliver. "There were a lot of references to expletive deleted, and it became clear that this man, who sat happily with conservative family

PROFESSOR KENDRICK OLIVER

Kendrick Oliver is a professor of American history and also director of The Center for Imperial and Post-Colonial Studies at the University of Southampton. He specializes in the history of the US from 1945-1980, particularly modern political, social, and cultural issues.

values, was swearing quite a lot and could certainly talk a blue streak. He often engaged in anti-Semitic language as well. The tapes revealed this complex and dark character."

Ultimately, though, Nixon's resignation set the Republicans on a very different path to where they are now. After democrat Jimmy Carter surprised everyone by winning the 1976 election, the Republicans shifted considerably to the right, something that might not have happened with a Nixon second term.

"You wouldn't necessarily have seen a scenario in which Ronald Reagan was a successful candidate in 1980," explained Professor Oliver.

President Ford
Gerald Ford becomes president, having served eight months as vice president. He causes controversy when he pardons Nixon for any crimes.
August 9, 1974

Spring Offensive
With little US resistance, North Vietnam invades the South, ultimately leading to the Spring Offensive and the Fall of Saigon in 1975.
December 1974

Carter Elected
Jimmy Carter pulls off an unlikely victory and becomes the 39th president of the United States, running his campaign on an anti-Watergate ticket. **November 2, 1976**

Ronald Reagan Elected
Ronald Reagan becomes US president after crushing Jimmy Carter—seeking a second term—by 489 Electoral College votes to 49.
November 4, 1980

Trump
Donald Trump defies all the odds to become US president, riding on a wave of conservative values in the Republican Party.
November 8, 2016

No Spring Offensive
With a resurgent US, there is no Spring Offensive in Vietnam. The South never falls, and the North and South remain divided.
April 1975

Second Term Ends
Nixon ends his successful second term, leaving a Republican Party largely more liberal than it is in reality today.
January 20, 1977

Democrats in Disarray
Struggling with a progressive Republican party, the Democrats are forced to shift ever more to the left.
1984

US Re-Enters Vietnam
Attempts by the North Vietnamese to expand into the South are met with swift air resistance ordered by President Nixon.
December 1974

Carter Fails
Jimmy Carter loses his presidential election bid, with many voters citing his inexperience in office as a main cause for concern.
November 2, 1976

Reagan Who?
With the Republican Party now leaning more towards the left, Ronald Reagan never gets the chance to run for president.
1980

Trump Trumped
Without the rise of more right-wing views in the Republican Party, Donald Trump never becomes the 45th president of the United States. **2016**

War & Battles

Discover how nations could have risen and fallen if the scales had been tipped the other way

90

76

52

80

66

62

58

82

What if . . .

Constantinople didn't fall to the Turks?

ROMAN EMPIRE, 1451-1521

What Really Happened...

Today, it's known as Istanbul in Turkey, but Constantinople was first founded in AD 330 as the capital of the Byzantine Empire (the eastern continuation of the Roman Empire). It endured several sieges over the course of its 1,000-plus years as capital.

However, once the Ottoman Empire was established in 1299, the Byzantine Empire began to lose its territories to the Turks, and by 1450, its territories only spanned a few miles outside the city's gates.

After Mehmed II rose to power in the Ottoman Empire in 1451, he started preparations to attack Constantinople—ruled by the last Roman emperor, Constantine XI Dragases Palaiologos—and further strengthen his forces. The siege began on April 6, 1943, with 7,000 Byzantine forces defending the city against 50,000–80,000 Ottoman soldiers. By May 29, 1453, Constantinople was claimed.

On May 29, 1453 Sultan Mehmed II, the leader of the Ottoman Empire conquered Constantinople. The last Byzantine Emperor, Constantine XI, died fighting to defend his city against the Turks. Mehmed followed this victory by waging wars against Christian powers in the Balkans and the Aegean. In 1481 he began his invasion of Italy at Otranto, but died before he could carry it out. But what would have happened if a war fleet dispatched from Venice to defend Constantinople had not been delayed, but had instead made it in time to save the city?

With the Venetian fleet occupying Constantinople's harbor, Mehmed is unable to bring his own vessels overland into those waters, which allows the defenders to focus their efforts on the land walls. After months of failure, Mehmed is forced to retreat to his capital at Edirne. In retaliation, he declares war against Venice in April 1454, focusing his attacks on Venetian territories in the Peloponnese. The commander, Cristoforo Moro, defeats the Turks at the Battle of Negroponte in June 1455. Six months later, a revolt of Anatolian beyliks forces Mehmed to leave Greece In 1456 Moro captures the island of Lesbos and the port city of Piraeus, and on May 1, Venetian and Greek forces conquer Athens. Meanwhile, the Genoese at Galata manage to capture Mehmed's castle of Rumeli Hisari. The sultan is unable to make another attack on Constantinople.

How would it be different?

Preparations
Mehmed sends a large force to the Peloponnese to intercept any aid that might try and reach Constantinople.
October 1452

For the Faith
Although official help is slow to arrive, wealthy Christians start to reinforce the city with small bands of soldiers.
1453

Real timeline

Real timeline

1451

A Sultan Rises
Sultan Mehmed II succeeds his father as ruler of the Ottoman Empire, but many have reservations about his ability.
1451

Any Means Necessary
The Byzantine Emperor agrees to a Union of the Eastern and Western Christian churches in exchange for military aid.
December 12, 1452

The Venetians Sail
The Venetians delay sending a fleet for a few months which meant they would miss the battle and arrive too late.
April 1453

Alternate timeline

Fortify the Bosphorus
Sultan Mehmed II builds Rumeli Hisar, a massive fortification that commands the Bosphorus strait and the heights just north of Constantinople. **April 1452**

The Turks Retreat
The Turkish siege of Constantinople fails after Venetian vessels cut off supplies to the besiegers making their way from the north. **June 30, 1453**

Harbor Blockade
The Venetian Fleet blockades the harbor of Constantinople, stopping the Sultan Mehmed from gaining access with his own vessels. **1454**

After Mehmed's death in 1481 his two sons, Bayezid and Cem, fight a decade-long civil war for control of the empire. They divide it, with the former taking the European territories and the latter the Asian. Emperor Manuel III of Constantinople exploits the division, winning concessions from both sultans, but little territory.

In April 1512, Selim I becomes sultan in the West after poisoning his father and brother. He immediately invades Anatolia. The war ends with the execution of Cem and the reunification of the Ottoman Empire under Selim. Given the sultan's power and reputation for cruelty, the Genoese give him Rumeli Hisari in exchange for a promise to leave the Genoese colony in Galata unharmed.

Over the next two years Selim brings land and sea forces to Constantinople, preparing for another siege. It begins in March 1515 and ends with the fall of the city on May 15. The last emperor, Constantine XII, flees the city. He is given an apartment in the papal residence in Rome, where he sets up a government in exile. On his deathbed he joins the order of the Knights Hospitaller.

In 1520 a new sultan, Suleiman I, issues his Edict of Grace to the rulers of Serbia, Bosnia, Wallachia, and Albania, allowing them virtual independence in return for tribute payments. Suleiman focuses on the repopulation and rebuilding of Constantinople, which is in a severely dilapidated state.

In Germany, the newly elected Charles V calls the Diet of Worms. With the Turkish threat neutralized, the emperor moves against the Protestant princes. When Martin Luther refuses to recant his heresy, he is burned at the stake. Between 1521 and 1523 imperial forces hunt down the last of the Protestant leaders in Germany. Relations between Charles and Pope Clement VII thus remained cordial. This gives Clement the freedom to respond favorably in 1527 when Henry VIII requests an annulment to Catherine of Aragon. The Protestant Reformation is fizzled out, limited to a few isolated pockets in Switzerland and Scotland.

THOMAS F. MADDEN

Thomas F. Madden is Professor of History and Director of the Center for Medieval and Renaissance Studies at Saint Louis University. He is a Fellow of the renowned Medieval Academy of America and the John Simon Guggenheim Foundation.

The Siege Begins
The Sultan Mehmed arrives with the last of his troops and begins the siege in earnest. The defenders take to the walls.
April 5, 1453

Naval Clashes
Unable to get past the great chain, Ottoman ships busy themselves attempting to stop any Christian ship from reaching the city.
April 20, 1453

All-out Attack
Overwhelmed by the sheer number of invaders, the Christian garrison can't stop the Ottomans from beaching the walls and gaining access to the city. **May 29, 1453**

Church Schism
Even hundreds of years after its fall, Constantinople is still a divisive topic in the Russian Orthodox church.
17th century

Istanbul not Constantinople
Despite being named Istanbul shortly after its conquest, the name did not become official until the 20th century. **1930**

Battle of Negoponte
The Venetian commander Cristoro Moro deals the Turks a crushing blow at the Battle of Negoponte.
June 1455

Ottoman Empire Reunited
Sultan Selim I defeats his uncle, Cem, at the Battle of Smyrna. Cem delivers control of the Asian territories to Selim.
April 10, 1513

To the Flames
Emperor Charles V comes to the Diet of Worms determined to end the Lutheran movement. Martin Luther refuses to recant and is burned at the stake.
April 21, 1521

Venetian-Turkish War
Mehmed II's war against the Venetian Peloponnese flounders when he is forced to divert forces to Anatolia to quash a revolt of Turkish beyliks.
April-May 1454

Brother Against Brother
Beyazid claims the throne. His brother, Cem, contests the claim leading to a bloody civil war until peace is reached in September.
1481-1491

Fall of Constantinople
Selim attacks Constantinople. When the land walls crumble on May 15 the few defenders flee to a Venetian fleet.
March 12—March 15, 1515

© IAN HINLEY

What if...
The Aztecs weren't conquered?

MEXICO, 1519

What Really Happened...

NOTABLE NAMES:
• Moctezuma II
• Hernán Cortés

IMPORTANT DATES:
February 18, 1519
November 8, 1519
May 22, 1521
August 13, 1521

Between 1325 and 1521, the Aztec Empire flourished, as did its capital city, Tenochtitlán. By 1951, it was led by Moctezuma II and the prospering city contained a population of between 200,000 and 300,000 people. But while it prospered, their religious and monetary demands caused resentment from surrounding city-states.

On February 18, 1519, Hernán Cortés began an unauthorized expedition to Mesoamerica to further Spain's colonization in the Americas, convert people to Christianity, and plunder the region for gold. After he arrived, his crew, local allies, and acquisitions grew. They made their way to Tenochtitlán on November 8, 1519, where Moctezuma initially welcomed them, but Cortés later placed him under house arrest. By then, Spanish forces were sent to arrest Cortés for insubordination and as the trouble unfolded, the residents of Tenochtitlán demanded the Spanish be removed from the city.

Driven away, the Spanish later returned with a fleet of ships, 200,000 Indigenous warriors, and better weapons. While also suffering from the smallpox epidemic, Tenochtitlán fell under attack between May 22, 1521, and August 13, 1521. Within a matter of 93 days, it was conquered by the Spanish.

What would have happened if the Aztecs hadn't been conquered by the Spanish?

Helen Cowie: It's easy to imagine that the conquest of the Aztecs was inevitable thanks to the superiority of the weapons used by the Spanish conquistadors (steel swords, crossbows, harquebuses and cannons against obsidian swords, slings, and bows and arrows). If we look in detail at the events of the conquest, however, it becomes clear that Cortés's victory was by no means certain, and that his expedition could quite easily have ended in failure. On several occasions the Spanish stared defeat in the face—most dramatically during the so-called 'Noche Triste', when they were forced to flee Tenochtitlán after an ill-judged massacre of Aztec nobles. Without the continued support of indigenous allies such as the Tlaxcallans, the conquest could not have been achieved. It was also the devastating effects of disease, as much as technology and horses that destabilized Aztec society politically. But for luck at several critical junctures, Cortés could easily have lost.

Matthew Restall: The invasion campaign led by Hernán Cortés came very close to failure. Most of the men who crossed to Mexico from the Caribbean in 1519 and 1520 died during the war against the Aztecs, and Cortés himself narrowly escaped death. But if Cortés had perished before the Aztec defeat, the final outcome of the war would surely have been very similar: one of his fellow captains, such as Pedro de Alvarado, would have continued the campaign in much the same way.

Nevertheless, it is also possible that the high mortality rate of the conquistadors and their allies, combined with the death of key captains and a failure of leadership, might have forced the survivors to retreat back to Cuba.

What effect would it have had on future attempts from the Old World to conquer the New?

Cowie: It's hard to imagine the Spanish would have abandoned attempts to conquer the Aztecs had Cortés been defeated. Further expeditions would probably have been mounted, perhaps with larger numbers of troops. Assisted by the effects of disease—a fatal legacy of Cortés's expedition—they would probably have won through in the end, although possibly at a much higher cost. Whether they would have been able to attract indigenous allies as easily as Cortés did in the wake of his defeat is another question. The Spanish attracted [indigenous] supporters because they appeared to be a successful fighting force, capable of standing up to their Aztec enemies. Had Cortés been defeated or killed, this aura of invincibility would have been lost, making indigenous backing harder to find.

What would the Aztecs have learned from the Europeans? Would they have modernized over time using European technology such as guns to their advantage?

Restall: Yes, they would certainly would have done so, just as other indigenous or Native American groups

If the Aztecs had withstood the Spanish conquest, they could have begun to use new weaponry

"Spanish conquistadors would surely have ended up facing Aztec warriors armed with steel weapons and possibly even guns"

INTERVIEWS WITH...
MATTHEW RESTALL

Matthew Restall is a professor of Colonial Latin American History at Penn State University. His areas of specialization are Yucatán and Mexico, Guatemala and Belize, Mayan history, the Spanish conquest, and Africans in Spanish America. He has co-authored four books published in 2011 and 2012, including *2012 and the End of the World: The Western Roots of the Maya Apocalypse*, and *Latin America in Colonial Times*.

HELEN COWIE

Helen Cowie is a lecturer of History at the University of York. She is the author of *Conquering Nature in Spain and its Empire, 1750-1850* and *Exhibiting Animals in Nineteenth-Century Britain: Empathy, Education, Entertainment*. She has also published a book on the cultural history of the alpaca.

did in later centuries—think of the warriors of the northern plains riding horses and using rifles, both to great effect. Indeed, during the Spanish-Aztec war, Aztecs captured and used Spanish weapons and armor. Had the war turned into a series of campaigns over years or decades, Spanish conquistadors would surely have ended up facing Aztec warriors armed with steel weapons and possibly even guns.

Cowie: There is evidence the Aztecs were already starting to learn how to counteract European weaponry and tactics during the course of Cortés's campaign. To avoid the projectiles fired by Spanish cannon and harquebuses, for instance, Aztec soldiers moved from side to side while marching, rather than in straight lines. To neutralize the advantage of Spanish cavalry, they erected barricades in the streets and avoided combat on flat, open terrain, which favored horses. Had Cortés lost, it is possible the Aztecs might have adapted

their military tactics further and become more capable of defeating European soldiers. They might also have learned something of the Spaniards' aims and mentality in war and adopted a more aggressive strategy in dealing with future attempted invasions.

Would the Aztecs have expanded and conquered the rest of the continent?

Restall: It is interesting to speculate on how the Aztec acquisition of horses and Spanish technologies of war might have allowed them to consolidate and expand their empire. The Aztecs appeared to have been poised to expand south into the Maya area by 1519, and [there is] no doubt they would have been able to achieve that.

Cowie: This is doubtful as the Aztec Empire was quite loosely structured. Rather than imposing their own systems of government, language, and religion on the people they conquered, they tended to leave existing

Fierce fighting broke out in Tenochtitlán during the conquest. Despite having better weaponry, the Spanish could have been defeated if deadly smallpox hadn't spread throughout the Aztec nation

"The fact the Aztec Empire collapsed after two years of warfare has influenced how we see the Aztecs"

leaders in place and simply extract tribute (a form of taxation) from them. There's little reason to imagine this system of government would have changed following a failed Spanish conquest, though the Aztecs would probably have exacted punishment on those former allies who proved disloyal and re-doubled their efforts to crush the Tlaxcallans. Though they traded across a wide region for luxury items such as jade, feathers, and jaguar pelts, it seems unlikely the Aztecs would have been able to enforce a more formal empire of conquest.

Would they have become a trading partner to the European powers?
    Restall: Had the Aztecs been able to fend off the Spaniards for generations, another factor would have complicated imperial interaction in the New World: the increased presence there of the Dutch, French, and English. In later centuries, the Spanish, French, and English used alliances with indigenous groups to wage war against each other and compete for territory and colonial control.
    Cowie: This seems unlikely. The Aztecs did trade extensively across Mesoamerica, but it is questionable whether the Spanish would have settled for a commercial relationship of this kind. The Spanish wanted vast quantities of gold and silver, which had to be mined, and souls to convert to Christianity, neither of which could have been achieved without formal conquest.

How would a failed invasion have affected Europe?
    Restall: I think a failed Spanish invasion of the 1520s would have been followed by further Spanish invasions, and that the impact of epidemic disease and repeated invasions would have destroyed the Aztec Empire by the end of the decade. However, let us imagine the Aztecs survive such attacks, borrow Spanish technology, and maintain their empire through

How would it be different?

Real timeline

1428

● **Discovery of the New World**
In search of new land and trading opportunities, Christopher Columbus becomes the first to discover the New World. After this, many Europeans make the journey across the Atlantic.
October 12, 1492

● **Beginning of the Conquest**
Cortés lands in Yucatán again after having set sail from Cuba with 11 ships and 500 men. He desires to claim this part of the New World for himself.
March 4, 1519

● **Cortés Arrives in Tenochtitlán**
The conquistadors arrive in the Aztec capital, receive gifts from Aztec leader Moctezuma II, and take residence in his palace.
November 8, 1519

Real timeline

● **Aztecs Become the Dominant Force**
With victory over the Tepanec at Azcapotzalco, the Aztecs become the major civilization in Central America with their culture, architecture, and language dominating the region. **1428**

● **Severe Flooding**
The Aztec capital Tenochtitlan is ravaged by severe flooding. This, in addition to famines and more floods, weakens the Aztecs before the Spanish conquistadors arrive. **1510**

● **Comet Spotted**
A comet is reportedly spotted flying across the sky on this date. In Aztec culture they are an omen, believed to signify impending doom and worried emperor, Montezuma. **1517**

● **First Cortés Landing**
The Spanish Conquistadors arrive in the Yucatán with a small force that is easily beaten after clashing with natives. They vow to return with a larger force. **February 1517**

Alternate timeline

the 16th century. That would have drawn intense interest from other European powers, such as the English. It might seem like a stretch to imagine the English conquering the Aztecs in the 17th century. But then consider that the English (later British) did establish a considerable empire in regions to the north, east, and south of what had been Aztec Mexico. Furthermore, the heirs to part of the empire—the United States—conquered and permanently acquired half of the nation that was the heir to Aztec Mexico.

Cowie: Failure to conquer the Aztecs (and subsequently the Incas) would have had serious implications for Spain, which came to rely on American silver to finance its military campaigns in Europe. Within the context of the Reformation and the religious wars then raging in the Old World, it would also have had a significant impact on the global spread of Catholicism.

How might we look at the Aztec civilization differently today?

Restall: The fact the Aztec Empire collapsed after two years of warfare has certainly influenced how we see the Aztecs. The Spaniards justified their invasion and colonization of the region by portraying the Aztec civilization as barbarian and bloody. In particular, they emphasized the Aztec practice of human sacrifice— even though the Spanish, English, and other Europeans also held public executions for political and religious reasons—and wrongly accused the Aztecs of practicing cannibalism. Although we now have a complex and more balanced understanding of the Aztecs' past, the negative stereotypes propagated by the Spaniards have survived in the popular imagination. But had the Aztecs survived the Spanish invasions of 1519 to 1521, especially if their empire had lasted long enough to establish alliances or diplomatic relationships with other European powers, we would probably now know much

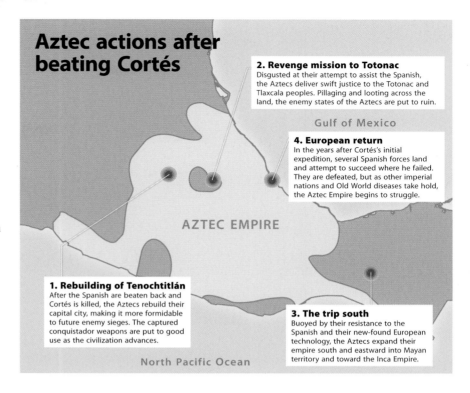

Aztec actions after beating Cortés

2. Revenge mission to Totonac
Disgusted at their attempt to assist the Spanish, the Aztecs deliver swift justice to the Totonac and Tlaxcala peoples. Pillaging and looting across the land, the enemy states of the Aztecs are put to ruin.

Gulf of Mexico

4. European return
In the years after Cortés's initial expedition, several Spanish forces land and attempt to succeed where he failed. They are defeated, but as other imperial nations and Old World diseases take hold, the Aztec Empire begins to struggle.

AZTEC EMPIRE

1. Rebuilding of Tenochtitlán
After the Spanish are beaten back and Cortés is killed, the Aztecs rebuild their capital city, making it more formidable to future enemy sieges. The captured conquistador weapons are put to good use as the civilization advances.

3. The trip south
Buoyed by their resistance to the Spanish and their new-found European technology, the Aztecs expand their empire south and eastward into Mayan territory and toward the Inca Empire.

North Pacific Ocean

more about life in the Aztec world and see it in less stereotypical terms.

Cowie: This is very difficult to say; it depends to a considerable degree upon whether the Aztecs were subsequently conquered by another Spanish expedition or whether they remained independent into the 19th century, when they would likely have become victims of a later wave of European imperialism. Either way, it is likely the negative images of human sacrifice would endure, assuming that at least some of the conquistadors survived to communicate them, but we might perhaps have greater respect for the Aztecs' military capability and realize the conquest was a close-run thing.

Battle of Cempoala
Cortés and his forces briefly leave Tenochtitlán to fight, and eventually defeat fellow Spaniard Diego Velázquez, an old enemy of Cortés. **April 1520**

La Noche Triste
The two forces assault the Aztecs but are driven back despite the death of Moctezuma. This escape from Tenochtitlán results in many Spanish deaths. **July 1520**

Tenochtitlán Falls
A combination of smallpox, horses, and Spanish steel defeat Tenochtitlán after a three-month siege as the population is routed. **August 1521**

Birth of Mexico City
Tenochtitlán is rebuilt as Mexico City, the new capital of New Spain. Cuauhetemoc serves as a puppet ruler before his execution. **1522**

Death of Cortés
Immediately wary of the Old World invaders, Moctezuma instructs a full-on attack on the Spanish. Surprised and overwhelmed, Cortés is killed and his forces scattered. **November 8, 1519**

Cortés Allies with Tlaxcala
The Spanish ally with the sworn enemy of the Aztecs, the Tlaxcala. They want their civilization to crumble as much as Cortés desires gold and riches. **July 1520**

Religious Changes
With Mexico still resisting invasion, the spread of Catholicism is halted while traditional Aztec religion and culture flourishes. **June 1525**

Spread of Smallpox
This Old World disease is brought over by the European raiders and becomes an epidemic, wiping out swathes of the Aztec population. **August 1520**

Further Expeditions
Further Spanish excursions, along with the introduction of Old World diseases, gradually wears down the civilization. **1640**

Death of Cortés
Hernán Cortés dies at the age of 62. The conqueror of the Aztecs, he is remembered as a great explorer but also as a man of greed. **1567**

New Technology
Using trial and error and interrogating Spanish prisoners, the Aztecs gain the knowledge of horse riding, making steel weapons and using guns. **January 1520**

Financial Effects on the Old World
Having no Aztec gold to speak of, Spain struggles financially and thus modernizes at a slower rate. **February 1520**

Destruction of Tlaxcala
As punishment for allying with the Spanish, the Tlaxcalans are completely massacred, ensuring they will never trouble the Aztecs again. **April 1520**

Cancellation of Pizarro Conquest
The planned occupation of Peru and the Inca Empire is canceled, as the Spanish cannot afford it. **1532**

Further Advancements
Having mastered steel, the Aztecs incorporate other Western technology into their military such as musket and cannon. **1781**

Fall of the Aztecs
After repeated Spanish invasions, continuing disease and even French and British involvement, the Aztecs fall. **1819**

© ILLUSTRATION BY IAN HINLEY

What if . . .

The Jacobite rising succeeded?

BRITAIN, 1745

NOTABLE NAMES:
- James Edward Stuart
- Charles Edward Stuart

IMPORTANT DATES:
April 16, 1746

What Really Happened...

The Jacobites—supporters of King James II of England/VII of Scotland—sought to restore the House of Stuart to the British throne. The Jacobites first arose in 1689, but the most famous uprising occurred in 1745 when James Edward Stuart's son, Charles Edward Stuart (also known as Bonnie Prince Charlie and the "Young Pretender"), attempted to snatch the throne from his father. While the Young Pretender was gaining support, the Jacobite army lacked it and James Stuart went home to Scotland.

On April 16, 1746, the Battle of Culloden occurred, where Bonnie Prince Charlie's army defeated the Jacobites, and, as a result, there was a crackdown among Scottish communities with many Jacobites being attacked or executed. Eventually, James died in 1766, and Charles passed in 1788 after the Jacobite cause had long fizzled out.

If the Jacobites had reached London, they would have needed French assistance to succeed. Bonnie Prince Charlie's forces only numbered 5,000 men, and even if they had defeated the British Army, they then had a city of 500,000 people to dominate. "However, the French were preparing to invade and planning on landing in Essex. So if Charlie gets to London and the French land, you have a potential Jacobite restoration," says Professor Szechi.

The Jacobites would have required constant French support, but they were fully behind the Young Pretender and were hopeful that a victory in London would knock the British out of the War of the Austrian Succession. It wouldn't have been all plain sailing for Charlie though, and King George II, who would have fled to Portsmouth, wasn't going to let go of the throne that easily. "The Hanoverians would have set up an alternative capital in Birmingham or Bristol, and England would have become the seat of a major war. There is a range of opinion that the Hanoverian regime would have collapsed if they had lost London. Its support was intrinsically brittle and there would have been widespread defections by people who would have been otherwise neutral. I think there would have

How would it be different?

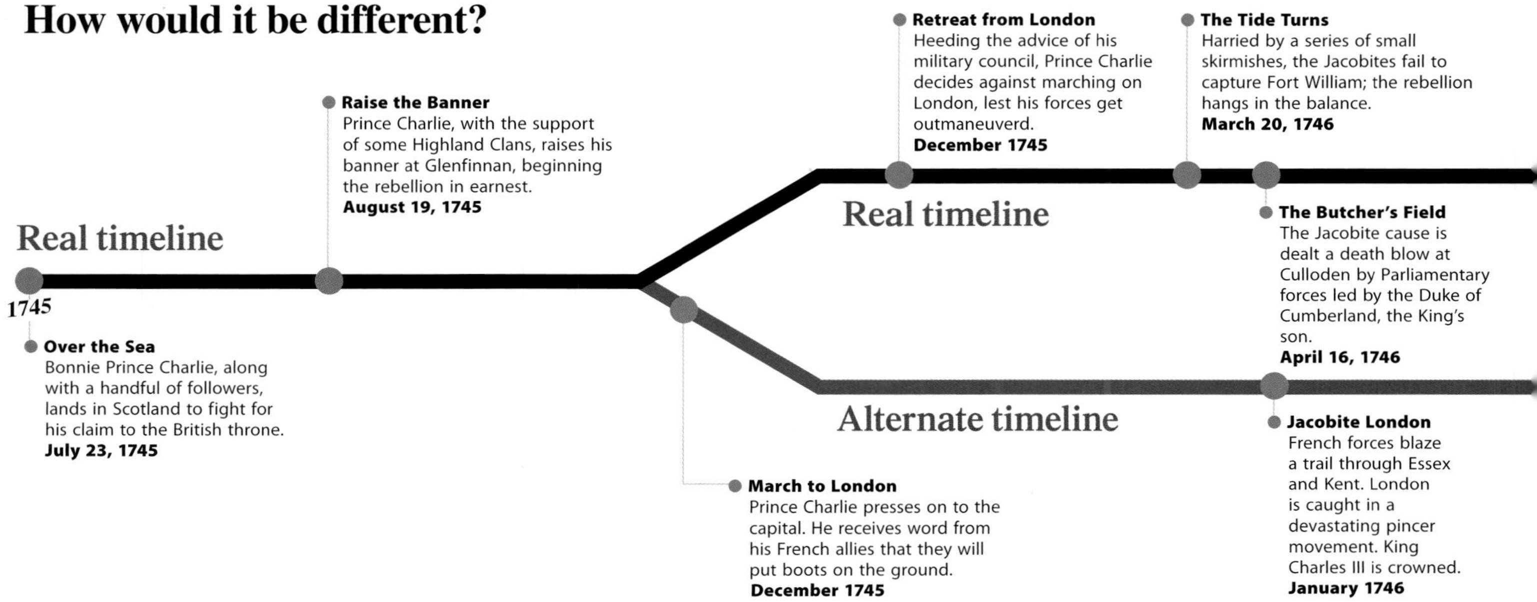

Real timeline
1745
Over the Sea
Bonnie Prince Charlie, along with a handful of followers, lands in Scotland to fight for his claim to the British throne.
July 23, 1745
Raise the Banner
Prince Charlie, with the support of some Highland Clans, raises his banner at Glenfinnan, beginning the rebellion in earnest.
August 19, 1745
Retreat from London
Heeding the advice of his military council, Prince Charlie decides against marching on London, lest his forces get outmaneuverd.
December 1745
The Tide Turns
Harried by a series of small skirmishes, the Jacobites fail to capture Fort William; the rebellion hangs in the balance.
March 20, 1746
Real timeline
The Butcher's Field
The Jacobite cause is dealt a death blow at Culloden by Parliamentary forces led by the Duke of Cumberland, the King's son.
April 16, 1746
Alternate timeline
March to London
Prince Charlie presses on to the capital. He receives word from his French allies that they will put boots on the ground.
December 1745
Jacobite London
French forces blaze a trail through Essex and Kent. London is caught in a devastating pincer movement. King Charles III is crowned.
January 1746

Not a real photo, has been altered.

PROFESSOR DANIEL SZECHI

Daniel Szechi took his first degree at the University of Sheffield and his PhD at the University of Oxford. He is currently professor of Early Modern History at the University of Manchester. He has published extensively on the history of Jacobitism and his book, *Britain's Lost Revolution?* (Manchester University Press) was published in 2015.

THE MARCH OF THE FORTY-FIVE

After a number of failed uprisings, the Jacobites rose once again in 1745. Led by Bonnie Prince Charlie, their objective was to initiate a Stuart restoration to the British throne. By December, the Jacobite army had reached as far south as Derby and faced a dilemma: press on to London or return north?

been full-scale civil war . . . It would have been very, very hard to say but Charlie and his supporters would have had the support of French regular troops so they could fight and defeat the British army in a straightforward face-off."

There's a Jacobite king on the throne and a strong Anglo-French alliance—international relations start to look a bit different. Firstly, Charlie, not being a religious man, maintains Protestantism in England and maybe would have even converted to Anglicanism himself. This accelerates religious toleration in the British Isles by about 100 years. Over in the New World, there are even bigger upshots: "The American Revolution was on the verge of collapse when the French intervened. The French saved America. No French intervention, no US. It would just have been a brief rebellion that the British government would have crushed." This in turn would have prevented a revolution in France as the people would have been satisfied with this new fruitful alliance with their neighbors over the Channel. This alternative timeline would have had profound effects on the rest of Europe too. "The combination of British naval power and French land power might have made for a more peaceful Europe. It would have been daunting for Prussia, Austria, or Spain to take on the combination." Conversely, would this new Anglo-French alliance have had

aggressive tendencies itself? "It's possible Britain and France could have ploughed eastward, but the French didn't have territorial ambitions against the Austrians. They just wanted to make sure they didn't become powerful enough to threaten the eastern frontier of France."

If the March of the Forty-Five had succeeded and held off an inevitable Hanoverian counter-attack, it would have had a profound outcome. No Napoleonic Wars and no US are two potentially huge changes, and going into the 20th century, we may have seen a very different, and potentially more peaceful, world.

Blood in the Glens
The government forces brutally sack the highlands, earning Cumberland the nickname 'Butcher'. Highland culture and dress are suppressed. **1746**

The Drunk Pretender
Charles flees to Europe and never makes another attempt for the throne. He grows drunk and bitter in his old age. **1746-1788**

American Revolutionary War
Fighting against British repression, the Thirteen Colonies, aided by the French and Spanish, gain their independence as the United States of America. **April 19, 1775**

Britain vs France
After the abolition of the French monarchy, Napoleon becomes Emperor and plunges Europe into a bloody series of conflicts. **1803-1815**

Statue of Liberty
A gift of solidarity from France, the statue is constructed in Manhattan and symbolizes America's freedom from Great Britain. **1886**

Major Border Changes
Without Britain, the Dutch and Austrians are defeated in the War of the Austrian Succession against France, Prussia, and Spain. **July 1746**

American Revolution Crushed
With French aid, the Thirteen Colonies are soon crushed. The Redcoats aren't kind to the rebels and enact even harsher constraints than before. **February 1776**

Europe at Peace
Napoleon remains just a revolutionary idealist. Austria, the Holy Roman Empire, and Prussia never pluck up the courage to strike against the Anglo-French alliance. **April 1792**

Victoria Statue Commissioned
To celebrate their ongoing alliance, the French begin work on the Queen Victoria statue that will stand in New York. **1877**

Second Civil War
The Jacobites initially struggle to keep order. With French support, Charles III convincingly beats down any resistance as George II is executed. **February 1746**

Long-Term Alliance
Britain and France become the strongest military bloc in the world on both land and sea and are universally feared. **18th Century**

No French Revolution
A much healthier and a happier population means Louis XVI and Marie Antoinette rule on under an extended and rejuvenated House of Bourbon. **January 1793**

Germany Backs Down
After a fair amount of saber rattling, Germany decides against challenging the overwhelming military power of the Anglo-French Alliance. **1914**

© THINKSTOCK

What if...
The Spanish Armada was victorious?

ENGLAND, 1588

NOTABLE NAMES:
- King Philip II of Spain
- Queen Elizabeth I of England

IMPORTANT DATES:
May 28, 1588
August 8, 1588

What Really Happened...

After years of hostility between England and Spain, King Philip II of Spain established the largest fleet in European history at the time. Known as the "Invincible Armada," the fleet consisted of 130 ships and 25,000 men with the intention of picking up 30,000 more in Belgium on its route to invade England, dethrone Queen Elizabeth I, and reimpose a Catholic monarchy. The Armada set sail on May 28, 1588.

However, the attack didn't go to plan and the fleet wasn't even able to reach Belgium, let alone England. Between poor strategy and leadership, bad weather, and faster English ships that eventually defeated them in the Battle of Gravelines on August 8, 1588, the Armada retreated to Spain in defeat. By the time they arrived home, nearly half of the ships had been lost.

This massive Spanish upset was the pinnacle of Queen Elizabeth I's reign, signified England's superiority of the seas, solidified Protestantism in the country, and led to the rise of the British Empire.

What if the Spanish Armada had been victorious?
Then I don't see why they shouldn't have been able to land at Margate and make it to London marching along the south bank of the Thames and perhaps getting to Kingston where there's a bridge and then turning back, marching into London and taking the capital. It had no walls worth speaking of and [the Duke of] Parma would have had a siege train. I think once they got ashore, the Spanish would have been irresistible.

So if the Spanish had played their hand differently they could have landed on British soil? Yes. Obviously it's always dangerous to speculate with what-ifs. What we need to do is ask ourselves two questions: the first is a minimal re-write . . . you can change little things. Second, you have to ask yourself in the end, even if all these changes were made, whether the long-term picture would have been different. What you might call a 'second order counterfactual.' The English are defeated, but what happens in the long term?

I think we have some pretty good indications. It was thought the Spanish would land in Essex, where the big army is, and neglect Kent, which is in fact the spot where Parma is going to land. You can't have your troops everywhere and the English make a guess—and it's wrong. In 1592, the Duke of Parma had a similarly difficult operation to understand and that is to get his troops in to France and relieve the town of Rouen,

which is about 80 miles away. They do it in seven days against a hostile enemy.

I do have a parallel for you: the Germans at D-Day had a very similar calculation to Elizabeth Tudor. That is to say, do you as Rommel wanted, spread the troops evenly out along the shore. Or do you as Von Rundstedt, spread a few troops along the shore and have a main reserve?

The Spanish Army of Flanders was on the other side of the Channel—what was the plan to get it to England? Here's the re-write, you see. The fleet would have come up from Spain, somehow communicate to Parma [the head of the Spanish army] that it's on its way so that Parma's troops are already in their little boats. They know the Dutch [England's ally] will be waiting so there are four very powerful 'galleasses' [battleships]. These had done very well in previous operations—they had 50 guns so were as powerful as Queen Elizabeth's galleon. The idea is that these galleasses, which are very shallow draft, go right in and bring Parma's fleet out. The Dutch can't do anything to stop it because none of their ships are armed in a way that could possibly stop the galleases doing their job. Once you get them into the middle of the Armada, it sails across and the galleasses do the same thing on the Kent shore, preventing anything from intercepting the landing craft.

INTERVIEW WITH... GEOFFREY PARKER

The award-winning professor of history and an associate of the Mershon Center at The Ohio State University has written about the social, political, and military history of early modern Europe. His best-known books are *The Military Revolution* and *The Grand Strategy of Philip II*. His new biography of Philip II, called *Imprudent King*, is available online.

The Army of Flanders Philip II had mustered was large, highly trained, and had a fearsome reputation. Could this army have prevailed on British soil? I don't think there's any doubt that, man for man, the Spanish army is superior. The one thing it doesn't have is cavalry. But the English don't have much cavalry either and however well trained the English are, if they're not superior man-for-man, 28,000 will overwhelm 7,000. The English have no field artillery, no fortifications south of the Thames. Even London's walls are primitive.

30 years before there is a rebellion by someone called Thomas Wyatt against Philip II which starts in Kent. Wyatt and his troops march exactly the route Parma would have taken. They cross the Thames at Kingston and they get right up to the walls of London. The only reason why they stop is that they have no artillery and in the end the rebellion crumbles. But Parma would have had a siege train of about 20 guns—London's walls would have come crashing down.

Philip II's ideal goal was to take Westminster with Elizabeth and the Parliament in it. Was this likely? I think we're getting to fantasy land. As soon as the Armada lands, the English Catholics would be up and one of them would have murdered her. I don't think they would capture Elizabeth, there would be an assassination. Then you have a Tudor state like a headless chicken.

Could Philip II have mustered support from the natives if his army had landed? They themselves [the Spaniards] assume nothing. They assume there will be no Catholic uprising or, if there is a Catholic uprising, it will be in the Northwest, not as they would need it to be in the South and the East. Protestantism is a new religion and even Elizabeth goes to mass in 1559 until she's absolutely sure she has peace with France, that her sister's war with France has been extinguished, so she still pretends to be Catholic.

I think there are people who would like to go back to being Catholic but in terms of a fifth column, in terms of there being a resistance similar to the one in June 1944 in Normandy, I don't think there would have been enough supporters of the invasion to make a difference.

The Duke of Parma had a history of bribing commanders to give up their strongholds. Would many towns in England have done the same? We do know some of the Anglo-Irish commanders in the Netherlands are bribed. Is that possible in England? Why not? The Anglo-Irish commanders in the Netherlands are all

"London's walls would have come crashing down"

The Spanish Armada could have sailed up the Thames and taken London by force

Attack and defense
How the invading and defending forces matched up

English defense

Spanish Armada

| 130 ships | 200 ships | 28,000 soldiers | 7,000 soldiers | 2,500 guns | 1,200 guns |

"They're terrible men [. . .] They're going to rape your women, flog you, then force you to go back to mass"

handpicked by Elizabeth. If she chose people who were ideologically unsound as allies, she might well have made the same mistake back in England. We do know the third-in-command, a man called Roger Williams, had spent three years fighting with the Spaniards himself. He was an admirer of the Spaniards and who's to tell whether he might have [defected] if push came to shove, especially if [Elizabeth] is dead. I mean, who are you fighting for? She has no heir—her heir was Mary, Queen of Scots and she had her executed the year before the Armada arrived. So it's hard to see who would have served as the rallying point. Would you really want to fight for James VI of Scotland? I don't think so. But again, Philip and Parma can't count on it—they reckon overwhelming force will do the job.

Elizabeth gave her famous 'Tilbury' speech during the Spanish offensive. To what extent did a successful defense of Britain galvanize her reign? The first written account of it is 1623, we don't hear about it until then and then someone says "I remember, when I was a boy . . ." How do we know she made that speech and what she said? Cate Blanchett's version is about as likely as the one recorded by Lionel Sharp in 1623!

We're thinking in 20th-century terms. A speech like Churchill's speech in the 1940s: "We will fight them on the beaches [. . .] we will never surrender." That's broadcast by radio, but Elizabeth doesn't have radio. What you do have is the pulpits. What the pulpits insist is that when these Catholics come, you're going to be very sorry: they're terrible men, they're bringing Jesuits with them, they're bringing whips. They're going to rape your women, flog you, then force you to go back to mass. So I think if you're looking for something that galvanizes resistance, it would be the religious card, not the political card.

How much of a knock-on effect do you think this would have had on the following century of Britain's history? I don't think the Gunpowder Plot would have happened, because if Elizabeth gives up some

---

How would it be different?

Real timeline

1558

● **Elizabeth Crowned**
England's Catholic queen, Mary I, wife of Spanish King Philip II, dies. Her successor is Elizabeth I, who denounces the faith in favor of Protestantism in 1559. Devout Catholic Philip II is furious.
1558

● **New Calendar**
The ancient (and inaccurate) Julian calendar is thrown out and the new Gregorian calendar is introduced in several European countries. Being a Catholic innovation, Protestant England refuses to adopt it until 1752, putting its dates out by 11 days.
1582

● **Mary Executed**
Elizabeth lights the touch paper of war with Spain when she has her Catholic cousin, Mary, Queen of Scots, beheaded. Philip makes plans to invade England and overthrow the Protestant regime.
1587

● **The Fleet Sets Sail**
A fleet of 130 ships sets sail from Lisbon. On board are 20,000 soldiers and 2,500 guns, with a siege train to take down London's walls. The Army of Flanders, numbering nearly 30,000, awaits the Armada in the Netherlands.
May 28, 1588

Real timeline

Alternate timeline

● **Attack on Plymouth Harbor**
Pressing the obvious advantage, the Spanish Armada sails into Plymouth Harbor and rains hell down upon a large portion of the English fleet. Anchored in harbor and the tide against them, many English ships are destroyed and scattered, leaving the Navy crippled.
July 19, 1588

The battle with the Spanish Armada claimed thousands of lives, more from storms than gunfire

concessions to Catholicism, there's no reason for the Catholics to hate James VI.

But we're concentrating on one side. We also have to consider that Philip II is still Philip II. His son Philip III is the child of Philip and his niece. There are already a large number of what we would call incestuous unions [in the family]. So Philip II dies and Philip III is left, a weak leader. His grandchildren will eventually lose Spain and the dynasty dies out in the 17th century. Even if Spain wins, they're going to have more to lose, they can't defend what they have. Having England as

a satellite and regaining the Netherlands—yes, in the short term, a great success. But the Hapsburgs are still Hapsburgs, they will breed and marry with each other. You can't change that and I think in the long term that England, if it had remained independent, if the Tudor dynasty had survived, you still get James VI, so you get reconciliation with Spain. Philip II remains a Hapsburg so his son will not have the skill to keep the empire together. However successful the Armada is, you still get Philip III who will lose whatever gains his father would have made.

Peace Negotiations
The same day the Armada sails, English ambassador Valentine Dale meets with Spanish negotiators in Warburg. Unknown to England, Spain has already chosen war and is using the negotiations to distract Elizabeth. **May 28, 1588**

The Armada is Sighted
Bad weather works in England's favor for the first and not the last time during the attempted Spanish invasion. It delays the Armada and forces several ships to return to Spain. The rest of the fleet is finally sighted off Cornwall in Southwest England.
July 19, 1588

The tide turns
While the Armada takes harbor on the French coast, the English fleet sends eight fire ships, filled with explosive pitch and gunpowder, into the anchored Spanish fleet, scattering them. **28 July 1588**

Battle of Gravelines
The English fleet returns with a larger naval force and decisively beats the Spanish at Gravelines, northern France.
August 8, 1588

Negotiations Abandoned
News of the Armada's approach reaches England and peace negotiations are called off. Elizabeth's fleet is poorly prepared and sorely outgunned. The knowledge that the powerful Army of Flanders is on the other side of the Channel does little to allay England's concerns. **July 16, 1588**

First Blood
Under direct orders from Philip II, the Spanish fleet forsakes an opportunity to attack part of the English fleet while it is anchored in Plymouth Harbor. Instead, the Armada faces Francis Drake's weaker but faster ships—this results in a stalemate.
July 21, 1588

Back to Sea
Another engagement with the English fleet further east of Plymouth, off Portland, is intended to gain the Armada a temporary harbor between the Isle of Wight and England. But a successful defense forces it back out to sea: instead, it heads for Calais. **July 23, 1588**

Safe Haven
Flush with its first success, the Armada moves into the Solent where it's able to create a safe harbor between the Isle of Wight and England.
July 23, 1588

Escort
Using a small but powerful part of its fleet, the galleasses, the Spanish sail to the Netherlands, where the Army of Flanders awaits in barges. They escort the remaining men across the Channel. **August 9, 1588**

Marching In
The Army of Flanders makes landfall in Kent and begins an irresistible march through the English countryside, capturing and pillaging towns as they go. London is only a week away.
August 10, 1588

Elizabeth I Assassinated
With news of the Spanish reaching London, the Catholics begin to revolt. Elizabeth's fate is sealed regardless, but whether for the sake of revenge or to make sure she has her comeuppance for Catholic repression, she is assassinated. **August 11, 1588**

England Beaten
Spain reaches London. With a flotilla of Spanish ships on the Thames, the Duke of Parma's siege train makes short work of London's ancient walls and fortifications. The city falls and the battle is won.
August 17, 1588

What if...

Britain won the War of Independence?

NORTH AMERICA, 1775-1783

NOTABLE NAMES:
• George Washington

IMPORTANT DATES:
April 18, 1775
July 4, 1775
September 3, 1783

What Really Happened...

Before the American Revolution began, tensions between the 13 colonies and Britain were mounting for more than a decade. A group of delegates met in September 1774 to voice their grievances against the British and arranged to meet again in May to consider further action. But on April 18, 1775, violence broke out when British troops marched from Boston to Concord, Massachusetts, and clashed with colonial militiamen. The American Revolution had begun.

June 17, 1775, marked the official first battle between British forces and the Continental Army, with George Washington as its commander-in-chief. By June 1776, the war was in full swing and on July 4, 1776, a "Committee of Five" appointed by the Continental Congress drafted and signed the Declaration of Independence.

The war continued for years until finally, on September 3, 1783, Britain formally recognized America's independence and signed the Treaty of Paris, officially ending the American Revolutionary War.

What if Britain had won the American War of Independence?

Stephen Conway: The American colonies would have remained in the British Empire, at least for the time being. Perhaps the colonies would have reconciled themselves to a restoration of British control and gradually have moved towards greater home rule and eventual independence in the same manner as many countries in the later British Commonwealth. But it's equally likely that the rebellion might have flared up again in a few years, or the British government might have taken the view that it was far too expensive to maintain a large army of occupation in the conquered colonies and de facto independence would have been granted.

Is it likely that victory for Britain would have merely delayed American independence? Or could the US still be part of the Commonwealth today, like Canada?

Robert Allison: Either one is possible. [Benjamin] Franklin thought that independence would come naturally; he anticipated something like the British Commonwealth. He thought it would be impossible, when the American population was far greater than the population of England, for the government of America to continue to be administered in London.

John Ferling: Franklin thought America's population would surpass that of Great Britain by the middle of the 19th century, and he based his calculation on natural increase alone. When immigration is factored in, America was certain to have had a far larger population by 1850. I don't see how London could have avoided extending far greater autonomy to the Americans [over] the course of the 19th century.

What might have become of the 13 colonies post-war had Britain been victorious, as well as revolutionary leaders like George Washington?

SC: The leaders of the rebellion might well have been treated in the same manner as the leaders of the rebellion of 1745-6 in Scotland, who were executed for treason.

JF: If Franklin is to be believed, the British public was enraged toward the colonists at the time the war broke out; years of war only stoked those passions. Had the rebellion been crushed, retribution would have been the order of the day. Some leaders would have been executed, some imprisoned for long terms, and the colonists likely would have had to pay fines or faced some sort of economic punishment.

And what do you think would have happened to the rest of America—beyond the 13 colonies?

JF: The French Revolution might have been America's opening for attempting once again to gain independence. But assuming that had not been the case, I think London would have continued pushing towards the west. It almost certainly would have taken the British longer to reach the Pacific than it took the United States. British merchants looked askance at settlements beyond the Appalachian barrier, but Britain would have gotten there eventually.

"I don't see how London could have avoided extending far greater autonomy"

INTERVIEWS WITH...
PROF. STEPHEN CONWAY

Stephen Conway is a professor of history in the History department at University College London. His teaching focuses on 18th-century British and colonial American history and his publications include *The British Isles and the War of American Independence* (2000) and *A Short History of the American Revolutionary War* (2013).

PROF. EMERITUS JOHN FERLING

A specialist in early American history, John Ferling has written several books around this subject area, such as *Struggle for a Continent: The Wars of Early America* (1993) and *Almost a Miracle: The American Victory in the War of Independence* (2007).

PROF. ROBERT ALLISON

Robert Allison has taught American history at Suffolk University in Boston, Massachusetts , since 1992, when he earned his doctorate at Harvard University. He chairs Suffolk's History department and also teaches history at the Harvard Extension School. His books include *The American Revolution: A Concise History* (2011) and *The Boston Tea Party* (2007).

The first cornerstone of the White House was laid in 1792—nine years after the War of Independence ended

Not a real photo, has been altered.

RA: Spain claimed the territory west of the Mississippi [River], but hardly controlled it. Britain probably would have kept the Native Americans of the Ohio Valley and the territory that is now Alabama and Mississippi, as they were trading partners. This might have stymied the spread of American settlers to the west. Then again, it might not have, as the Royal Proclamation of 1763 had not done so.

The real impetus for American settlement of the Great Plains—the area between the Mississippi River and the Rocky Mountains, much of it wrested from Mexico in the [mid-19th century]—was to connect the east coast with the west. In the 1840s the United States and Britain nearly went to war over what is today British Columbia [in Canada]; '54°-40 or Fight' was James K. Polk's campaign slogan in 1844 [before he became the 11th US president]. Britain, with its naval superiority, would have controlled the American west coast.

Spain would have been squeezed out. It's not clear if Mexico or the other Latin American countries would have developed in the same way had there not been an independent United States in North America.

What benefits—or disadvantages—might victory have brought Britain?

SC: The benefits, if such they were, would have taken the form of greater economic control of the colonies, and especially of their overseas trade, which was subject to the restrictions of the 17th-century English Navigation Acts. But that advantage was unlikely to have been very much greater than the British reaped from defeat. The independent United States remained in a semi-colonial economic relationship with Britain for many years after 1783, consuming vast quantities of British manufactured goods and sending to Britain enormous quantities of raw materials. Had the British won the war, they would have been burdened by the costs of governing and defending America, so we can say that defeat left Britain with many of the benefits but few of the costs of empire.

JF: A great challenge would have been to somehow win back the hearts of the colonists. It would not have been easy. A victorious America largely hated the British for a century after the Revolution. Hatred would have lingered longer and burned more deeply in a defeated America.

The Battle of Nassau was an American naval assault on the then British-ruled island in the Bahamas that took place in March 1776

How might nations, other than Britain and the US, have been affected if the war had gone the other way?

RA: France, Spain, and Native Americans [would have been] most notably [affected]. France supported the Americans, but primarily as a way to weaken Britain and protect France's West Indian colonies. Would the French Revolution have happened without the successful example of the American Revolution—or the huge debt France incurred by [participating in] it? Granted, France was reeling from an ineffective government overladen with aristocracy and political inefficiency, and the defeat in the Seven Years' War. Spain was fortifying its Mexican borders in the 1770s and 1780s; its main interest in the war in America was to get back Gibraltar.

The Native Americans were the big losers in the war though. The British were their allies, though allies the British sold out when it served their interests. I'm not singling out the British for doing this, as most nations tend to seek their own self-interest. The British had proposed an Indian buffer state in the Ohio Valley, and they were trading partners with the Iroquois, Creek, and Cherokee tribes—one reason they supported the British rather than the Americans.

Could a one-nation unification with Canada have been on the cards for North America?

SC: The Americans tried to conquer Canada in 1775, and wanted it ceded to the United States in the peace negotiations of 1782-3. But the British were determined to keep Canada, which was now increasingly gaining the Protestant population British governments had wanted since 1763, thanks to the exodus of American loyalists from the US. If America had lost, then the loyalists may have stayed in the old British colonies, leaving Canada overwhelmingly francophone and Catholic, in which case it would have remained very different from the rest of the mainland British colonies.

JF: I think Britain would have opposed unification, at least for a very long time after it crushed the American rebellion. During the Seven Years' War it had sought to keep the 13 colonies from unifying under one government, as Franklin had proposed in his Albany Plan of Union. Had it defeated the colonists in the Revolutionary War, Britain might have divided some colonies to keep them weak. Furthermore, the changes it sought to impose in Massachusetts' government in the Coercive Acts in 1775 probably would have been the rule of thumb in every colony.

How would it be different?

Britain Rejects Peace
In the summer of 1775, King George III ignores the Second Continental Congress's Olive Branch Petition, and the war continues apace. In May 1776, King Louis XVI of France solves the Americans' munitions problem by granting a huge donation. Soon after, the US Declaration of Independence is voted in on July 4, 1776. **1775-1776**

Continental Congress Held
The First Continental Congress is formed and they agree to oppose the Intolerable Acts. From early on there's a sense that conflict is both inevitable and imminent. **1774**

Real timeline

Real timeline

1774

Alternate timeline

Intolerable Acts Passed
The Intolerable, or Coercive, Acts are passed by the British government in early-1774 in response to the perceived lawlessness of the Boston Tea Party—a colonial uprising many years in the making. **1774**

War Begins
The first shots are fired in the war, with the opening conflict at Lexington involving local Massachusetts militia (the formation of which had been suggested by the First Continental Congress in 1774) and British forces. **April 19, 1775**

Battle of Bunker Hill
In this major battle, Patriot troops bravely resist a repeated British assault, only to be eventually worn down by the sheer numbers and persistence of the enemy—plus a lack of ammunition. The British lose massive numbers but prevail to take Bunker Hill. **June 17, 1775**

Do you think Australia would have still been developed as a penal colony if the 13 American colonies had remained under British control?

SC: New South Wales in Australia was established as a penal colony, but if the North American colonies had remained British, there would have been less incentive to ship convicts so far. America was the cheaper option by a long way. Incidentally, the idea of imprisonment and reformation of convicts would have suffered a blow, as it was the end of transportation to the American colonies that provided an opportunity for reformers who argued that criminals should be incarcerated and improved, rather than executed or exported. More broadly, we can say that the loss of America saw a shift in British imperial focus towards the East—especially Asia. This so-called 'swing to the East' has perhaps been exaggerated, but there was undoubtedly a recalibration of imperial w. That said, expansion in India had already started, and would probably have continued, though not perhaps at the same pace.

RA: Probably. Britain's real colonial interests in the 1770s were not America, but India, Jamaica, and Barbados. And so Britain wanted control of sea routes to India, and also direct trade with China. Australia would be useful to both.

If Britain had retained control of America, how might this have impacted 20th-century events like WWI?

SC: If we assume that the British had won the war, and the colonies had remained subject to the British crown, they would no doubt have entered World War I in the same manner as the British Dominions in 1914. Whether that would have tilted the balance in favor of the Allies and against Germany/Austria-Hungary is impossible to say; maybe a still-dependent America would not have industrialized so quickly and its population would have been smaller, with the result that the addition of strength was nowhere near as great as it was in 1917-18 [when they actually entered WWI].

JF: My understanding is that Britain made a concerted effort to smooth relations with the US beginning around 1890, which proved helpful during World War I. How that war would have been seen in an America that was tied to Britain as colonies or in a Commonwealth arrangement is difficult to know. Canada did not need any prodding to back London in 1914. However, there was a deep strain of resentment in America in 1776 (one can find it in Thomas Paine and Benjamin Franklin) at the colonies having been dragged repeatedly into that 'old rotten state's plundering wars' (Franklin). Such a sentiment might only have hardened over time and, as for many in Ireland, a European war might have been the spark for many Americans to rise up in favor of breaking away from Britain.

Canada Canada's French Catholic influence remained strong and France threatened Britain with war, but lack of support and finance prevented this. Lower Canada, Upper Canada, and most of America would likely unite into one legislative state.

The 13 British colonies A heavy British military presence would have been necessary in the 13 colonies in order to retain control. The situation would have possibly resembled Northern Ireland, with violence and unrest—both political and social—never far away.

Gun control After defeating the rebels, American colonists would no longer be permitted to carry firearms, in an effort to try and 'de-claw' any separatist movements in areas like Boston and New England.

Native Americans Native Americans would receive generous terms for allowing western expansion through their territory because of the overstretched British troops being unable to guard the east and conquer the west at the same time. Large areas of America remain firmly in tribal control well into the late-19th century.

Southern states The Southern colonies become more and more difficult to control due to the British abolition of slavery in 1833. Southern cotton lords fear for their livelihoods if their workforce is set free. Britain is forced to commit ever more troops and resources to guard its American colonies as the Southern states become more militant.

Washington for the Win
George Washington carries out a surprise attack on the British contingency at Trenton, NJ. The Patriots claim a decisive victory, boosting morale. **1776**

British Surrender
The British army surrenders at Yorktown on October 19, 1781. In February of the following year, the British government decides to abandon the war. **1781-1782**

Another War
The US declares war on Britain, reopening the conflict. The prior conflict has overshadowed the 1812 War, but "The Star-Spangled Banner" anthem dates from this time. **1812-1815**

US Enters WWI
Having preferred a policy of neutrality, and with concern for trade with Britain in mind, America enters WWI, and US soldiers fight alongside the Brits. **April 1917**

Battle of Long Island
Sir William Howe, C-in-C of British forces, claims victory at Long Island. The Americans try to escape to Manhattan, but the British cut them off. George Washington is killed. **August 27, 1776**

Britain Faces New Enemy
Support for America grows in Europe, particularly in France, and on July 10, 1778 France declares war on Britain. The French navy plays a key role. **1777-1778**

Penal Colonies
The 13 American colonies along the Atlantic coast serve as the main destination for UK transportation. Far fewer convicts are sent to Australia. **1790**

France Invades Spain
King Louis XVIII, angered by what was seen as Spain's gross betrayal in selling 'French' Louisiana, orders the invasion of Spain, but retreats when Britain weighs in. **1823**

American Population Booms
Controlled immigration into British North America has gradually increased, with transportation of criminals to both America and Australia ending in 1868. **1868**

Anglo-American Agreement
This pact officially ends the war. Patriot supporters who don't flee are imprisoned or hung, including key leaders like John Adams and Benjamin Franklin. Britain goes on to cement her hold of the colonies. **1776**

Louisiana Purchase
With France effectively bankrupted by its support for the American Revolutionary War, Spain is courted by the British government and persuaded to release Louisiana. Britain purchases the territory at a discount. **1803**

Act of Union
Lower Canada, Upper Canada, and the American colonies are united into British North America. The British government appeases the French by granting trade with the regions that France had ceded. **1840-1867**

What if...

Napoleon won the Battle of Waterloo?

WATERLOO, JUNE 18-19, 1815

NOTABLE NAMES:
• Napoleon Bonaparte

IMPORTANT DATES:
March 20, 1815
June 18, 1815
June 22, 1815

What Really Happened...

Napoleon Bonaparte was a French soldier who climbed the military ranks, proving himself to be a skilled and bold leader. In 1799, he gained political power, then in 1804 he crowned himself as the emperor of France. He went on to conquer much of Europe through the Napoleonic Wars, but after a series of defeats, he abdicated his throne on April 6, 1814, and was exiled.

Not long after, he escaped and returned to Paris on March 20, 1815. The king, Louis XVIII, fled and Napoleon began his Hundred Days campaign, raising a new army and preparing to fight his enemies—the Austrians, British, Prussians, and Russians.

On June 18, 1815, the Battle of Waterloo began, but Napoleon made the crucial mistake of waiting to attack the British army. This decision allowed Prussian troops more time to join. Ultimately, the French lost 40,000 men, while the British and Prussian forces lost 22,000. Napoleon's defeat at Waterloo marked the end of his decorated military career, and he abdicated the throne for the second time on June 22, 1815. He was then exiled in October to a remote island and died on May 5, 1821.

What would have happened if Napoleon had won the Battle of Waterloo?

Alan Forrest: He would certainly have taken Brussels and he might have tried to advance toward the boundary of the Rhine and Schelt. But there was no possibility of long-term success. He would surely have gone on to lose within weeks or months, because although the British, Dutch, Belgians, and Prussians were involved at Waterloo, neither the Austrians nor the Russians were, and they had armies of 150,000 to 200,000 waiting in the wings. In particular, the Tsar wanted Napoleon destroyed: he didn't believe Europe could remain at peace if Napoleon remained at large.

Mark Adkin: I wouldn't have thought [that Napoleon would have enjoyed success for] more than a few weeks. If he had won the battle, Wellington would have withdrawn what was left of his army and Napoleon would have had to hurry back to Paris. The Allies would have waited until the Austrians and Russians had arrived and the British and Prussians had recovered, then would have teamed up together. Napoleon wouldn't have had much chance at all.

Why did Napoleon lose at Waterloo?

MA: Napoleon had a big problem because he was surrounded by various countries that were desperate to get rid of him. There were four main threats once he established himself back in Paris: The Anglo-Dutch Army under Wellington in Belgium, the Prussians under Blücher in Germany, the Russians under Barclay De Tolly, and the Austrians under Schwarzenberg. That's nearly [a] half million men under arms and they all planned to converge on Paris. The only way he could possibly win was to make the maximum use of the time it was going to take Russians and the Austrians and so on to get there. While they were marching, he had to deal with the others, in particular Wellington and Blücher. He wanted to defeat the Prussians at Ligny, while Wellington was held off by a smaller force. Once the Prussians were defeated, he could turn the combined strength on Wellington. He succeeded partially at Ligny—his strategy worked and he split the two Allies, turned on the Prussians and defeated them, but he didn't crush them. He let them withdraw and recover. That was a mistake. Napoleon allowed them to withdraw north instead of east, and by withdrawing north they were able to turn and then rejoin Wellington's forces.

AF: Napoleon had no possibility of finding large numbers of additional soldiers because he was now reliant on the French population alone, and while he was on Elba, France had abolished conscription. As long as the Allies could unite their forces against him, he was hopelessly outnumbered, and his failure to drive home his advantage after Ligny proved to be a fatal mistake.

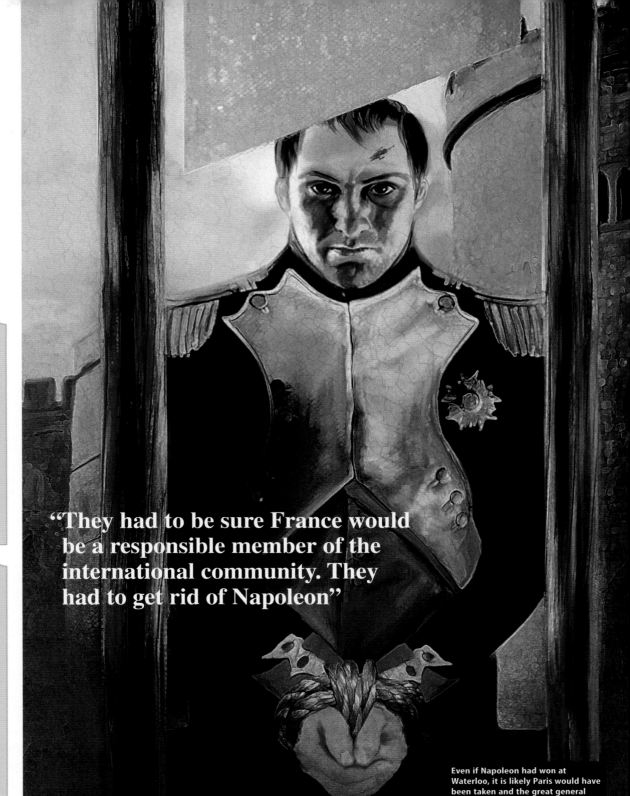

INTERVIEWS WITH...
ALAN FORREST

Alan Forrest is emeritus professor of modern history at the University of York. He has written widely on French revolutionary and Napoleonic history. His books include *Napoleon's Men: The Soldiers of the Revolution and Empire*, and a biography simply called *Napoleon*. He is currently working on a three-volume Cambridge History of the Napoleonic Wars.

MARK ADKIN

Mark Adkin is a military historian who took up writing after serving in the British Army for 18 years and over ten years working in the Colonial Service in the Pacific. He is the author of *The Waterloo Companion: The Complete Guide to World's Most Famous Land Battle*, and has more recently written *The Western Front Companion*. He also wrote *The Sharpe Companion*, which placed Bernard Cornwell's *Sharpe* novels in historical content.

"They had to be sure France would be a responsible member of the international community. They had to get rid of Napoleon"

Even if Napoleon had won at Waterloo, it is likely Paris would have been taken and the great general would have been executed

So if Napoleon had stopped the Prussians at Ligny, he would have defeated the British at Waterloo?

MA: Wellington knew the Prussians were coming; he had been promised that they were coming, which is the actual reason why he stood at Waterloo and defended that bridge. If he knew the Prussians were not coming, then he would probably have withdrawn until he could join the Prussians and therefore the battle would not have taken place, not there anyway. So the crucial thing is the Prussians and their arrival clinched it [the battle].

Did the people of France support Napoleon's return from Elba?

AF: The most important thing to remember is that the French people were war-weary in 1815; they wanted peace above all else and few believed Napoleon could deliver that. On the other hand, there was no enthusiasm for the Bourbons and certainly no desire to go back to the Anción Regime. The fear was that the Bourbons would try to restore the kind of aristocratic and clerical authority that had existed previously.

The armies at Waterloo

French	British	Prussian
Commander	**Commander**	**Commander**
Napoleon Bonaparte	Duke of Wellington	Field Marshal Von Blücher
Troops	**Troops**	**Troops**
55,000	56,000	49,000
Guns	**Guns**	**Guns**
256	156	134
Cavalry	**Cavalry**	**Cavalry**
14,000	11,000	19,800

> "Most of the old soldiers were tremendously loyal to Napoleon [. . .] he gave them good pay"

Napoleon had surrounded himself with luxury and riches at the height of the empire, but when he returned from Elba in 1815 he sought to present himself as the little corporal of the army who had risen through talent to be its commander, but who remained essentially a man of the people, true to the ideals of the Revolution of 1789. This proved a clever tactic.

MA: Most of the old soldiers were tremendously loyal to Napoleon. Napoleon had raised the standing of the ordinary French soldier during all those campaigns. He was extremely generous and gave them good pay. When he came back from Elba, I think thousands of these men, who had been thrown out of the army by the Bourbons coming back, had nothing and were no longer the number-one citizens like they used to be, so they rejoined Napoleon in their thousands.

If he abandoned his imperial ambitions, could Napoleon have negotiated to stay in power in France rather than the Allies restoring the Bourbons again?

MA: He tried to at the beginning, after escaping from Elba. He tried to convince the European powers he wanted to avoid war and that he renounced all claims to Belgium, Holland, Germany and Poland. He was unsuccessful, of course.

AF: This was never realistic. Russia wouldn't allow it and I'm not sure that Britain would, either. Britain did, however, want France to remain a viable European power since it was an important part of the balance of power structure on which peace depended. Britain was aware of the possibility of a rampant nationalistic Prussia and was very aware of the threat posed by Russia, especially in the Balkans and the eastern Mediterranean. Britain particularly needed to maintain lines of communication with India. Remember that Britain was an emerging global power in 1815 and that the Russians were aware of that. So they needed to protect France's position, but that also meant that they had to be sure France would be a responsible member of the international community. For that reason they had

How would it be different?

Real timeline

1813

Battle of Leipzig
Napoleon is decisively beaten in battle for the first time by a coalition including troops from Russia, Prussia, Austria, and Sweden. He is forced to return to France but the coalition continues to pursue him.
October 16, 1813

Napoleon Abdicates
After being defeated by the Allies of the Sixth Coalition, Napoleon is exiled to the island of Elba. The pre-revolutionary Bourbon monarchy is restored and Louis XVIII becomes King of France. **April 11, 1814**

Beginning of Napoleon's Hundred Days
Napoleon escapes Elba and after landing on the French mainland convinces the regiment sent to incept him to join him and march on Paris. As he moves north, more soldiers defect to join him. King Louis XVIII flees to the Netherlands.
February 26, 1815

Congress of Vienna
Representatives of Austria, Britain, France, Russia, and Prussia declare Napoleon an 'outlaw', marking the beginning of the War of the Seventh Coalition.
March 13, 1815

The Waterloo Campaign
Napoleon battles the Prussians at Ligny as marshal Michel Ney and Wellington fight the inconclusive Battle of Quatre Bras. This battle was crucial because if Napoleon won, he could concentrate on the British.
June 16-18, 1815

Real timeline

Alternate timeline

Napoleon Defeats Wellington
After defeating the Prussians, Napoleon waits for the battleground to dry before maneuvering artillery and cavalry to attack the Anglo-Army at Waterloo. Facing substantial loss of life, Wellington retreats to the British garrison in Brussels.
June 18-19, 1815

to get rid of Napoleon. It didn't really matter who else was there, the Bourbons would do, but they were sure that they did not want Napoleon to play that role.

If they wouldn't accept him as a ruler of France, would the Allies have still exiled him to St Helena and risk him escaping again?

AF: Napoleon himself was much more terrified after Waterloo of falling into the hands of the Bourbons, who might have done just that. He chose to surrender to the English in the hope that he would be allowed to live as a prisoner under house arrest in England; in other words, the British would treat him decently, with a modicum of respect. As we know, the British rejected that option and exiled him to St. Helena, a remote island in the South Atlantic, far removed from Europe, from which there was little possibility he could escape. In France he could have faced a trial for treason and possible execution, as happened with Michel Ney and others of Napoleon's loyal lieutenants. But that course was not without its dangers. The regime would have risked turning Napoleon into a political martyr and, given the devotion in which he was held by his followers, it surely would have got one. I think you could make the point that the Allies had to deal with Napoleon a little delicately in 1815, because there was a real danger that they would create a martyr, in the process dividing French opinion and risking lasting instability.

Napoleon was exiled to the Italian island of Elba but returned to Paris and declared himself emperor

If France did destabilize and wasn't able to balance power in continental Europe, how would this have changed history?

AF: The United Kingdom would definitely have become the most dominant world power of the 19th century—which is what did happen anyway. The next challenge, except for the colonial wars in taking place in China and so on, is going to be the Crimean War, which essentially means that the balance of power that was established with events in 1815 more or less holds.

Wellington Defeats Napoleon
Napoleon attempts to wipe out Wellington's center troops with attacks before the Prussians arrive. However, he engages too late after waiting for the ground to dry and Blücher arrives. Napoleon retreats. **June 19, 1815**

Paris Turns on Napoleon
Napoleon returns to the capital in defeat three days after Waterloo to find the public no longer support national resistance. While his brother Lucien believes he can still seize power by dissolving the Parliament, Napoleon senses the change and abdicates his throne in favor of his son. **June 22, 1815**

Napoleon Sent to St. Helena
Napoleon is banished to the remote island of St. Helena without any of the perks he enjoyed on Elba. He dies of natural causes in 1821. **October 23, 1815**

Michel Ney Executed
Napoleon's long-time ally and marshal at the Battle of Waterloo, Michel Ney, is executed as a warning to Napoleon's supporters. **December 7, 1815**

Austro-Russian Invasion
The Austrian and Russian armies' combined siege of Paris overwhelms the French, with Barclay de Tolly drawing on his experiences of capturing the city the year before. **July 1815**

Hundred Days Ends
After the president of the provisional government intimates he should leave Paris, Napoleon exits the capital. Soon after, Graf von Zieten's Prussian I Corps enters Paris and defeats the French. Louis XIII is restored. **July 8, 1815**

Napoleon Surrenders
After the British Navy blocks his attempt to take a ship to America, Napoleon surrenders himself to Captain Frederick Maitland of HMS Bellerophon and is transported to England. **July 15, 1815**

Emperor Again
Returning triumphant to Paris, Napoleon is unopposed as he dissolves Parliament and assumes dictatorial powers to better defend Paris from attack. **June 21, 1815**

Napoleon Executed
After his surrender the Allies allow Louis XVIII to execute Napoleon, believing he is too great a threat to Europe's peace. However, the move divides France and Napoleon becomes a martyr. **July 1815**

The Bonaparte Spring
Bonapartists inspired by Napoleon's promises of constitutional reform during his Hundred Days are outraged at his execution and protest against Bourbon rule in Paris. **July 15, 1815**

Outbreak of Civil War
Disillusioned Napoleonic generals and officials seize on pro-Bonaparte feeling amongst the masses to make a grab for power. Events escalate and civil war erupts across France. **September 1815**

Rise of the British Empire
Britain seizes neglected French colonies and with a self-destructing France unable to balance European power, the Crimean War between Britain and Russia is possibly hastened. **Mid-19th century**

© AMRO ASHRY

What if...

The slave states won?

NORTH AMERICA, 1865

NOTABLE NAMES:
• President Abraham Lincoln

IMPORTANT DATES:
April 12, 1861
January 1, 1863
January 31, 1865
April 26, 1865
December 6, 1865

What Really Happened...

For decades, there was great tension between the northern and southern states over slavery, states' rights, and westward expansion.

In 1860, seven southern states seceded and formed the Confederate States of America. Later, four more states would join them. The first shots of the Civil War were fired on April 12, 1861, and a series of bloody battles followed for the next four years.

The Emancipation Proclamation, signed by President Abraham Lincoln, went into effect on January 1, 1863, freeing enslaved people within the Confederate States. However, it wasn't until January 31, 1865, that Congress passed the 13th Amendment, which was ratified on December 6, 1865, that slavery was officially abolished everywhere in the United States.

The Confederacy surrendered on April 26, 1865, and while the conflict was over, it was the deadliest and bloodiest war ever fought on American soil, with over 620,000 killed, millions injured, and the South left in ruins.

What would have happened if the slave states had won? There were two major accomplishments of the civil war, and they are the preservation of the Union and emancipation. If the Union hadn't stayed together—that is, if the United States had broken into two—then it's likely that other regions of the US would have taken advantage of Confederate seccession or would have seceeded themselves, either from the then-existing North or the South. So you could certainly see an independent Midwest, and the area from California through to Washington state probably could have made itself its own place. Even within the Confederacy, there were certainly sections like East Tennessee that were vigorously Unionist during the war, and which might have pulled away. This was one of the major arguments against seccession to begin with—where did it stop? So I expect that it would have continued; that process of creating smaller autonomous republics within the space that is today the continental United States.

So, the United States would have been a series of smaller countries rather than one whole one?
Yes—the United States is bigger than continental Europe, so there's no reason why it couldn't be 45 independent republics. We tend to look at the shape of the US and regard it as somehow inevitable that it would go from the Atlantic to the Pacific, but there's no reason that it's inevitable.

Would slavery still have been abolished?
The question of emancipation has broader global implications, including that slavery would not have ended in 1863. There's no reason to think that if the Confederate states had won the war—not necessarily conquering the North, but at least fighting to a draw—they would have voluntarily given up slavery. Certainly not any time in the rest of the 19th century. World opinion could have turned to the point that they would voluntarily relinquish slavery in the 20th century, but even that is hard to imagine playing out. That then has implications for Brazil and other nations holding power in the Western hemisphere, some of which emancipated their slaves after the US civil war, because they had seen what happened in the US and wanted to avoid that kind of bloody confrontation. So instead, you've got a very different future where slave labor has a new lease of life. We're talking about a 20th century in which slavery is a vital part of the labor scheme and the social and political structures of large countries in the Western hemisphere.

If the US had permanently divided into North and South, could either have thrived?
In global terms, from the perspective of Britain and France, it would have been a very good thing to divide the US in half. Both those empires would have breathed a sigh of relief, because by 1860 the entire US already had the largest economy in the world, but separately the North and South didn't. The South would have needed to buy a huge amount of manufactured goods from the North, so there might have been some kind of agreement between the two, although the unpleasant war would have left the South turning towards European manufacturers, pursuing trade agreements with European nations, sooner than it would have turned to the North. In 1860, while the South was rich and productive, it was apparent that the development path the North was on—towards more

"Lincoln's fortunes are tied to the war, the difference between a great president and a terrible one hinged on the fate of the armies"

Presiding over a war that ended poorly, Lincoln would have gone down not as one of the best presidents in history, but one of the worst

Not a real photo, has been altered.

INTERVIEW WITH...
PROFESSOR AARON
SHEEHAN-DEAN

Aaron Sheehan-Dean is the Fred C. Frey Professor of Southern Studies at Louisiana State University. He is the author of titles such as *Why Confederates Fought: Family and Nation in Civil War Virginia* and the *Concise Historical Atlas of the U.S. Civil War*, and is also the editor of several books. He teaches a number of courses on 19th-century US history, including the Civil War and Reconstruction and also Southern History.

intensive industrial and urban development—was the recipe for future success. By 1890 or 1900 it would have been apparent that basing your economy around the production of staple crops, like the South had done with cotton, rice, sugar, and tobacco, was not a good long term strategy, so the North would've been in a much better position.

Would the US still have entered World War I?
If the South had started making trade agreements with Britain, it would have soured relations between the North and the UK, and that might well have reduced the likelihood of them entering World War I. Whether a South that's loosely tied to Europe would have felt compelled to enter is hard to say; they wouldn't have

been nearly as much help unless they dramatically expanded their industrial base, and that was a big part of why the US involvement in World War I was so valuable—it was the combined economic power of the whole US and its industrial capacity. So that would have played out on the world stage very differently by the early 20th century.

How would the North losing have affected Britain?
It was pretty apparent that the leadership of the British government wanted to mediate for peace, although I don't think that was entirely altruistic. I mean, they came very close to recognizing the Confederacy as it was in September 1862, and it was only really the Battle of Antietam that stopped them from doing

that. They were interested in re-establishing trade negotiations; they wanted cotton to begin flowing again by that point because the Confederate embargo on cotton had begun to really pinch in Britain. I think they also imagined that a weakened North was a better proposition for them in the long run. The Union victory is credited with helping pass the various reform acts in Britain during the 1860s as well as the liberalization of voting rules. Without that global victory for democracy as they saw it, those things might have never happened, or would have happened much later.

What were the turning points of the war?
The twin victories of Gettysburg and Vicksburg were essential to forestalling the Northern peace movement, which had gained strength in early 1863. The Democrats had regained seats in the Congress in the fall of 1862 and Lincoln was facing a very unhappy electorate in 1863, so those victories were essential. Another turning point was the fall of 1864, when Lincoln anticipated he wouldn't be re-elected and that [General George Brinton] McClellan, who had returned as the Democratic presidential candidate, would be elected in his stead on a platform of negotiating an end to the war, and probably abandoning the emancipation as a Northern war policy. Lincoln believed that he was going to lose until as late as the end of August 1864, and it was only the victories of General Sherman at the Battle of Atlanta [July 1864] and Admiral Farragut at the Battle of Mobile Bay [August 1964] that saved the Union. It also saved the Republican party's electoral votes, so Lincoln was soundly re-elected and the war ended with him at the helm. Certainly if he'd not been re-elected that would have produced a very different outcome.

Border patrols between the Northern and Confederate states might not be too dissimilar to those between the US and Mexico today

How would it have gone without Lincoln in charge?
McClellan was not a sympathetic character in the pantheon of civil war generals, but he was in a parked position because radicals in the Democratic party had nominated him on a platform that called to start negotiating for peace. Even though he did his best to disavow that aspect of his platform, there would have been a lot of pressure within the party as soon as he was inaugurated in March 1865 to negotiate for peace. Without Lincoln's military victories, the war still wouldn't have been over: [General Ulysses S.] Grant would have still been fighting against [General Robert E.] Lee outside Petersburg, and it may well have been that McClellan came into office and immediately suspended fighting, and started negotiating for peace. It would have been hard for him to do that, though, given the sacrifices soldiers had made. The little support he had was among soldiers who felt he was their true commander, but had he negotiated for peace then it might have said to them that their sacrifices had been in vain. It's very likely that he would have stopped emancipation, and even if slavery had ended he would have presided over a much faster reconstruction, which probably wouldn't have involved the enfranchisement of black men.

> "The Union victory is credited with helping pass the various reform acts in Britain during the 1860s"

How would it be different?

The Battle of Gettysburg
General Gordon Meade ends Confederate General Robert E. Lee's invasion of the North with victory in Gettysburg, Pennsylvania.
July 1, 1863

The Battle of Vicksburg
Vicksburg, the last Confederate stronghold on the Mississippi River, surrenders to the Union. The Confederacy is now split in two and faces defeat in the war.
July 4, 1863

Bombardment of Fort Sumter
The Confederacy opens fire on the Union's garrison of Fort Sumter in Charleston, South Carolina, often known as the "shot heard around the world."
April 12, 1861

Real timeline

Real timeline

1861

The South Secedes
Numerous Southern states, including Florida, Alabama, and Georgia, secede from the Union, setting in motion a chain of events that would eventually culminate in the American Civil War. **January 1861**

Civil War
Battles break out across North America, including the bloodiest day in US military history—the Battle of Antietam in September 1862—which leaves over 22,000 people either dead, wounded, or missing.
June 1861— December 1862

Emancipation
President Lincoln issues the Emancipation Proclamation, making the abolition of slavery in the Confederate states the ultimate goal of the Civil War.
January 1, 1863

Alternate timeline

So does this mean Lincoln would not have been assassinated?

Given how much venom John Wilkes Booth had for Lincoln, he would have been happier to see him disgraced and essentially abandoned by the Northern electorate—there's no point killing him any more. So Lincoln then goes down not as one of the best presidents, but as one of the worst, having presided over a civil war that ends poorly, if at all. Lincoln's fortunes are infinitely tied to the fate of the war, and the difference between being a great president and a terrible one really hinged on the fate of the armies.

Without a unified United States, would other nations like Russia have grown more in the 20th century?

Russia is an interesting example because they had emancipated their serfs in 1861, and so there was some degree of friendship [between Russia and the North]. Certainly Russia was a vigorous supporter of the North; they never even contemplated supporting the Confederacy in this fight. Lincoln saw a friendly rivalry between the Russian and American empires, and he talked famously about how the Russian empire in the East and the American empire in the West would be forces for good and spread over the globe. But it would have been a substantially weakened North America and so it's likely that you would have seen other empires, both the British and French but also the Russian, growing stronger without that kind of counter-balancing force of the US.

What would it be like in the modern day?

It depends on the future of slavery in the South. Enslaved people had been pushing against the system of slavery from the very beginning in North America,

when the Spanish empire was there, but it depends on the degree of success. A successful Confederacy would've no doubt ramped up slave patrols and the federal protection of slaves. The question is whether that encourages the British Empire to pursue [slave] labor in India and in other parts of its empire more vigorously, as it has essentially received a sanction of success. That portends to a very different globe, as opposed to one that gradually liberalizes its treatment of workers and improves working conditions, which certainly happened over the second half of the 19th century in the West and then much later in the East. Instead, the trajectory would have gone in the other direction. I suspect it would have been much worse if the Confederacy had been successful and then stood behind [slave] labor as a viable strategy for decades after that, or who knows how long.

How the world would have changed

United States of America The North grows into a nominal power, but soured ties with Europe due to Southern trading mean it is unlikely it joins WWI.

Confederate States of America With slavery still rampant, the Southern states struggle to compete with the industrialized North and must rely on trade with Europe to prosper.

Britain Like Brazil, a Confederate victory gives countries like Britain an excuse to continue slavery in other parts of the world, such as Africa and India.

Russia Russia keeps strong ties with the United States of America, but is able to grow into a bigger power without a unified North America in its way.

Brazil Without the Emancipation Proclamation, Brazil and other countries in South America continue with slavery well into the 20th century, at least.

Europe Countries such as Britain and France are able to expand and control their empires much more vigorously without a victory for the Union.

Offensive
A massive coordinated campaign of all the Union Armies begins, once and for all, to defeat the Confederacy, starting with Lee's Army of Northern Virginia.
May 4, 1864

Lincoln Assassinated
President Lincoln is shot by John Wilkes Booth and dies the next morning. Thanks to Lincoln's resolve, slavery is abolished in December 1865.
April 14, 1865

Lincoln Re-Elected
Abraham Lincoln is re-elected as president, defeating Democrat George McClellan and allowing him to continue fighting for victory, rather than peace.
November 8, 1864

Lee Surrenders
General Robert E. Lee surrenders the Confederate Army to General Ulysses S. Grant in Virginia. The remaining Confederate forces surrender the following month and the war finally ends.
April 9, 1865

World War I
The entry of the powerful US into World War I greatly helps bring the war to a swift conclusion and allows the Allies to emerge victorious on November 11, 1918.
April 1917

McClellan Elected
Democrat George McClellan is elected president of the Union, defeating disgraced former president Lincoln after Confederate victories at Gettysburg and Vicksburg.
November 8, 1864

Peace
The North seeks peace with the South and eventually ends the fighting. The Union and Confederacy remain two separate nations, with slavery still prevalent in the South. **May 1865**

Relations
By 1900, the South has struck strong trading relations with Europe, while a prosperous North remains embittered to European countries like Britain but allies with Russia in the East. **1900**

World War I
Without a unified US it is unlikely either the North or South would enter The Great War, leaving the Allies without the crucial aid they needed to win the war in 1918. **April 1917**

What if . . .
Britain & Russia went to war over Afghanistan?

CENTRAL ASIA, 1893-2015

NOTABLE NAMES:
- Habibullah
- Amanullah
- Babrak Karmal

IMPORTANT DATES:
1838-1922
December 24, 1979

What Really Happened...

The "Great Game" was a long-standing rivalry between Great Britain and Russia as their power moved closer together in South-Central Asia, but they never went to war with each other over Afghanistan. Beginning in 1830 and lasting throughout the 19th century, Britain was concerned with Russia's growth into Central Asia, and Britain considered Afghanistan to be a buffer state. These concerns led to Britain invading Afghanistan for control, in the First Anglo-Afghan War (1838-1842), the Second Anglo-Afghan War (1878-1880), and the short-lived Third Anglo-Afghan War (May 1919).

Eventually, the Anglo-Russian convention was held in 1907, which divided Afghanistan into areas of British and Russian influence. Afghan ruler Habibullah still wished for total independence, but he was assassinated in 1919 and his son, Amanullah, took the throne.

After the third war ended, Britain lost control of Afghanistan's foreign affairs. Amanullah established diplomatic relations with Russia in 1919, and then with Britain in 1922. But years later, on December 24, 1979, the Soviet Union invaded and infiltrated Afghanistan, poisoned the president, installed puppet leader Babrak Karmal, and triggered a nine-year-long Afghan civil war.

Britain launched two invasions of Afghanistan in the 19th Century in order to abort a perceived Russian incursion into the buffer state that separated British India from the Russian Empire. This was Great Gamesmanship at its most extreme: the two wars cost Britain nearly 30,000 casualties, failed to alter the status quo, and were undertaken on false intelligence, equivalent to the dodgy dossier of the day. But what if Russia had taken the fatal step of dispatching an army into Afghanistan?

How would it be different?

Real timeline

1839

The Game Begins
Imperial British forces march into Afghanistan, beginning the First Anglo-Afghan War. The result is a humiliating defeat for the British.
1839

The British Raj
After the Indian Rebellion the East India Company transfer power to the British crown, beginning the rule of the British Raj.
1858

Real timeline

The Durand Line
An agreement between the Emir and Raj is signed with the Durand Line finalizing British and Afghan spheres of influence.
November 12, 1893

The Red Revolution
White and Red factions vie for supremacy as Russia exits WW1. Britain supports the monarchist Whites and supplies them with more arms than any other country.
1917

Hindu-German Conspiracy
The Niedermayer–Hentig Expedition fails to bring in Afghanistan on the side of the Central Powers but did create political turmoil that led to the assassination of the Emir.
1915-1916

Alternate timeline

An Agreement is Made
Emir Rahman and the Raj amicably agree on demarcation line between both countries. This precludes the need for the Durand Line to safeguard defensive access to India. **November 12, 1893**

A Mission is Rejected
Abdur Rahman's son, the new emir, rebuffs a secret German mission sent to Kabul to persuade the Afghan ruler to invade British India in WWI.
March 1, 1916

Let's imagine what our alternate history would be if this war had taken place: Empires must expand to survive. Stagnation behind closed borders poses a continual danger to security. The tsar's subjugation of Tashkent, Samarkand, and Khiva has taken Cossack cavalry to the banks of the Oxus River, within striking distance of British India. The gate of entry is Afghanistan. Russian foreign minister Count Karl Nesselrode, emboldened by Britain's catastrophes of 1839 and 1879, decides to move from brinksmanship to action. In the summer of 1880 tsarist armies launch a two-pronged assault, north from the Oxus and east from Herat, to secure Afghanistan's military objectives before Calcutta can mobilize sufficient troops to counter the attack.

The viceroy, Lord Lytton, at his summer residence in Simla, learns of the attack from friendly Afghan agents in Kabul. He immediately telegraphs the commander-in-chief, General Sir Frederick Haines, ordering him to dispatch two columns through the Khyber and Bolan passes. As a veteran of the Crimean War, Haines is an experienced hand in confronting the aggression of the Russians.

Nesselrode's rather reckless adventure triggers an interesting chain of events that eventually relegates Russia to the status of a second-rate power in Asia. Britain, having annexed the Punjab in 1849, has military units garrisoned on the North-West Frontier abutting Afghanistan. Russian military supply lines stretch hundreds of miles through hostile territory. They are effectively fighting a two-front war against a seasoned, well-equipped British Indian Army and an Afghan insurgency determined to oust the invader. It is absolutely no contest, as the tsar's troops are routed in a matter of weeks by the superior firepower of the Raj. The way is now clear for Britain to 'liberate' the

JULES STEWART

Jules Stewart is a former journalist for Reuters who has reported from more than 30 countries. He is the author of ten books that deal mainly with the Anglo-Afghan wars of the 19th Century and the North-West Frontier. His latest book, *Gotham Rising: New York in the 1930s* is out now.

Russian-occupied khanates on Afghanistan's northern border, with the connivance of Abdul Rahman Khan, the 'Iron Emir', whose foreign policy has been under British control since the end of the Second Anglo-Afghan War.

For Russia, it is a downward spiral. Still smarting from defeat in Afghanistan, its next military humiliation comes in 1905 with the sinking of the fleet in the Russo-Japanese War. The Raj adds vast buffer territories to its empire, rendering even more remote the risk

of a Russian attack. However, the real winner is undoubtedly Afghanistan. Freed from the menace of a hostile Russia and consequently the threat of preventive military action by Britain, the Soviet invasion of 1979 does not take place. There is no US-backed Mujahedin, no Taliban to put order in the civil war between rebel factions. A politically stable Afghanistan, for the first time in its turbulent history, is allowed to benefit from its strategic position on the Asian trade route.

● Soviet Invasion
Fearing the loss of influence with the Amin regime, the Soviet Union deploy troops to oust him and install a Soviet sympathizer. **1979**

● The Enemy of My Enemy
US President Reagan meets with Mujahideen fighters at the White House to discuss aid and Soviet atrocities. **1982**

● 9/11
Al-Qaeda carry out terrorist attacks on American soil, the US responds with an invasion of Afghanistan with a goal of ousting the Taliban. **September 11, 2001**

● Operation Neptune Spear
Osama bin Laden, the mastermind behind the 9/11 terrorist attacks, is killed by US special forces in Pakistan. **May 1, 2011**

● Lingering Presence
Although hostilities have formally ceased, thousands of US Army troops remain in the country, spread across four garrisons. **2017**

● Negotiations are Made
The Afghan Army is defeated, but in peace negotiations at Rawalpindi, Amanullah obtains the return of Afghan sovereignty in foreign policy from the British. **August 19, 1919**

● The Soviet Union is Powerless
The Soviet Union, in its weakened state and lacking access through Turkmenistan and Uzbekistan, is powerless to contemplate an invasion of Afghanistan. **24 December 1979**

● The Durand Line is Abolished
The Durand Line is abolished by agreement between Afghanistan and Pakistan, who work out a new line of demarcation to the satisfaction of the Pashtun tribes living on both sides. **November 9, 2015**

● An Attack is Launched
King Amanullah, under pressure from extremist religious leaders at his court, launches an attack on British India, which becomes the Third Anglo-Afghan War. **May 1, 1919**

● A Regime is Installed
Mohammed Daoud Khan overthrows King Zahir Shah in a peaceful coup, and installs a regime focusing on developing Afghanistan's vast natural resources and modernizing the country's infrastructure. **July 17, 1973**

● A Fortune is Discovered
Afghanistan signs bilateral co-operation treaties with the US and European Union, who send trade missions and engineers to Kabul. The US Geological Survey announces a discovery of $1 trillion in mineral wealth under Afghan soil. **September 11, 2001**

What if...
Germany won WWI?

WORLD WAR I, 1914-1918

What Really Happened...

Tensions had been brewing throughout Europe for years before World War I broke out, but the catalyst was on June 28, 1914, when Archduke Franz Ferdinand of Austria was assassinated. Ferdinand was heir to the Austro-Hungarian Empire, and Austria-Hungary blamed the Serbian government for his murder. Russia supported Serbia, and Austria-Hungary was seeking support from Germany.

On July 5, 1914, German leader Kaiser Wilhelm II pledged his support, and World War I began with Russia, Belgium, France, Great Britain, and Serbia on one side—the Allies—and Austria-Hungary and Germany on the other. The United States would remain neutral until German U-boats sank U.S. commercial and passenger ships. When Germany sunk the ocean liner, the Lusitania, as it was traveling from England to New York with hundreds of American passengers on board, President Woodrow Wilson called for a declaration of war against Germany on April 2, 1917.

Eventually, after several battles on both land and sea, 40 million military and civilian causalities, and 20 million deaths, Germany was forced to sign an armistice on November 11, 1918. The Allies had won, and World War I was over.

What would have happened if Germany had won World War I? It depends on when they win it. If they win a short war in 1914, with the Schlieffen Plan [the plan to quickly defeat the French first to avoid fighting on two fronts] working, it's different than if they win a negotiated victory after a long, hard fight at the end of 1916 or early in 1917, which is the other possibility. Either way, you get a large German Empire dominating central and Western Europe. What is likely to happen is you get a very strong and dominant Germany, [but one] that is not quite as bad as Hitler's Germany in two respects. One is that it doesn't have a plan for the genocide of the Jewish population of Europe—at least we don't think it would have—and it doesn't have a plan for global domination. With those two exceptions, you get a very nasty, racist, expansionist state with enough power in terms of economic and political power to dominate Europe, which means it can do something no power had ever been able to do: it can afford to have an extremely large and extremely good army, and it can also afford to have an extremely good navy, large enough to defeat the Royal Navy. They don't actually have to invade Britain, although they probably would, but they can just starve it into submission.

Would this have led to another war? If Germany wins World War I, they get into a strong position [against the rest of Europe] and then there's almost certainly a war about ten years later, in which the British are defeated. So the British have absolutely no motive for letting this happen. In 1914, the British have three things that nobody else on the planet has got:

they've got the world's only global empire with massive resources, they've got dominant control of the world's financial systems through London, and they've got the biggest and most powerful navy in the world. So, why should they sit there doing nothing while a country that will almost certainly defeat them in the next war ten years on establishes that position [to leapfrog them]?

Without a German defeat, is there any chance of someone like Hitler still rising to power? The short answer is yes. Mussolini came to power in Italy and Italy was on the winning side in World War I. The Treaty of Versailles was [Hitler's] excuse, no reputable historians believe that World War II leads inevitably from World War I. The idea that a botched peace treaty in 1919 inevitably leads to World War II is not historically accurate.

What might a victorious German Empire have looked like in practice? Again, it depends on when it happens. At the start of the war in 1914, the Germans have no real concept of any war aims except reaching the enemy capital, which had been their experience in the Franco-Prussian War from 1870 to 1871, for example. When that fails in September 1914, they realize they're going to need some war aims so they come up with something called the 'Septemberprogramm'. This is a plan for a domination of Belgium as a client state, the Netherlands, which is neutral, the annexation of large parts of northern France with its industry, an absorption of parts of the Austro-Hungarian Empire and the establishment of a German

"What is likely to happen is you get a very strong and dominant Germany that is not quite as bad as Hitler's Germany"

frontier further to the East. All of this would produce a German-dominated super-state that would reach roughly from Calais to as far east as Kiev.

Could Germany have won the war with the entrance of the United States? As it happened, the Germans made the conscious decision instead to try to go for another total win by introducing unrestricted submarine warfare in January to February 1917 in an attempt to starve the British out and that was the principal decision that brought the US into the war. Once the US is in the war as well, it's difficult for the Germans to come up with any kind of win; they make a last attempt with their spring offensives after the collapse of Russia, in spring 1918, but these do not succeed.

What would a German victory in World War I have meant for the United States? A dominant Germany in Europe does not pose a direct threat to the United States, and given the physical distances involved with the Atlantic it is entirely possible that the United States would simply accept this position. President Woodrow Wilson had been re-elected in 1916 on the basis of having kept the United States out of World War I, but when German submarines started sinking American transport ships on the high seas in early 1917, they are compelled to enter the war. So in the short term, the United States might well have taken the view that this was no threat to it. What might then happen half a century on is an open question, but if Germany had developed into the kind of powerful, aggressive state

WWI saw true industrial warfare for the first time in history

A company believed to be the Public Schools Battalion (16th Battalion), prior to the Battle of the Somme, 1916

most historians think it would, it's entirely possible it would have challenged in South and Central America, or it might have challenged in the Atlantic or the Pacific [Oceans]. We might well have seen a war against that kind of German empire, going to war with the United States in a manner not too dissimilar to World War II.

How would Britain have responded? Even if there is a complete and spectacular German victory in 1914, which is not likely, as people have been trying to make a quick German win with the Schlieffen Plan work perfectly more or less ever since the battle actually took place. Even if that happens and France surrenders as it did in 1914, the imperative for the British to avoid the domination by any one power of Europe is so great that you would get a situation similar to that which the British faced with France under Napoleon a century

> "We might well have seen a war against that kind of German empire [. . .] in a manner not too dissimilar to WWII"

How would it be different?

The Schlieffen Plan
Germany must decide whether to try for an immediate outright victory in Western Europe with their Schlieffen Plan, or engage in a longer war with the Allied nations. **September 1914**

Declaration of War
After Austria-Hungary declares war on Serbia, Germany in turn declares war on Russia and, two days later, also on France. After Germany invades Belgium, Britain feels forced to enter the war as well.
August 1, 1914

Real timeline

1914

Real timeline

Alternate timeline

Franz Ferdinand Assassinated
The heir to the throne of the Austro-Hungarian Empire, Franz Ferdinand, and his wife Sophie are assassinated while on a visit in Sarajevo, Bosnia.
June 28, 1914

Germany Offers Support
Kaiser Wilhelm II offers German support for Austria-Hungary against Serbia. This leads to Austria-Hungary ultimately declaring war on Serbia on July 28.
July 5, 1914

The Battle of Mons
The British Expeditionary Force (BEF) retreats after the Battle of Mons with the advancing German First Army making ground.
August 23, 1914

earlier, that they would just keep rebuilding coalitions against this hostile Germany. And you could envisage that the British could just about mount the equivalent of D-Day, taking a British counter-invasion, either of France, Belgium, or even the German coastline some time in 1916. So hypothetically you might have seen D-Day several decades before it took place.

If the US hadn't entered the war, would they still have grown into the global superpower they are today or would they be more isolated? The US entry into World War I established its position as an important global power. Indeed, one of the effects of World War I is that the new Soviet Union and the US emerge as non-European powers for the first time, playing a major role in the international system. And the effect of World War II is to establish the domination of those two non-European powers, the US and Soviet Union, with the European powers no longer playing the role they had played recently. This lasts through to the end of the Cold War in 1990 and 1991. Would the US have emerged into its assumption after 1945 of global interests without its involvement in World War I? I would say it's unlikely. If Germany doesn't threaten the US or its interests you're going to see a more isolationist US. If a confident, expansionist, aggressive, and militaristic Germany starts to threaten the US, the US would almost certainly respond.

Would the League of Nations and, ultimately, the United Nations still have materialized under a German victory? No, the League of Nations was very much the ideal of President Woodrow Wilson. And of course the US itself doesn't join the League of Nations, but it is a product of the peace of Paris including the Treaty of Versailles in 1919. What you would see is something with some kind of form in Europe, an extension of what is known as the Zollverein, the pan-German Customs Union of the 19th century, forming into something which would bear some resemblance to the modern EU but only to the extent that it would

be a very large trading block. Its laws, traditions, and attitudes towards human rights would have been completely different. But no, with a German victory in WWI, the League of Nations and from it at the end of World War II the United Nations, I don't think there's any way this would happen.

Would Russia still have become the Soviet Union? Russia had its own problems. It had already had its minor revolution, the uprisings of 1905, leading to political reforms and the creation of a Russian parliament, the Duma. If France is defeated in 1914, Russia probably makes peace with Germany and Austria-Hungary fairly quickly. What basis that will be made on is very hard to say at the moment, but it will almost certainly have been a limited Russian defeat. But what happens after that is not particularly connected with the war; it is the strain of fighting the war over the three-year period that precipitates the Russian political and economic collapse, and without that the idea of a Russian revolution in the way it actually happened is not a certainty.

Do you think World War II would have still happened? If you got the Germany I've described, that has been successful in World War I and has achieved this kind of domination, who is going to fight it and why? The only thing that works is looking at the British strategy before, against revolutionary and Napoleonic France, where the British kept putting together alliances, kept being defeated, and just wouldn't give up until Napoleon was finally defeated, and that war lasted for a quarter of a century. So you could easily envisage the British drawing on the resources of their empire, simply refusing to accept German victory and carrying out a long and persistent war on the peripheries of Europe and around the world to prevent this domination, which could have gone on for decades. Whether Britain could have brought the US in on their side is hard to construct a scenario for, but that depends almost entirely on whether Germany tries to starve Britain into submission by cutting off its supply routes.

Blockade of Britain
In an attempt to starve the British, Germany begins unrestricted submarine warfare, sinking any vessels bound for Britain. **February 1915**

The US Enters the War
After continued sinking of vessels, the US enters the war, mobilizing troops immediately, while the Great German Withdrawal takes place. **April 6, 1917**

Brest-Litovsk
Russia agrees to a negotiated peace with Germany in the Treaty of Brest-Litovsk. **March 3, 1918**

Armistice Day
The war comes to an end as a battered Germany signs an armistice with the Allies. **November 11, 1918**

Trench Warfare
Scrapping the Schlieffen Plan, trenches are dug along the Western Front, foreshadowing a long stalemate. **November 1914**

Blockade of Britain
Germany attempts to starve the British island nation through their extensive U-Boat submarine campaign. **February 1915**

Invasion
Germany attempts to invade Britain after annexing large parts of Western Europe. **September 1915**

Battle of the Somme
In the bloodiest day of fighting in British military history, 60,000 Allied soldiers are dead, wounded, or missing after a disastrous battle. **July 1, 1916**

US Troops Arrive
The first US troops arrive in France and the Allies begin significant advancements against the Germans. **June 25, 1917**

Spring Offensive
The German Spring Offensive fails to break down the Allied front line. **April 1918**

Treaty of Versailles
The Treaty of Versailles is signed, imposing strict limitations on Germany following their defeat in the war. **June 28, 1919**

Germany Attacks
The Germans decide to go ahead with the Schlieffen Plan, planning sweeping attacks across Western Europe. **November 1914**

France Surrenders
The French surrender to Germany, with other countries in Western Europe soon following suit, apart from Britain. **December 1914**

Russian Peace
Russia enters into a negotiated peace with Germany before the war with Britain escalates further. **June 1915**

D-Day
After resisting a German invasion, Britain decides to launch a ground assault on Western Europe. **March 1916**

No US Help
With its resources floundering, Britain makes another failed attempt to bring America into the war on their side. **1917**

Britain Loses
Ultimately, after drawing on the resources of their entire empire, Britain loses the war, leading to a dominant Germany in Europe. **1924**

What if . . .

The Ottoman Empire joined the Allies in WWI?

OTTOMAN EMPIRE, 1914-1918

What Really Happened...

NOTABLE NAMES:
• Mehmed V

IMPORTANT DATES:
July 30, 1914
October 29, 1914
November 2, 1914

After months of remaining neutral and negotiating with both sides, the Ottoman Empire (established in 1299) had secretly formed an alliance with the Central Powers on July 30, 1914. They were declining in power at the time, but regardless, the Ottoman Empire officially entered World War I on October 29, 1914, when their ships—manned by German crews and admirals—carried out the Black Sea Raid against Russia.

As a result of the attack, Russia declared war on the Ottoman Empire on November 2, 1914, with Britain and France doing the same on November 5. The Ottoman Sultan, Mehmed V, declared war against Britain, France, and Russia on November 11.

While the Ottoman Empire had several armies tasked with different roles and missions, it struggled to supply and prepare them, and their weapons were outdated. Over 3 million Ottoman soldiers served in the war, but approximately 325,000 of them died.

By October 1918, the Ottoman Empire accepted its defeat. Between their loss in World War I, the Armenian Genocide, and other devastating events that were a direct result of World War I, the Ottoman Empire collapsed by November 1922.

Having stood on their own against several enemies in the Balkan Wars, the Young Turks in power vowed to actively seek an alliance in 1914. The Ottoman minister of war, Enver Pasha, orchestrated an alliance with Germany. However, had his request for a treaty been declined by Berlin, Russia would have quickly reconsidered allying with the Ottomans.

Suspecting Kaiser Wilhelm II would attempt to accept the Ottoman alliance offer with the intention of persuading Istanbul to declare jihad against the Entente,

How would it be different?

Real timeline

1861

● **Ottoman Military Reforms**
The Ottoman empire begins a long series of military reforms that sees its armies prepared for war in 1914.
1861-1922

● **Berlin-Baghdad Railway**
Construction begins on a vast railway that will connect the German city of Berlin with the then Ottoman-controlled Baghdad.
1903

Real timeline

● **Underhand Dealings**
Outwardly displaying neutrality, the Ottoman Empire had secretly signed an alliance with the Central Powers in the summer of 1914.
August 1914

● **Caucasus Campaign**
The Ottomans and Russia clash in the southern Caucasus. The Russians fight alone on the front for most of the war.
October 1914-1918

● **Attack on Russia**
The Ottomans launch the Black Sea Raid against Russian ports. The Allies declare war against the Empire in November.
October 29, 1914

Alternate timeline

● **Ottomans Join Allies**
Though leaning more towards siding with Germany and the other Central Powers, the Ottomans make an alliance with the Allies. **July 31, 1914**

● **Von Sanders Leaves**
Under pressure, Ottoman Empire asks the German military mission headed by General Liman von Sanders to leave Istanbul.
August 9, 1914

Sergei Sazanov, the Russian foreign minister, would convince London and Paris to sign an alliance, closing the deal just as war broke out. Despite Russia's allies seeing Turkey as a liability, Sazanov believed it was preferable to have Turkey on their side rather than the side of Germany.

With an alliance secured, the Ottomans declared mobilization, but because of inadequate industrialization and transportation, this took three months. The Allies would not have expected much, since their real aim would be to keep the Ottomans away from the Germans. Sharing no borders with Germany or Austria-Hungary, the Ottomans would eventually send a token expeditionary force comprising three army corps to the Western Front. Ottoman Mehmetçik ('Little Mehmed') in Europe would be armed and equipped by France and Britain. When the Russians found themselves bogged down against the German offensive in April 1915, they would have asked Istanbul for reinforcements against Austria-Hungary. When the Russian supplies and food ran short in the late summer of 1915, the Turkish Straits would have become a lifeline for Russia as Istanbul could allow supply ships to pass through, preventing another revolution in Russia like that in 1905.

When Syria, Lebanon, and Palestine were hit with a major locust plague in 1915, the Ottoman government, aided by its allies, would send foodstuffs to the region to avoid a major famine. Istanbul looking after its citizens in the Arab provinces would no doubt make the people of the region more loyal to the state. In fact, this would cause the small group of Arab nationalists who saw the war as an opportune time to declare a revolt for their independence to postpone their plans.

Undoubtedly concerned that the Allies had post-war designs on the empire, the Young

YÜCEL YANIKDAĞ

Associate professor of History and International Studies at the University of Richmond, he specializes in the late Ottoman Empire and the early Turkish Republic. His book, *Healing the Nation: Ottoman Prisoners of War, Nationalism, and Medicine In Turkey, 1914-1939*, was published in 2013.

Turks would endeavor to appear more useful to the war effort. Thus, upon persuading Bulgaria to join the Allies in October 1915, Enver Pasha would suggest a joint attack on Austria-Hungary through occupied Serbian territory. The plan would only be activated when Romania also joined the Allies. A small contingent of Ottomans would join its newest allies to invade Austria-Hungary from the south and east.

With no need to station troops in Egypt, London would send many more thousands—Anzac and Indian Army soldiers—to the Western Front. With a well-supplied and strengthened Russia on the Eastern Front and heavy concentrations of troops on the Western Front, Germany and Austria-Hungary would soon realize the futility of continuing. Just as the Americans were considering entering, the war would come to an end in 1917.

The Suez Canal
An Ottoman army tasked with expelling the British from Egypt are fought to a standstill at the Suez canal.
February 1915

Sorrow at Gallipoli
In an attempt to capture Istanbul, Allied forces are decimated by the Ottoman army after a disastrous amphibious landing.
April 25, 1915–January 9, 1916

The Arab Revolt
Eager to gain independence from the Ottomans, many Arab tribes revolt. They are given military aid from Britain and France.
June 1916–October 1918

Battle of Jerusalem
The city of Jerusalem is captured by British and Dominion forces. The capture was a "Christmas present for the British people."
December 30, 1917

Armistice of Mudros
The Ottoman Empire is stripped away when hostilities cease in the Middle Eastern Theater. Britain takes control of many Ottoman possessions.
October 30, 1918

Lifeline to Russia
Russian supplies and food run short in the face of a German offensive. Cargo ships pass through the Turkish Straits to relieve them.
Summer 1915

Bulgaria Joins Allies
The Ottomans had feared that Bulgaria might attack shipping to Russia. The news that they have joined the Allies is welcomed.
October 11, 1915

Attack on Austria-Hungary
The three Balkan allies attack Austria-Hungary through Serbia and Romania. Austro-Hungarians face great difficulty fighting both the Russians and their new enemies. **June 29, 1916**

Germany Surrenders
Germany decides that it cannot continue to fight on two distant fronts. The war comes to an end.
September 1, 1917

The Western Front
Ottoman Mehmetçik heads to the Western Front. The French discover the Germans had made significant advances in training Ottoman soldiers.
October 1914

Locust Plague
Locusts strip away all vegetation from Palestine to Syria, causing widespread famine. French and British ships join Ottomans in delivering supplies.
March-October 1915

Romania Enters War
After being put under pressure by Russia, Romania enters the war with hopes of gaining Austrian territory for its effort. **May 1916**

Sykes-Picot Agreement
Being on the winning side, the Ottoman Empire survives WWI intact. They cooperate with Britain in the Middle East.
1918

© IAN HINLEY

What if...

The Entente marched on Berlin in 1918?

GERMANY, 1918-1919

NOTABLE NAMES:
- President Friedrich Ebert

IMPORTANT DATES:
October 29, 1918
August 21, 1919

What Really Happened...

The Triple Entente (French for a friendly understanding) was an informal agreement between Russia, France, and Great Britain. It was this agreement that initially formed the Allied forces of World War I.

Around the time the Central Powers signed the armistice that ended World War I in November 1918, Germany was facing more internal problems—the German Revolution. With the Kiel mutiny, the Christmas Crisis, the founding of the Communist Party, the January Revolt, the Weimar constitution between adopted, and several other pivotal events, Germany was in turmoil between the fall of 1918 and August 21, 1919, when Friedrich Ebert was sworn in as Reich President.

As a result of this civil unrest, the federal constitutional monarchy was overthrown, and a democratic parliamentary republic was established.

In a railroad car at Compiegne, France, on November 11, 1918, the armed forces of Imperial Germany surrendered to the Entente, effectively ending World War I. Although the armistice brought an end to the fighting on the Western Front, civil unrest was already sweeping Germany, fomenting potential revolution at home and giving rise to the "stab in the back" theory that contributed during the interwar years to the rise of the Nazi Party and the coming of World War II. What if the Great War had continued in the autumn of 1918 and Allied forces had pushed to capture Berlin?

Our altered history would look something like this: Following the rejection of an ultimatum for surrender, General Erich Ludendorff, commander of German forces in the field, prepares as he can for the Allied onslaught that is sure to come. The Germans have spent their combat effectiveness during their failed offensive in 1918, and shortages of men and war material have

How would it be different?

Naval Mutiny
Many sailors refuse suicidal orders and are arrested. The blame falls on Ludendorff and he is removed from command. **October 26, 1918**

The Kaiser Flees
Germany is declared a republic with no resistance. Kaiser Wilhelm flees into exile in the Netherlands, never to return. **November 9, 1918**

Sue for Peace
Hindenburg urges Charles of Austria to begin moves towards peace but initial offers are rejected by the Allies. **September 10, 1918**

Real timeline

Real timeline

1918

Hundred Days Offensive
The last major offensive conducted by the Allies during the war. German high commanders realize the war is lost. **August 8, 1918**

Ludendorff Cracks
Bulgaria signed a separate armistice with the Allies and Ludendorff suffers a mental breakdown. Germany cannot mount an effective defense. **September 29**

Alternate timeline

Armistice Refused
The Allies outright reject the first German request for an armistice, demanding unconditional surrender. The Germans refuse. **October 4, 1918**

The Allies Advance
Allied soldiers cross into German territory after pushing the Germans back from defensive positions along the Franco-German frontier. **December 10, 1918**

reduced the army to a shadow of its former self. Desertion is a problem, and Ludendorff fears that military discipline will crumble in the face of renewed hostilities.

On November 15, the Allies unleash a massive offensive all along the Western front. British forces drive across the old battlefields of Flanders, through Belgian Wallonia and on to Liege, pausing briefly to resupply. Crossing the German frontier, the British encounter diminishing resistance from the enemy and complete the ejection of German forces from northern France and Belgium.

South of the British advance, French troops move into Alsace, threatening the German left flank as Ludendorff retires across the River Rhine. Meanwhile, American forces under General John Pershing race for the crossings of the River Meuse near Sedan. Fighting is very heavy, but the weather hampers the Allied offensive. By late December, the British, French, and American forces consolidate their front, drawing up along the west bank of the Rhine, poised to renew their offensive stance the following spring.

On March 12, 1919, the Allies, under the unified command of French Marshal Ferdinand Foch, launch the final offensive to capture Berlin. Rapidly crossing the Rhine, the British occupy the Ruhr, Germany's industrial heartland, and march into Cologne. The Americans jump off near the German city of Koblenz at the confluence of the Rhine and its tributary, the Moselle. Their advance on Frankfurt meets light resistance, and the city falls within days. Victory in the Twelve Days' Battles shatters German resistance.

British forces sweep across the plain of northern Germany to the gates of Berlin. A brief squabble develops among the Allied commanders for the honor of taking the German capital, however, when Kaiser

MICHAEL HASKEW

Michael Haskew has researched and written on military history topics for over 30 years and is the author of more than 20 books, including *West Point 1915: Eisenhower, Bradley, and the Class the Stars Fell On*, and *De Gaulle: Lessons in Leadership from the Defiant General*.

Wilhelm II abdicates on April 20, Berlin is declared an open city.

The Allies formally occupy Berlin the following day, enacting martial law and quelling the unrest between communist and right-wing paramilitary groups. Occupation zones are established, and a provisional German government is given limited autonomy. A decade of military occupation follows, and only when a democratic German government is deemed stable are Allied troops withdrawn.

Armistice Declared
On the 11th hour of the 11th day of the 11th month, The Great War comes to an end with the Allies and Germany signing the armistice.
November 11, 1918

Rhineland Occupied
Four allied nations send troops to occupy the Rhineland. French troops would continue to occupy the region until 1930.
December 1, 1918

Spartacist Uprisings
Ideological struggles between right and left wing groups erupt into violence as communists and right-wing paramilitary groups clash. **January 4–15 1919**

Treaty of Versailles
Seven months after the armistice was signed, the treaty would bring a formal end to the hostilities.
June 28, 1919

14 Points
Taken from his speech back in January 1918, President Wilson's 14 points became the basis for the Paris Peace Conference.
January 21, 1920

Wilhelm Pushed Out
A provisional government is established in Berlin, and Kaiser Wilhelm II has virtually no continuing role in the conduct of the war.
December 31, 1918

German Troops Crumble
During the so-called Twelve Days' Battles, Allied troops destroy the remnants of three German armies, and organized enemy resistance rapidly wanes. **March 12–24 1919**

Berlin is Taken
A multinational Allied contingent enter Berlin with a delegation of provisional government officials. Negotiations conclude with the surrender of Germany.
April 21, 1919

Martial Law Enacted
The capture of Berlin is virtually bloodless. The Allies impose martial law, arresting the leaders of prominent communist and right-wing factions.
April 30, 1919

Continued Fighting
Heavy losses are sustained on both sides as German troop formations begin to disintegrate. Civil unrest grows across Germany.
December 16, 1918

Berlin Coup
Communist revolutionaries stage an attempt to overthrow the provisional German government. Troops of the right-wing Freikorps quell the uprising with force.
January 6, 1919

Allies Smell Victory
Allied commanders meet as their forces approach Berlin. A squabble ensues as to whose command will be the first to enter the capital.
April 9, 1919

Occupation Begins
Germany is divided into British, French, and American occupation zones and the provisional German government is given limited autonomy.
May 21, 1919

© IAN HINLEY

What if...

The US invaded Canada?

NORTH AMERICA, 1904-1916

What Really Happened...

As a result of the Venezuelan debt crisis that began in 1901, Germany, Italy, and Great Britain threatened military intervention. President Theodore Roosevelt felt the European countries were justified, while President Cipriano Castro refused to negotiate and resolve the crisis. Eventually in 1903, Castro asked Roosevelt to help him reach a settlement. Eager to restore order, he did, and later created the Roosevelt Corollary in 1904. This was an imperialist doctrine, declaring the United States' right to intervene in the western hemisphere.

During this same time, Canada was split regarding their feelings towards their relationship with Britain, with many wanting to distance from their British mother country. Roosevelt wanted Canada to join the American union, but also expressed wanting to take the country by force as well. Nothing came to fruition, however, in particular because it was strategically unwise.

Originally titled, 'Assumption—war has broken out with Great Britain', the 1904/05 plan by the United States to invade Canada was the first of its plans for wars to be drafted. While crude by modern war-planning scenarios, it was audacious in its strategic thinking. Rather than fight Britain on its terms, the United States would strike where the nation was easiest to injure—Canada. Most likely this plan was devised after the tensions of the Venezuela Crisis of 1903-04.

The plan was aimed at crippling Britain economically. If Canada were taken from Britain, it would cut off nearly a third of the island's wheat and over 75 percent of the nickel. Better yet, with a mostly undefended border, Canada was ripe pickings. The only downside to attacking the US's neighbor to the north was its vast size—it was akin to sending armies into Russia.

Thus the US plan for attacking Canada was not an all-out invasion but rather a direct attack across the

How would it be different?

Real timeline

1902

● **Venezuelan Crisis**
A naval standoff in Venezuela heightens tensions between the US, Britain, and other major European powers like Germany.
1902-03

● **New Canadian Military**
The Canadian military is reformed with new corps being appointed and a new navy beginning to be constructed in 1911.
1904

Real timeline

● **WWI Begins**
After the assassination of Archduke Ferdinand, the major European powers declare war. The BEF is sent to France.
July 28, 1914

● **Battle of Mons**
Despite inflicting numerous casualties on the numerically superior Germans, the BEF is forced to give ground but retreat in good order.
August 23, 1914

● **Arms Supply**
The US, an industrial powerhouse, would supply Europe with over $2.2 billion worth of arms and munitions.
August 1914–March 1917

Alternate timeline

● **Protecting the Front**
British garrison forces reinforce Quebec to deter further American adventurism. Tensions remain high between Britain and the US as both sides build forts. **1905-14**

● **BEF Formed**
The outbreak of the Great War leaves Britain with a significantly smaller BEF force because of troops tied down in Canada.
Summer 1914

Saint Lawrence Seaway to seize Fort Erie, Niagara Falls, and the Welland Canal. Once secured, US cavalry forces would strike northward to Toronto, cutting off rail service and raiding at will.

Canada could do little to stop an invasion as the bridges across the Saint Lawrence were seized. With only roughly 12,000 militia and officers spread out across the vast territory, they would be fighting with limited ammunition, and only two batteries of artillery were posted in the Niagara area where the fighting would be the heaviest. The Canadians had a total of 12 machine guns in their entire defensive force, so defending Canada relied on arming private citizen gun clubs with Lee Rifles and giving them almost no formal training. With the US striking quickly, the closest professional military help for the Canadians was five hours away by rail (The Royal Canadian Dragoons). By the time they arrived, the invasion force would have taken its objectives—cutting off the Saint Lawrence Seaway, Fort Erie, and forming a compact defensive line around Niagara.

The US would be deploying a full division of troops along with an additional division's worth of artillery and cavalry in reserve. US machine guns would be concentrated in the drive of seizing the canal and securing Toronto. The US army would have had little opposition in securing Ontario as a whole, cutting Canada in half.

Britain would respond, the US knew that. But by the time any British relief forces would have arrived, the US would be deeply entrenched and reinforced. The clashes by British troops to attempt to retake Toronto would have taken on a Great War effect, with troops rushing massed artillery and machine guns. With the US massing troops in Maine, threatening to cut off Halifax and resupply,

Great Britain would have to face losing a significant and strategic portion of Canada.

Ontario would have become the 46th American state, while Britain would be forced to garrison the rest of Canada as a peace settled in.

BLAINE L. PARDOE

Blaine Pardoe is a New York Times bestselling author of military history. Two of his books deal with speculative history—*The Fires of October* on the Cuban Missile Crisis and *Never Wars*—the *US War Plans to Invade the World*. In *Never Wars*, he draws on a US plan to invade Canada.

Sinking the Lusitania
The sinking of the Lusitania is a major diplomatic incident and brings US public opinion around to the idea of war.
May 7, 1915

US Declares War
After the release of the Zimmermann Telegram, President Wilson asks congress to help "make the world safe for democracy."
April 2, 1917

The Doughboys Arrive
By 1918 large numbers of American troops are pouring into Europe, much to the chagrin of the beleaguered Germans. **1918**

End of War
On November 11 at 11 a.m. the armistice was signed between the Allies and Germany in a train car in the Forest of Compiègne.
November 11, 1918

Treaty of Versailles
The peace treaty signed with Germany by the Allies placed the blame of war squarely on Germany's shoulders.
June 28, 1919

The Rout of Mons
The BEF is driven back, causing a collapse of the French lines. The Allies fall back, giving Germany significant territorial gains.
August 23, 1914

Battle of Paris
A defensive arc around Paris is formed. The British and French hold the line, which quickly devolves into a bloody stalemate.
November 24, 1914

Unrestricted Naval Warfare
The US selling and shipping of munitions to Germany forces Britain to call for unrestricted naval warfare.
February 4, 1915

Quebec Independence Movement
In retaliation, the US arms Quebec nationalists. Uprisings take place and the British garrison is soon under siege.
March 1915-16

US Refuses Neutrality
With a British army in the north, the US refuses to sell munitions to Britain but agrees to supply France and Germany.
August 4, 1914

Coastal Battles
The German armies swing north and secure strategic ports. Dunkirk and Calais fall and the Channel becomes a contested passage.
September 10, 1914

US Seizes RMS Lusitania
RMS Lusitania is laden with illegal munitions, and is seized in New York harbor. Tensions between Britain and the US escalate.
December 10, 1914

WWI Ends
France sues for peace as Britain sends the BEF overseas to cope with the uprisings. Britain and France are blamed for the war. **March 10, 1916**

© KEVIN MCGIVERN

What if...

Germany won the Battle of Britain?

THE BATTLE OF BRITAIN, UK, 1940

NOTABLE NAMES:
• Adolf Hitler

IMPORTANT DATES:
July 10, 1940
October 31, 1940

What Really Happened...

During World War II, the Battle of Britain lasted from July 10, 1940, until October 31, 1940. With Britain's Royal Air Force on one side and the Luftwaffe—Nazi Germany's air force—on the other, it was the first-ever battle fought entirely in the air. The goal was to win control of the airspace over Great Britain, Germany, and the English Channel.

By October 1940, Adolf Hitler called off his invasion and the Battle of Britain was over. While both sides suffered tremendous losses, Britain had managed to weaken the Luftwaffe and prevented Germany from further occupation. It would be Hitler's first large defeat in the war and a major turning point. And while Britain stood their ground on their own, many RAF pilots were from Poland, the United States, Australia, Belgium, France, South Africa, and several other countries.

**INTERVIEW WITH...
STEPHEN BADSEY**

Stephen Badsey is Professor of Conflict Studies at the University of Wolverhampton. An internationally recognized military historian, he has written or edited more than 90 books and articles. His writings have been translated into five languages and he appears frequently on television and in other media.

What would have happened if Germany had won the Battle of Britain? Most people define winning the Battle of Britain as the defeat of RAF Fighter Command and achieving air superiority over Southeast England. That was considered the essential first step for the planned German invasion called Operation Sea Lion. However, they didn't only have to defeat Fighter Command; they would also have had to defeat the Royal Navy, which would have sailed into the English Channel and cut off the German invading forces. And that battle the Germans could not win. They had not nearly big enough a navy. The Luftwaffe could have attacked the Royal Navy but it couldn't be everywhere at once, so while it was doing that it couldn't be supporting the invasion. After three or four days the German force that makes it across the Channel and lands, and it's pretty certain they could have done that, has its communications across the Channel cut and runs out of fuel and ammunition. If you want an actual successful German invasion and a defeat of Britain, it can't be done purely in military terms; you have to look for some reason the British would have surrendered.

What were Germany's aims with the Battle of Britain? The Germans were trying to do two things simultaneously with the air battle. One was to achieve aerial superiority over Southeast England, and they were getting close to that in the course of the battle. They had forced the RAF to abandon some of its critical airfields in Southeast England, and that's more important than it sounds, because these were pre-war established airfields. But [the Germans] were also working on a theory that was very popular before World War II, that bombing by itself would so frighten an enemy civilian population that they would rise in revolt and demand their government makes peace. Now, that theory turned out not to be true, even with the massive bombings that took place during this conflict, but nobody knew if that was true or not [at the time].

What was the turning point in the battle? Critically, in the middle of the battle there was this German decision to switch from attacking the fighter airfields to bombing London. There's always been a strong theory and suspicion that cannot be proven that this was a fundamental error. It was based very much on the [mistaken] idea that Fighter Command had been worn out and that now was the time for the shock tactic of bombing the civilian population. One of the things they neglected and weren't very good at is what's called military intelligence, which is understanding what the other guy is doing, and they could never get an accurate count on how many aircraft the British actually had and what kind of losses they were suffering. One of the reasons they couldn't do that is that Fighter Command kept harboring its reserves, feeding them into battle in small units, so the Germans thought RAF losses were much higher than they were. There's a lovely comment by one hard-bitten German fighter pilot towards the end of the battle, watching yet another RAF formation come up to meet them. He said over his radio [exhaustedly]: "Here they come, the last 50 Spitfires." It's got that kind of feel to it.

If Germany had won the Battle of Britain, Hitler would have invaded, and Nazi soldiers could have been marching through the streets of London soon after

What would it have taken for Britain to lose? First of all, at some unspecified time before the war, the Germans could have developed a real amphibious capability, which they didn't have. If the Germans had developed proper landing craft and all the doctrines and training that go with them so they could actually mount a major amphibious assault quickly and effectively with well-trained troops, that would have made a big difference. Then, as I said, the German Navy was much smaller than the Royal Navy but you can construct scenarios in which it's a bit stronger. They lose some ships in the invasion of Norway, and the British sank the French Mediterranean fleet when

France surrendered in French North Africa. If that hadn't happened and the Germans had been able to get hold of the French battle fleet, it's still not enough to defeat the Royal Navy, but that would improve the German chances. Then if the invasion does take place, you've got a matter of days to come up with some kind of political shock to convince a British government it has to surrender.

Would Britain have surrendered? It's unlikely that would happen with Churchill as prime minister, but of course he nearly didn't become Prime Minister. When France collapsed virtually the day the German attack

British troops just before D-Day. If Germany had won the Battle of Britain, the series of landings at Normandy would not have occured

Could Britain have held out? Presuming the British don't surrender, the Germans would try to bypass London. The next main defensive line after that is for the industrial heartlands of the Midlands, the Stratford-upon-Avon canal, which runs roughly speaking southwest to northeast a short distance south of the Birmingham area. If the Germans go through that, the last line of defense is to the northwest of that, between Wolverhampton and Telford. If the British lose that, they are pretty well defeated.

Would the remnants of the British Army have fought on like the Free French Forces did in France? What the 'Free British' would have looked like we don't know, but the Royal Navy would still be very much intact and you can envisage a scenario in which transports filled with troops and some civilians escorted by the Royal Navy actually head westwards in the expectation that they would be able to continue the war from the British Empire. In terms of Britain itself, in addition to the famous Home Guard, there were also small units that were effectively assassination squads. These were highly motivated people and some of them are quite surprising; George Orwell and Michael Foot were among the people who volunteered for this. Their job was essentially a suicide mission to try and kill the highest-ranking German they could find. That probably would have happened. So you would have probably had a British resistance to German occupation in the same way you got a French resistance.

With Britain defeated, what would happen next? We can never be certain, but it probably means that Germany has won the war in Europe. It is hard to construct any reasonable course of action whereby the United States would become involved in a war with Germany, and it is incredibly hard looking at a map to see how military operations to liberate German-occupied Europe could have been mounted from the far side of the Atlantic. What would almost certainly happen next is what did happen; the following year [in

on France starts, May 10, 1940, Chamberlain resigns and Churchill becomes prime minister, but it was nearly Lord Halifax and he was a much less pugnacious person than Churchill. Whether with Halifax in charge of the government the British would have offered surrender just with the threat of a German invasion we don't know. It's a possibility, but [for Britain to lose] it needs to be that kind of thing; Britain needs to collapse in the way that France did in May and June 1940, as much a political collapse as a military one.

Assuming the invasion did go ahead, what was Hitler's next move? The British chiefs of staff had advised Churchill that if the Germans did get ashore in strength the army was not strong enough to defeat them and drive them back. The first line of defense of the British is something drawn halfway between the invasion area round about Dover and London which is called the GHQ Line [General Headquarters Line]. Regarding London itself, Churchill's view was that if it came to that he was intent on making the Germans fight for it house to house. So if you had this Battle of London, it would absorb a massive number of German troops, which was the intention.

How would it be different?

German Expansion
Hitler's march continues unabated as Germany invades Denmark and Norway. **April 1940**

Battle of Britain
In the summer of 1940 the first major campaign to be fought in the air begins. The Luftwaffe and RAF planes meet in the skies as the Germans target bombing radar stations and airfields. **July 1940**

Targets Switch
Believing the RAF to be on the brink of defeat, Germany switches their attacks from airfields to major cities. **September 7, 1940**

Real timeline

1939

War Declared
An increasingly aggressive and confident Germany ignores warnings and invades Poland on September 1. Two days later both Britain and France declare war. **September 1, 1939**

New Prime Minister
Neville Chamberlain, the prime minister who had believed in appeasement, resigns. Winston Churchill, the former First Lord of the Admiralty, is chosen as his successor. **May 10, 1940**

France Surrenders
France signs an armistice with Germany. Shortly after France's surrender, Churchill famously says: ". . . the Battle of France is over. I expect that the Battle of Britain is about to begin." **June 22, 1940**

Real timeline

Alternate timeline

Attacks Continue
Germany decides to keep attacking airfields and further weaken the RAF. Two days later, they make plans to invade mainland Britain. **September 7, 1940**

1941] Hitler's Germany and the Axis members would have attacked the Soviet Union. That was always the big Nazi ambition and to that extent the war in the West was viewed almost as not quite a mistake, but something that they had not been aiming for. Without a hostile Britain remaining to the West, the German attack on the Soviet Union is more likely to succeed.

Would Japan and America still have gone to war?
Whether the Japanese would have attacked the US at Pearl Harbor is extremely difficult to answer, but it doesn't look as if this scenario makes it less likely. There probably would have been some kind of Japanese-American Pacific war, which would probably have played out pretty much as it did; the Japanese didn't really have a chance of winning that war. But that would have been a separate war. In terms of Europe, if the Battle of Britain is won [by Germany] and Britain is invaded successfully, the next German attack on the East on the Soviet Union establishes the German Empire throughout Europe.

Would Germany and the US ever have come to blows? Most historians believe that the ultimate objective of Hitler was world domination. So after establishing this great European power and absorbing within it not just the French colonial empire but the British colonial empire, the largest empire in history, then at some point in the future Hitler's Germany might have made a war of conquest, attempting to seize the Americas as well as the US.

Why do you not think it was possible? It's a matter of global transport. For Germany to build such a global transport system is a step too far in terms of our speculation. What they could have done, and people were very concerned that they might have done, was build an Intercontinental Ballistic Missile [ICBM], capable of reaching one continent from another. If the Germans could have and did build a workable atomic bomb—which is possible—and if they built an ICBM to

Aircraft spotter on the roof of a building in London. St. Paul's Cathedral is in the background

fire it, they could have hit American cities which would have been hit with bombs equivalent to those that hit Hiroshima and Nagasaki. That is plausible.

What might things have been like in the modern day? As a personal view, I don't believe in economic terms that the Nazi state was viable for more than a few years. In order to feed the German people they were basically stealing the grain supplies from every country they invaded, and I just don't believe it's viable. It would have just collapsed in revolution in a few years' time, having done a great deal of damage.

"Most historians believe that the ultimate objective of Adolf Hitler's war was world domination"

Battle of Britain Day
The Luftwaffe suffers their greatest losses since mid-August. A reconsideration of tactics is needed and, two days later, the planned invasion of England (Operation Sea Lion) is canceled. **September 15, 1940**

Operation Barbarossa
Hitler decides to attack the Soviet Union, despite still having Britain as a foe in the West. The decision will ultimately prove disastrous. **June 22, 1941**

Germany on Back Foot
With the arrival of the United States into the war, a belligerent Britain, and a stubborn Soviet Union, Germany's prospects of winning the war dwindle. **December 1943**

D-Day
The Allies stage a series of landings at Normandy, ultimately wrestling control of Western Europe back from Germany. **June 6, 1944**

Operation Sea Lion
With the RAF crippled and the Royal Navy kept at bay, the invasion of Britain, Operation Sea Lion, begins. **October 1, 1940**

Invasion of the Soviet Union
Hitler carries out Operation Barbarossa. With no hostile Britain in the West, he is able to focus the majority of his forces on the Soviets and successfully invade. **June 22, 1941**

America Under Attack
Germany builds Intercontinental Ballistic Missiles and atomic bombs. They strike major US cities. **1944**

Victory in Europe Day
The war comes to an end with the Allied forces accepting the unconditional surrender of Nazi Germany following the fall of Berlin and Hitler's suicide. **May 8, 1945**

Royal Navy Subdued
The French Mediterranean fleet has not been sunk and the German Navy manages to prevail. **September 1940**

Britain Surrenders
By the end of the month, despite fighting in London continuing, Germany controls large parts of Britain, including the industrial heartland in the midlands. Britain has no choice but to surrender. **October 31, 1940**

German Empire
Nazi Germany controls almost the entirety of Europe, in addition to absorbing the empires of Britain and France and in turn creating a new formidable global empire. **December 1943**

Nazi Victory
The remaining Allied forces accept defeat and surrender, enabling the Nazi empire to claim victory in Europe. The war with the United States rages on as Hitler attempts to control the world. **1945**

Empire Crumbles
Despite its victory the Nazi empire begins to crumble under the sheer weight of people it has to both feed and control. **1950**

© ALAMY, CORBIS; LUKAS BALANDIS

What if...

Japan didn't attack Pearl Harbor?

ASIA, 1941

NOTABLE NAMES:
- President Franklin D. Roosevelt
- Admiral Isoroki Yamamoto (Japan)
- Captain Minoru Genda (Japan)

IMPORTANT DATES:
December 7, 1941
December 8, 1941
December 11, 1941

What Really Happened...

In 1941, the United States was providing support to Great Britain during World War II, while also pressuring Japan to cease its military expansion. At this point, the U.S. was not actively involved in the war, but offering supplies to the Allies.

On the morning of December 7, 1941, Japan carried out their surprise attack on the United States Naval Base at Pearl Harbor with the goal of crippling the US Navy and their efforts in sending supplies to Great Britain. The attack began at 7:55 am and was over by 9:10 am. In that short amount of time, 2,403 U.S. personnel, including 38 civilians, were killed, and 1,178 people were wounded. Among the wreckage, 19 U.S. Navy ships, including eight battleships, were completely destroyed or damaged, along with 328 U.S. aircraft.

This attack is what finally pushed the U.S. into WWII with the support of the American people. The next day on December 8, President Franklin D. Roosevelt asked Congress for a declaration of war against Japan, and it was granted. On December 11, Japan's allies, Germany and Italy, declared war on the United States, and thus began America's official boots-on-the-ground involvement in World War II.

What would have happened if Japan had not struck Pearl Harbor? History would have turned out very differently. For a start, it would mean Japan was not going to expand its empire into Southeast Asia—because that is what provoked Pearl Harbor. Instead, they would have been concentrating their war efforts solely in China, which was a conflict that began in 1937. Now, China proved to be more than Japan could chew in diplomatic and military terms. Plus, the US had its own interests in China and that was what, ultimately, set them to war with Japan. The US had imposed a trade and financial embargo against Japan. As a result, Japanese financial assets in the US had been frozen and they did not have the means to buy anything from abroad. So to avoid Pearl Harbor, Japan would need to do something to accede to American demands—including pulling out from China. My guess is that the Chinese nationalist government, under Chiang Kai-shek, would have come to terms with Hideki Tojo's government in Tokyo to beat the communists. History would still need to be quite different—for instance, the Japanese would have had to maintain more control over the troops in Nanjing, and not let them massacre an entire city of people, but if things had been less brutal, we can imagine a possible peace treaty between the two countries. Chiang Kai-shek's nationalist government deeply feared Mao and so did the Japanese. So you would not have had Mao—and China would be totally changed. I think Japan would also have demanded access to Chinese markets. It would be a much more influential and powerful country after the end of the war. And, of course, you would not have had the atomic bomb.

Do you think the US would have eventually dropped an atomic bomb somewhere anyway? At the time, Eisenhower was eager to test it out. Churchill, let us not forget, was considering battling Stalin immediately after the Nazis surrendered. Perhaps Eisenhower would have used it against Stalin after the formation of the Soviet bloc in the wake of the fall of Berlin? I don't know if I can make a reliable judgement on that but you are correct—the Americans were thirsting to try the bomb out in a real situation and the idea that they could do it as a pre-emptive strike against the Soviet Union is certainly plausible. Japan would not be the Japan that has the resentment it has now—as the sole country to have been subjected to atomic war, but I suspect it would probably have realized that its economy could win them peace and influence rather than the use of empire and force. I do believe democracy would have won in the end.

At the time, Japan had also conquered Taiwan and Korea. Of course, Chiang Kai-shek fled from China to establish a modern Taiwan that exists, to this day,

If Japan had not struck Pearl Harbor, the US may have dropped an atomic bomb on Moscow instead of Hiroshima and Nagasaki.

Not a real photo.

in a state of uncertainty as a broadly unrecognized 'nation' while Korea was thrust into war. **If Pearl Harbor had not happened, how would this have changed?** Taiwan and Korea would eventually have become independent but under tight Japanese control. As with all empires, the Japanese one would crumble, but I suspect Taiwan and Korea would have become de facto puppet states—possibly even today. Of course, there would have been no Korean War and no split between the North and the South. And modern Taiwan would not be recognized as a rogue Chinese province by Beijing.

Hypothetically, could Japan have found a way to expand its empire into Southeast Asia without attacking Pearl Harbor? Japan would have been very vulnerable in the rest of Southeast Asia if it had not

conquered the Philippines—and that country was an American protectorate at the time so they had to hit the US. Burma was also attractive because it allowed Japan to cut off supplies to the Chinese from the UK. But if you take on Burma you are taking on the British and that means you needed to take on Malaysia and Singapore as well. Japan's strategy had to be all or nothing—they had to take all of Southeast Asia, except Thailand, who were a close ally because there was nothing strategically useful about them. However, French Indochina and Dutch Indonesia were definitely going to be invaded. For Japan, Pearl Harbor was really the sideshow—they were trying to get rid of the US fleet of ships and attempting to stop supplies to the British. It was not about taking Hawaii. Their interest was in expanding to Southeast Asia and removing the Western powers.

**INTERVIEW WITH...
PROFESSOR
ROBERT CRIBB**

Professor Cribb is a lecturer at ANU College of Asia and the Pacific in Canberra. His research interests have covered the changing face of Asia in the wake of World War II, in particular Indonesia and its war of independence with the Dutch after the fall of Japanese rule. His projects include the origins of massacre in Indonesia, *Puppet States Revisited: Empire and Sovereign Subordination in Modern Asia* (with Li Narangoa), and *The Trial and Release of Japanese War Criminals, 1945-58* (with Sandra Wilson, Beatrice Trefalt and Dean Aszkielowicz).

Troops of Chinese 179th Brigade departing Taiyuan, Shanxi Province, China for the front lines in 1937

Japanese soldiers crossing the border from China into the British colony of Hong Kong in 1941

Let's try another hypothetical situation—Japan decides not to attack the Philippines but withdraws from China. Might the US have come to terms with loosening their trade embargo? And might Japan have retained its empire in Southeast Asia? I think this is very unlikely. The Philippines is in the middle of the South China Sea and it was able to block Japanese supply routes so it really had to fall. But let's imagine a situation where Japan is just battling against the European colonial powers—it wants them out of there and Tokyo wants to run things. The British were not strong at the time and they did not fight a strong war in Burma. In the end they were only able to battle the Japanese because of help from the Americans. The French, certainly, would not have been able to fight back until 1945, so Vietnam, Cambodia, and Laos would have remained Japanese. In Indonesia, the Japanese invasion was transformative because it broke down Dutch power. It also increased Indonesian confidence and the movement for independence, which would have happened, but they would have been fighting the Japanese. In the end, if this had transpired—and we take out the Philippines and Pearl Harbor—you have another very different history. The Vietnam War, for instance, does not take place. The Viet Minh would have fought the Japanese and, I suspect, have won. The Japanese were not good with insurgencies. They tended to react brutally, which alienated the populations they were trying to rule—again, look at China. So I think Japan would have handed over independence in these areas, but they would have given the power to people they saw as safe. In turn the local revolutionary movements probably would have overthrown them anyway, such as Ho Chi Minh in Vietnam, and the Western colonial powers would not have returned. Malaysia, I suspect, would have fallen to the communists without the British back in power.

How would it be different?

Pearl Harbor is Struck
A surprise attack on the naval base in Hawaii, an attempt to cripple the US Navy and halt supplies, gives the White House full public support to enter World War II—in Asia and Europe. **December 7, 1941**

Japan Creates the Puppet State of Manchukuo
After the 1931 invasion of Manchuria, and believing that all of Asia should be unified under the rule of Emperor Hirohito, Japan creates a new state, Manchukuo, located in inner (Chinese) Mongolia. **September 15, 1932**

Real timeline

Real timeline

1895

Japan Invades Taiwan
Believe it or not, the road to Pearl Harbor begins here. The East Asian island is invaded by the Japanese, whose empire begins. **May 29–October 21, 1895**

The Outbreak of the Sino-Japanese War
Although tensions between the two countries had been high after the invasion of Manchuria and creation of Manchukuo, it is the increasing number of Japanese soldiers deployed to the mainland that finally breaks Chinese patience. When a Japanese private fails to return to his post, his squad demands to enter the walled town of Wanping. When the Chinese refuse, the Japanese respond with force. What may have been a simple disagreement was the spark that lit a brutal eight-year war. **July 7, 1937**

Alternate timeline

The Outbreak of the Sino-Japanese War
Japan's most challenging battlefront since its annexation of Taiwan and Korea many decades prior begins. However, the army—despite its reputation for brutality—attempts to win over hearts and minds. Nanjing is treated especially carefully. **July 7, 1937**

Would the US have become involved in the war without Pearl Harbor? Yes, I think they would have. Roosevelt saw the Nazis as evil and he did want to get involved—but it was winning over the American public that was his problem. I think he would eventually have found a way to justify fighting in Europe. I think it is possible that the US would not have become involved in Asia, which means—as we just touched upon—you would not have the 20th century as it currently existed, right down to Pol Pot in Cambodia.

Stalin had a non-aggression pact with the Japanese. But on August 9, 1945, he also declared war on the territory. Was this too little too late? How could the Russians have influenced the outcome of all this? It is interesting because, until Pearl Harbor, the Japanese army felt their next war was going to be with the Soviet Union. They fought them on the borders of Manchukuo and they were chastened by that experience. The outbreak of war with China was in many ways not what the Japanese expected. I think they were anticipating that Stalin would break that pact at some point.

Finally, can you think of any way that the US and Japan might not have gone to war with each other? I think we can imagine a possible circumstance where Japan concentrates its troops in China, and sets up puppet administrations that actually function. The US, at the time, wanted free trade in Asia, and Japan was looking to create closed areas of financial interest. So let's imagine that Japan did just enough in China for the US that the White House relaxed its trade ban. In theory, that could have stopped Pearl Harbor. But the main thing that would have stopped the attack on Pearl Harbor is Germany. At the time of the attack, Germany looked as if it was winning in Europe. Japan felt it was going to be on the winning side of the war and it was part of this all-conquering fascist Axis. Six months later, though, Germany was in retreat. If that had happened I don't think Japan would have launched an attack on Pearl Harbor.

The USS Arizona burning after the Japanese attack on Pearl Harbor

"For Japan, Pearl Harbor was really the sideshow—they were trying to get rid of the US fleet of ships"

● **Invasion of the Philippines**
With their sights on the oil-rich Dutch East Indies (now Indonesia), the Japanese attack and conquer the American protectorate of the Philippines. Manila becomes one of the biggest victims of the whole of World War II. **December 8, 1941**

● **Fall of Hong Kong**
The British colony of Hong Kong surrenders to Japan. Churchill considers it a disaster as this marks the very first British territory to surrender to fascism. Burma (now Myanmar), British Borneo, Malaysia, and Singapore would soon follow. **December 25, 1941**

● **Dropping of Atomic Bombs in Hiroshima and Nagasaki**
Eager to test out the power of nuclear warfare, President Eisenhower makes the controversial decision to engulf two of Japan's major cities in a mushroom cloud of death and radiation. The cost to civilian lives remains controversial. **August 6 and August 9, 1945**

● **Tokyo Surrenders and Retreats from its Colonies**
The war in Asia comes to a conclusion. Japan retreats from all of its territories, but fighting between the Western powers and their 'liberated' populations continues for years, and in some cases decades. **September 2, 1945**

● **Talks with Chiang Kai-shek**
Hideki Tojo's government speaks to Chiang Kai-shek about joining forces against the communist army of Mao. Once the communists fall, Japan agrees to leave China. **December 28, 1941**

● **Eisenhower Drops a Nuclear Bomb on Moscow**
With Stalin's forces brutally occupying Taiwan and Korea, the president's flirtation with nuclear weaponry becomes a reality. Moscow surrenders all territories. **August 6, 1945**

● **'Comrade Godzilla'**
Inspired by the bombing of Moscow, the creation of 'Comrade Godzilla'—a mutated red lizard that trashes the Russian capital—thrills viewers all across the world. **June 9, 1955**

● **The US Threatens to Freeze Japanese Assets**
The US requests that Japan withdraw from China or else all assets will be frozen. Japan begins talks with the White House about a resolution regarding China. **July 26, 1941**

● **Japan Removes Itself From Hitler's Sphere of Influence**
With rumors that Stalin is prepared to tear up his non-aggression pact with Tokyo, Japan proclaims it is no longer aligned with fascism. **August 20, 1941**

● **Defeat of the Chinese Communists**
One of the bloodiest struggles of the war comes to a close. Japan wins cautious plaudits for assisting Chiang Kai-shek in his vision for a unified, Western-friendly China. **March 1, 1944**

● **Stalin Becomes Involved in the War in Asia**
Aghast at Japan's aggression towards the Chinese communists, Stalin orders the Red Army to strike Taiwan and Korea, hoping to gain a foothold in the continent. **May 31, 1945**

What if...

The Allies lost the Battle of the Atlantic?

BATTLE OF THE ATLANTIC, 1939-1945

IMPORTANT DATES:
September 3, 1939
May 8, 1945

What Really Happened...

The longest military campaign of World War II, the Battle of the Atlantic between Axis and Allied forces lasted from September 3, 1939, until May 8, 1945, when the Germans surrendered and were defeated. It's been called the "longest, largest, and most complex" naval battle in history.

This naval, submarine warfare was an effort to control shipping lanes, involved thousands of ships and aircraft, and spanned thousands of miles. Over the course of the battle, the power dynamic shifted from one side to the other, until 1943 when Allied forces took and maintained the upper hand with the innovation of the Hedgehog, a forward-throwing anti-submarine weapon. The battle peaked between February and May—nicknamed "Black May"—and Nazi Germany's U-boat losses were devastating. They eventually withdrew and the Allies had won the Battle of the Atlantic.

What if the Allies had lost the Battle of the Atlantic?
Britain would not have been able to carry on its war effort for very long. In 1939, Britain was dependent for at least half of its food imported from overseas, so it would have been in a very serious situation in this regard. Also, Britain's economy in 1939-40 is pretty much export-based, so to survive economically it needed to import raw material and export finished goods. It would have been virtually impossible for Britain to survive if it had not been able to use the sea. The Germans reached the French coast in the summer, so Britain would have that year's harvest.

If the Germans had put the squeeze on Britain in the winter of 1940-41, which they tried to do, I think it would have been just a matter of weeks, perhaps months, before the British government would have had to make a decision about accommodating German requests. I don't see a great surge of Germans coming across the English Channel, at least not initially, because the Germans could not have launched an invasion at the same time they were trying to do an effective blockade of Britain. The big question for the British would have been, apart from accommodating Hitler's wishes and succumbing to the pressure, the extent to which it would have been an occupied country. That would certainly have been an interesting situation.

How would it have been possible for the Germans to have won the war in the Atlantic? Most people tell me that if the Germans had had 300 U-boats in 1939 they would have won the Battle of the Atlantic. My response is always that if the Germans had had

300 U-boats, the Brits would have had 250 destroyers, sloops and frigates. You can't change one variable and expect the others to remain unchanged. The Brits built for the threat — Germany's surface fleet. The rest could be — and was — improvised in a time of crisis. Simply put: the Germans could never have won the Battle of the Atlantic, but Britain could have lost it.

The greatest threat to imports in 1940-41 was the bombing and closure of key British ports and that's a Luftwaffe responsibility, nothing to do with the Kriegsmarine. Many historians make a facile and erroneous link between import decline and sinkings at sea in this period, but it's just not that simple. The Germans did not have the power in 1940-41 to inflict a knockout blow at sea. 'Death by a thousand cuts' was a more plausible scenario, but even that could not be done fast enough to ensure the death of the victim. The Germans are really the engine of the Atlantic War because if the Germans don't do anything, the Allies win. It is just that simple.

So, if Germany were to have won the war in the Atlantic, it would have been in the winter of 1941 when Britain was standing alone in Europe?
Yes. Someone said that Britain had 500 million people around the world backing it up, but it really is the little Dutch boy with his finger in the dike in the winter of 1941. That's the only moment when the Germans have a clear, measurable, obtainable objective in the Atlantic War — and that is to blockade Britain and force it to surrender. But the problem for the Germans is that they don't have the resources to do it. One of the biggest

INTERVIEW WITH...
MARC MILNER

Marc Milner is Professor of History and Director of the Gregg Center for the Study of War and Society at the University of New Brunswick, Canada. He has published extensively on the Battle of the Atlantic and the history of the Royal Canadian Navy. A contributor to the official histories of both the RCN and the RCAF in World War II, Milner's book, *Battle of the Atlantic*, won the CP Stacey Prize for the best book on military history in Canada in 2004. Other recent works have focused on the Normandy campaign, including *Stopping The Panzers: The Untold Story of D-Day*, which won the US Commission on Military History's 'James Collins Book Prize' for 2014-15.

What if Nazi Germany had won the Battle of the Atlantic and invaded Britain?

Allied tanker Dixie Arrow torpedoed by U-71 in 1942

1941 there are only eight German submarines at sea that are operational. You can't win the Battle of the Atlantic with eight submarines. The Germans pushed out as many surface vessels as they possibly could.

It is a very dangerous period for Britain in the winter of 1941 because Scharnhorst and Gneisenau, the two big battlecruisers, are loose in the North Atlantic. [Admiral] Hipper and Admiral Scheer are out in the North Atlantic. There are long-range Condors and Blohm & Voss flying-boats doing patrols. Some of the Condors are attacking shipping at sea, particularly in the east Atlantic. The Germans are beginning to use U-boat wolf packs and achieve some dramatic successes. But it's never quite enough. They spent the winter of 1941 pulling the lion's tail and tweaking its ears, but when the fair weather of spring comes in April and May and they send Bismarck out, it is a totally changed operational environment.

If Britain had succumbed, could America have found another staging post for its entrance into the war in Europe? Yes. In 1942 the Allies invade French North Africa, and the landings along the Moroccan coast are staged directly from the US eastern seaboard as part of Operation Torch. So the way back into Europe would have been, in some ways, the way that NATO subsequently planned to get back into Europe should Western Europe and Great Britain fall to the Soviet Union. That is to work their way through North Africa and then eventually through the Iberian Peninsula.

Presumably, though, without Britain as an ally, America might not have declared war on Germany in December 1941? From what we know of the Americans in 1939-41, it is not clear whether they might have made an accommodation with the new regime in Europe and lived with it. America had not begun to mobilize, seriously, by the summer of 1941. It was still building up its fleet and the infrastructure for the huge army that would appear in Europe in 1944. It is just not in place at this time, so I think America would have had

impacts on British imports in the winter of 1940-41 is the Blitz. Most people don't associate that with the Battle of the Atlantic, but the bombing and closure of ports along the English south and east coasts promptly cuts into British imports far more than anything that is done at sea because all of a sudden the major import harbors are closed and they have to reorient longshoremen and rolling stock and railways and the handling gear to the West Country ports, and that takes almost a year to do. The net result is a sharp decline in imports to Britain — they just don't have the port handling capability. But Germany does not have enough submarines. In January

"The question becomes, does Britain capitulate, or does the British government go into exile and continue the war from the Empire and the Commonwealth?"

How would it be different?

The Happy Time Begins
U-boats carry the war to America's eastern seaboard and enjoy huge success as the US Navy fails to organize effective convoys, resulting in the loss of thousands of tons of vital shipping. **December 1941**

Pearl Harbor Attacked
Carrier-based Japanese aircraft launch their surprise strike on the US Pacific Fleet. A day later, the United States declares war on Japan. Three days after this, the US declares war on Germany. **December 1941**

Arctic Operations Begin
When Britain begins running supplies of raw materials and finished hardware to Russian ports under the Lend-Lease deal, U-boats, shore-based aircraft, and surface vessels commence operations in Arctic latitudes. **June 1941**

Real timeline

Real timeline

1939

The Outbreak of War
Only 27 of Germany's 57 U-boats are capable of long-range Atlantic operations. Germany's Z-plan aims to build 300 U-boats, enough to strangle Britain. It takes a further 20 months to reach this tally. **September 1939**

Capture of French Atlantic Ports
U-boats now enjoy easy access to the eastern Atlantic. Despite the delineation of a neutral zone where American ships will sink marauding subs, the Germans soon extend operations to the central and western Atlantic. **June 1940**

Alternate timeline

Z-Plan Hits Target
The Kriegsmarine beefs up production and hits its target of 300 U-boats, with most capable of long-range Atlantic voyages. The blockade of British ports puts enormous pressure on Churchill. **June 1941**

German U-boat bases in France were hundreds of miles closer to the Atlantic than the bases on the North Sea

to make a serious decision. My best guess — and it can be no more than that — is that they would have made an accommodation with Nazi Europe and made every effort to make sure that Britain was as far as they got [on their westward expansion].

If Britain had fallen, do you think Churchill would have been able to continue fighting from bases in Canada and other parts of the Empire and Commonwealth? Canada declared war against Nazi Germany, not as part of the British Empire but as an independent, self-governing nation. So it is entirely conceivable that the war would have continued. There were certainly plans to move the British fleet to Canada, and ports along the Canadian east coast were surveyed to see just where the Royal Navy could shelter. So the question becomes, does Britain capitulate like the French did and make accommodation, or does the British government go into exile and continue the war from the Empire and the Commonwealth? That would also change the situation for the Americans.

If Britain had fallen in 1941, how would that have affected Russian resistance to Nazi Germany?

The assumption is that Britain would have fallen in the spring of 1941 because it is difficult to figure the scenario before or after that. And by then Brits have already signed the Lend-Lease deal and are already trans-shipping vast amounts of goods destined for Britain like American fighters, P40-Warhawks, and Tomahawks straight to Russia. Britain is also sending a large number of its tanks to Russia in the autumn of 1941. I have read recently that perhaps as much as upwards of 40 percent of the tanks that stand between the Germans and Moscow in the first week of December 1941 were Matilda and Valentine tanks from British factories. If that's the case, there is a very narrow window in which British production and Lend-Lease material, including Hurricane fighters, get to Russia just at the most critical moment of the German advance on Moscow. And many historians assume — though I don't know that it's a fair assumption — that had Moscow fallen, the Soviet Union would have capitulated. I am not entirely convinced of that but, if so, then the British aid to the Soviet Union in the autumn of 1941 might well have been one of the most singular, decisive things that Britain did to ensure the Allied victory in World War II.

Stalingrad Comes to an End
Arguably the single most crucial battle of the European war concludes with Germany's defeat in the ruins of Stalingrad. Thousands of German troops become POWs. **February 1943**

The Longest Day
Germany is stretched to its breaking point as Allied forces, including a vast American army, launch D-Day operations with the invasion of Normandy.
June 6, 1944

Hitler Commits Suicide
The war in Europe nears its end as Hitler takes his own life in his Berlin bunker shortly before the Red Army arrives. Unconditional surrender follows a week later on May 7. **April 1945**

The US Drops the Bomb
World War II nears its end after a B-29 bomber drops the world's first deployed atomic bomb on Hiroshima, destroying 90 percent of the city and instantly killing 80,000 people. **August 1945**

Royal Navy Moves to Canada/Ceylon
Churchill relocates the Royal Navy to Halifax in Canada, and Trincomalee in Ceylon, the only Empire-Commonwealth ports capable of handling such warships.
August 1941

The Allies Take North Africa
British Empire forces in Africa, supplied via the Suez Canal, have taken control of the continent. The invasion of Italy is planned.
November 1942

Second Battle of Moscow
The German Sixth Army takes Stalingrad and Hitler launches a second assault on Moscow. Yet Russia still stands.
March 1943

D-Day Launches via Iberian Peninsula
The Iberian Peninsula becomes the staging post for the Allied push into Western Europe.
June 1944

Britain Falls to the Reich With food supplies dwindling and the U-boat wolf packs emerging pre-eminent in the Atlantic, the British government goes into exile to continue the war from the Empire.
November 1941

The US Declines Germany Deal
Roosevelt strongly considers negotiations with Nazi Germany, but pressure from Britain, Canada, and Hitler's early success in Russia prompts him to enter the war in Europe. **December 1941**

D-Day Preparations Begin in Earnest
Operation Torch is no longer a requirement given Allied success in Africa. American GIs begin arriving in Morocco and Algeria in preparation for a strike at mainland Europe.
January 1943

Liberation of Great Britain
With his forces stretched thin following defeat at Kursk, Hitler withdraws from mainland Britain in a bid to shore up his defenses in France. Churchill returns to Whitehall. **February 1944**

What if...
North Korea won the Korean War?

KOREA, 1950

NOTABLE NAMES:
- Syngman Rhee
- Kim Il Sung
- President Harry Truman
- Mao Zedong
- President Dwight D. Eisenhower

IMPORTANT DATES:
June 25, 1950
July 27, 1953

What Really Happened...

In August 1945, Korea was divided in half with the Russians occupying the north and the United States occupying the south until 1948. By the late 1940s, anti-communist dictator Syngman Rhee was the leader of South Korea with reluctant support from the U.S., and communist dictator Kim Il Sung was leader of North Korea with full support from the Soviet Union.

On June 25, 1950, North Korea's soldiers crossed the border to invade South Korea. Out of fear over the expansion of communism, President Harry Truman readied troops to support South Korea. However, North Korea was well-trained and skilled, South Korean soldiers were afraid and prone to fleeing, and soon, America's role switched from defensive to offensive. Communist China got involved with Mao Zedong not only sending troops, but also threatening the United States with full-scale war.

Peace talks began in July 1951, but nothing could be negotiated until two years later on July 27, 1953, after Dwight D. Eisenhower became president and an armistice was finally signed by North Korea. It's from this agreement that a new boundary was formed, along with the 2 miles of demilitarized zone that exist today.

What if North Korea had won the Korean War?
It is impossible to answer this question, we can only speculate. But if—and it is a huge if—North Korea had won the war, then the massive devastation caused by the fighting, Chinese intervention, the 'scorched earth' retreat from North Korea, and the US air campaign would have been largely obviated and this, in turn, might have led North Koreans not to harbor such bitter memories of the war. Moreover, the stability engendered by a unified country might have led to a less paranoid regime and by defeating the US, the country would not have such a massive chip on its shoulder. Kim Il-sung's war aims were the unification of the peninsula and the end of the South-Korean state. The best example of what might have been had North Korea won is probably Vietnam, which had a similar historical experience; It was a nation on the flank of China, was colonized, divided, and it fought the Americans. But Vietnam defeated its French colonial power in battle and drove off the Americans, reunifying the country. As such, Vietnamese have decent international relations, a liberal economy, and relatively open society. Korea, on the other hand, was unable to free itself from Japanese colonial rule and North Korea was unable to defeat the US in war. North Korea has also shuttered itself off against the wider world and there are few signs of a liberalizing economy or society. Would a unified Korea look more like a unified Vietnam? Maybe.

How close was North Korea to winning the war? At the beginning, North Korea was very close to winning the war. Republic of Korea (ROK) units were smashed in the initial blitzkrieg attack that took place in the early hours of Sunday June 25, 1950, and then pushed into a headlong retreat southward. US combat units, rushing to the peninsula from Japan, had no more luck in stemming the onrush of the North Korean People's Army (NKPA) in the early July battles.

It was only when the remaining ROK units and massive US (along with British) reinforcements arrived that a 130-mile defensive front was established in the southeast: The Pusan Perimeter. If you had looked at a map during the summer of 1950, this little corner of South Korea—along with a number of offshore islands—was the only part of the peninsula painted blue; the rest was deepest red. However, by late summer, the NKPA had broken its teeth against the hardening ROK and UN defenses. When General Douglas MacArthur, in a brilliant but risky gambit, pulled his best troops, the US Marines, out of the line, embarked them on landing craft, and landed them 200 miles in the enemy rear in his amphibious descent upon Inchon—the port serving Seoul—the NKPA's bolt was shot.

When did the United States intervene? The US reacted very quickly and with a tremendous sense of urgency. The war broke out in the early hours of June 25 and US forces' air and naval units were committed

> "It would have been recognized internationally, in just the same way that Mao's Communist Party was eventually recognized as the government of mainland China"

North Korea was very close to winning the Korean War, which could have changed the global political landscape as we know it

Not a real photo, has been altered.

UNITED STATES

KOREA

INTERVIEW WITH...
ANDREW SALMON

Andrew Salmon is a Seoul-based reporter and author. He has written four books on Korea, including *To the Last Round: The Epic British Stand on the Imjin River, Korea, 1951*, which was named Military Book of the Year in the UK in 2009 and won a Korean Wave award in South Korea's National Assembly for its contribution to the literature of the conflict. In 2014 he published *All That Matters: Modern Korea*.

on June 27, soon followed by Australian and British units. In a model case of international consensus building, which would grant its intervention credibility, Washington went down the multilateral route and fought the war under the aegis of the UN. It is important to note that despite spirited and important roles of contingents from as far afield as Ethiopia and Columbia, the lion's share of the fighting was done by the ROK and US forces with the UK, the UN's third-largest contingent, also playing a critical role. Arguably, the UN has not mounted such an effective military intervention since.

If North Korea had won the war would the government and political elite of South Korea have escaped? Perhaps, perhaps not. Syngman Rhee

[South Korean president] and Kim Il-sung [leader of the Democratic People's Republic of Korea] never met but they were to-the-death rivals: if Rhee and his key aides and allies had not escaped, it seems likely that they would have been at best imprisoned, at worst, liquidated. They could possibly have established a government-in-exile on an offshore Korean island or in the United States. But whether he would have had the power or influence to convince the US to carry out a seaborne counterattack—probably from Japan—onto the Asian mainland is very questionable. First, the South Korean government of the Fifties was not the dynamic force it would become in the Sixties and Seventies, when it engineered the 'economic miracle' and while MacArthur was close to Rhee,

President Harry Truman was not, and the Bay of Pigs fiasco the US later engineered in Cuba would later show how dangerous such adventures could be.

If North Korea had won would there have been purges? North Korea has a poor history of human rights and a strong record of purging undesirables. During the war, both the South and North Koreans carried out numerous atrocities, including massacres of POWs, prisoners, and regime opponents. If the North Koreans had won the war, they would certainly have established Korea as a unified country: this was why Kim Il-sung, who was a nationalist as well as a communist, launched the war in the first place.

If it had been established as one unified country would it have been recognized internationally? I suspect it would have been recognized internationally, in just the same way that Mao's Communist Party was eventually recognized as the government of mainland China. It would certainly have been welcomed by its communist allies with whom it shared (and still shares) borders—China and the Soviet Union/Russia—and with the wider communist bloc. And with South Korea eliminated as a free-world nation, then the 'east' truly would have been 'red': The Northeast Asian mainland would have been communist, with just Japan and Taiwan, on their island fastnesses, holding out.

Would Kim Il-sung have been leader? Yes, there is no doubt that Kim was the man in charge. Indeed, several of his generals and other factions were purged after the war. As it is, North Korea's personality cult paints Kim as the greatest Korean and one of the greatest human beings who ever lived—even though his biggest gambit, the war to reunify Korea, failed. If he had succeeded, his standing would have been magnified, though it is difficult to imagine a personality cult stronger than the one in place today.

How would the worldwide balance of power changed? Korea has historically seen itself as a

American M-40 gun motor carriages provide heavy-artillery support to US Army's 25th Infantry Division in Korea, November 1951

'shrimp' between the 'whales' of China, Russia, and Japan. In the modern era—i.e., the late-19th century onward—it has tried to pit one power against another, though this has not always worked. To a large extent, the first Sino-Japanese War, and the Russo-Japanese War, were both fought over which of these powers would control Korea. What is often overlooked in 21st-century South Korea is that there were strong Korean factions at that time who favored Japan, just as there were other factions that favored China and Russia. As for the effect of a communist victory in Korea in 1950, arguably, the United States would have become more defensive and more hard line in defending free-world interests. But compared to China and the USSR, Korea is not that significant in terms of the communist bloc's economic, political, or military arms. North Korea has a formidable army for fighting on home turf, but beyond its special forces, it has no real expeditionary forces, so it doesn't affect the global balance of power. Currently, an isolated North Korea is creating nuclear weapons and strategic missiles: If it had won the war, it might not have felt the need for these programs.

How would it be different?

Real timeline

1910

● **Japanese Empire**
After the Russo-Japanese War (1904–1905), Korea became a protectorate of Japan. The Empire of Japan annexed Korea in 1910, leading to 35 years of colonial rule. **1910**

● **WWII Ends**
After World War II, Japanese occupation of Korea ends with Soviet troops occupying the north, and US troops the south part of the country. **1945**

● **KWP Formed**
North Korea's Communist Party Korean Workers' Party (KWP) is established. Soviet-backed leadership is installed, including Red Army-trained Kim Il-sung. **1946**

● **Russia Withdraws**
Russian troops begin leaving North Korea, leaving Kim Il-sung in charge. In the south the Republic of Korea is formed with Syngman Rhee as the country's first president. **1948**

● **American Withdrawal**
US troops begin leaving the south of the country, giving the north encouragement that they could unify the country. **1949**

● **Invasion**
North Korea invades the south, crossing the 38th Parallel, leading to a full-scale war. Two days later, their tanks reach the outskirts of Seoul. **June 25, 1950**

Real timeline

Alternate timeline

● **No Assistance**
The Americans decide that Korea falls outside their strategic sphere of influence, and the South Koreans, with their poorly armed troops, are overwhelmed in battle. **June 26, 1950**

How might Seoul have developed? Well, the 'economic miracle' of the Seventies—the extraordinary process of a backward, agrarian country transforming itself into an export powerhouse and heavy industrial player—would not have happened. In turn, the political miracle of the Eighties—when the country, through people-power protests, forced the military junta to accept democratic elections—would not have transpired either. And with the above developments absent, the ongoing social and cultural changes, under which Koreans have become high-tech, global citizens, overturning many of the autocratic, old-fashioned aspects of their society and developing internationally-admired entertainment products, would not have taken place. That having been said, Seoul, as the capital or sub-capital of a Korea unified by Kim, would probably not be as insular, isolated, and paranoid as Pyongyang is today. Again, we can look to the example of Hanoi's status as the capital of a unified Vietnam. Both Hanoi and Saigon today are far more open than Pyongyang in political, economic, and social terms. Perhaps a Kim-ruled Seoul would look like a cross between today's Pyongyang and today's Saigon.

How long would the new regime have lasted? As it is, the Kim regime has survived a devastating war, the collapse of European communism, famine, poverty, and the death of both its founding father and his son, yet has still managed to pass power on to the third generation. In gentler and kinder circumstances, it seems unlikely that the regime would have given up its grip on power. Then again, perhaps a more open, less isolated, and less totalitarian communist Korea would have been more vulnerable to (or open to) change and so would have collapsed. We saw this with the regimes in Eastern Europe and the Soviet Union. Militating against that speculation is the fact that in Asia—in Beijing and Hanoi—communist parties have actually survived in political power even while they have opened their economies and societies. So, my guess is that the Kims would have survived as leaders of a unified Korea. I also suspect that the government of a Kim-unified Korea

US Marines taking North Korean soldiers prisoner, Korea, 1951

would have been harder-line that the current governments in power in Hanoi and Beijing but not as hard line as the current regime reigning in Pyongyang today.

How might the world be different today? Not radically. Sure, there would be no Samsung smartphones or Psy, but none of these things can be said to have made a significant difference to humanity. However, the whole is greater than the sum of its parts. If South Korea had ceased to exist in 1950, we would not have witnessed the greatest national success story of the 20th century; the rise of South Korea from the ashes of war to become one of the most admired national benchmarks on Earth—an economic force, democratic polity, and an increasingly liberal society. More broadly, if there were not two opposed Koreas, a major causus belli would not exist in Northeast Asia. Absent this, perhaps the region—China, Korea, Japan, and the Russian Far East—would have achieved greater economic unity, like the European Union and the North American Free Trade Area.

American Assistance
After the invasion of the south and full-scale war, the US military intervenes extremely quickly with air and naval units engaged only a few days after the conflict breaks out. **June 27, 1950**

Stalemate
An armistice is called. The war has cost over 2 million lives and the country is split into two. The Demilitarized Zone is reset as boundary between communist North and anti-communist South. **July 27, 1953**

Economic Miracle
The country continues to experience economic and industrial growth but its government is still a long way removed from democracy and would be until the sixth republic. **1979**

Two Very Different Countries
Relations between the two countries are still strained and the demilitarized zone that separates the two countries stretches the width of the peninsula and into the Yellow Sea. **Present day**

Engage the Enemy
US ground units meet the enemy in battle. Although they are unsuccessful, it highlights how quickly American troops engage North Korea. USA gets international cooperation and legitimacy for the conflict through the UN. **July 5, 1950**

North Korean Purge
Relations with Russia and China and North Korea deteriorate but Kim remains in power and strengthens his grip by purging his enemies. **1958**

Cult of the Leader
The country is united under Kim Il-Sung with his face appearing all over the united country. Korea is recognized as one country with Kim as its leader. **1974**

North Korea Nosedives
North Korea's economy begins to deteriorate rapidly, propelled by the fall of the Soviet Union and the end of their favored trade and aid. In the mid-nineties famine ravages the country and possibly a million people die. **1990s**

Marching on Seoul
North Korean troops enter Seoul just a few days after the conflict has begun. Members of the South Korean government flee the country for the United States. **June 29, 1950**

Purges
The North Korean leader Kim Il-Sung orders a purge of those he sees as a threat to his government. Tens of thousands of people are killed. **1951**

Communist Borders
China and the Soviet Union welcome the new united country. Northeast Asia is now 'red' with just Japan and Taiwan not communist. **1952**

Bay of Pigs
After the Bay of Pigs invasion in Cuba ends in fiasco, the South Korean exiled government's hopes for a US-backed counter invasion of Korea are dashed. **1961**

Open Economy
Korea is still ruled by Kim's grandson in an authoritarian manner but China-style economic reforms are implemented. As market capitalism takes effect, hopes arise for a more democratic polity. **Present day**

What if...

The USA won the Vietnam War?

VIETNAM, 1955-1975

What Really Happened...

In total, the Vietnam War lasted 20 years, from November 1, 1955, until April 30, 1975.

Communist and political leader Ho Chi Minh formed the Viet Minh, and when he eventually gained control of the north, he and his supporters sought to unify north and south Vietnam as a communist nation. In 1955, anti-communist Ngo Dinh Diem became president of South Vietnam.

Diem began to arrest, torture, and execute southern Viet Minh sympathizers (the Viet Cong, or Vietnamese Communists), and by 1957, the Viet Cong began to fight back. The unrest continued to escalate, and Diem was assassinated in a coup by some of his own council members in November 1963. While the United States was technically involved in the war from the start, it wasn't until March 1965 that the U.S. sent combat forces with public support.

However, in November 1967, both the American public and soldiers began to oppose the war; between July 1966 and December 1973, more than 503,000 U.S. military members deserted. In January 1973, the United States and North Vietnam reached a peace agreement and ended hostilities, while North and South Vietnam continued to fight until April 30, 1975, when the North conquered the South.

What would have happened if the United States had won the Vietnam War? There are a lot of academics and historians who look at Vietnam as a part of something much bigger—namely the Cold War. So if the US had won, the Cold War would probably have ended a little sooner and the dawn of that unilateral superpower controlling things would have come quicker. In Southeast Asia, everything would be radically different—including a faster and more thorough confrontation between the US and China. I doubt China would have sat by and let an American victory happen without repercussion—even though they were not exactly fans of the Vietnamese either. I don't think Beijing would have invaded Vietnam to repel the Americans, as they did in Korea, but it certainly would have been the US against China and Russia. And it would have been a war that was not just cold but glacial. American politics would certainly have been more tumultuous as well.

If you look at the US presidential elections since the 1960s, every one of them has been fought over Vietnam to one extent or another. It is still the most controversial aspect of a controversial time period. Had they come out of that smiling, with another greatest generation on their hands, US politics would have looked quite different. For instance, it is hard to see the Republican revolution taking place. Republicans typically have an aggressive foreign policy, it is one of their tropes, but if Democratic policy had won in Vietnam—because it was the

Democrats who started the war in Southeast Asia—that would have taken a lot of heat away from their rivals.

Would they have become involved in more conflicts? Yes, I think the US would have been much less gun-shy during the 1970s and 1980s. Reagan tinkered with it, but that use of force to solve conflicts didn't really come back until the first Bush and then with Bill Clinton. The reason the US did not rely on its military, on any great scale at least, to solve problems during the 1970s and the 1980s was all down to the country's failure in Vietnam.

When the Vietnam War began to cross into Cambodia it created the environment in which Pol Pot and the Khmer Rouge came to power. What resulted was a four-year holocaust. Could this have been avoided? If the US was ever going to win the Vietnam War it would have been during the Tet Offensive of 1968. That was the turning point and that was when the public, back in the United States, saw the North Vietnamese were not just going to retreat and surrender—it was literally a fight to the death.

Of course, there was no big, magical American victory during Tet, but let's imagine there was. Let's imagine the US had repelled that attack quickly and conclusively and the war was essentially over as a result. At that point in time, the Khmer Rouge was not a big player in the conflict. It is only after the US

HA LONG BAY

McDonald's

BOOSTER

LIGHTNING

began its military incursions into Cambodia and the government in that country began to fall that everything became out of hand. A victorious US in Vietnam would not have required any entrance into Cambodia and, as a result, you almost certainly would not have seen the rise of the Khmer Rouge. They are intrinsically tied to how the Vietnam War progressed, no doubt about that.

Would we ever have seen a situation like in Korea where the communist North and the democratic South are split down the middle, even to this day? No, that was never going to happen. One side was going to

reunify the country, no matter what. So if there was a big American victory, one situation you have is reunification under non-communist rule. As a result of that, the turn towards Asia the US is presently taking would have happened then as opposed to now. We would have had an immediate conflict with China. Unlike the North Koreans, the North Vietnamese were much less likely to accept the scenario where the country remained split. If you look at their leadership, at their proclamations and their goals, they were not going to go for a 'tie.'

In addition, the tactical situation in Vietnam was much trickier. This is because the border between North

INTERVIEW WITH... DR. ANDREW WIEST

Dr. Andrew Wiest currently lectures at the University of Southern Mississippi and is the founding director of the Dale Center for the Study of War and Society. His books include *The Boys of '67: Charlie Company's War in Vietnam*, *Vietnam's Forgotten Army: Heroism and Betrayal in the ARVN*, and *Vietnam: A View From the Front Lines*. He has also organized trips for Vietnam veterans suffering from PTSD to visit the country they once fought in. Wiest has developed a 'study abroad' program for US students wishing to soak up life in Saigon or Hanoi.

An Alternative, Successful Campaign

CHINA

BURMA

LAOS

NORTH VIETNAM

Attention From the North
Having conquered Hanoi and North Vietnam, a new Cold War front is established at the northern border to China, whose government feels threatened by the US-allied Vietnam.

A Reversal of Fortune
A successful defense of the Tet Offensive in January 1968 spurs the US-backed South across the demilitarized zone into North Vietnam, resulting in a Westernized, unified Vietnam.

In the Balance
With two superpowers next door to each other, Laos and Thailand become fair game for the US and China's race for influence and allegiance in Southeast Asia.

THAILAND

Atrocities Averted
By avoiding a campaign in Cambodia, the Khmer Rouge don't gain traction in the country, avoiding the genocide under Pol Pot that would otherwise have taken place. Cambodia is stronger as a result.

CAMBODIA

SOUTH VIETNAM

"If the US was ever going to win the Vietnam War, it would have been during the Tet Offensive of 1968"

and South Vietnam is so long and porous that it would be very difficult to police—and that is why you had the Ho Chi Minh trail, the excursions into Cambodia and Laos, and all of that other stuff. So it might be convenient to think that we could replay the Korean War and end Vietnam with a stalemate, but that was never going to happen. People forget the wanted reunification too—just under different circumstances.

If John F. Kennedy had not been assassinated, would the Vietnam War have been avoided? That is a controversial question. There have been so many arguments about this—and, of course, Kennedy's legacy is such a sacred thing in the States that it is political kryptonite to touch it. The pro-Kennedy forces argue he wanted to withdraw most of the 16,000 military advisors that were over there. However, before Kennedy there were only 600 military advisors over there. He had begun a war over there and I think there are two things that still would have hamstrung him even if he had wanted out.

The first is that he still wanted his political party to win another term, and if the Democrats had wiped their hands of Vietnam there is a good chance they would not have achieved that. The second is that Kennedy wanted his brother to be the next man in the White House. To mess that up, by handing Vietnam to the communists, would have sunk this. I would also argue that Robert McNamara, who was Kennedy's confidant in the first place and the architect of the Vietnam War, was going to give him the same advice he gave Lyndon B. Johnson—which was to go in with all guns blazing. You have to remember that both Kennedy and Johnson faced

How would it be different?

The Geneva Conference
France agrees to the decolonization of Vietnam. Free elections are promised, but the US suspects the communist Ho Chi Minh may win. It installs a brutal dictator, Ngo Dinh Diem, in South Vietnam. He is viewed by Ho Chi Minh and the North as a puppet ruler. **July 21, 1954**

Real timeline

Real timeline

Assassination of Đình Diêm
Diem—whose anti-Buddhist policies famously caused the monk Thich Quang Duc to immolate himself—is murdered in a brutal but mysterious coup d'état. **November 2, 1963**

Real timeline

1945

Vietnamese Declaration of Independence
Based on the American Declaration of Independence, Ho Chi Minh asks the US and the West to oppose French colonial rule in Vietnam and support what will be "a free and independent country." **September 2, 1945**

Ho Chi Minh Contacts President Truman
The Vietnamese revolutionary writes to Truman asking him to "urgently interfere" in the foreign rule of his country. Truman fears Vietnam becoming communist and instead backs the French. **February 28, 1946**

Alternate timeline

US Reunites Korea
Fears that China would support the North prove unfounded. The US manages to push back the comparatively minimal army of Kim Il-sung and successfully reunites the two Koreas. Seoul aligns itself as a Western-friendly government. **July 27, 1953**

A man suspected of supporting the Viet Cong forces being arrested and detained by US forces

A convoy of US tanks in Vietnam

the post-World War II consensus: to fight a difficult, problematic, and long war against what they perceived as a communist threat or to embark on social changes back home—in particular the civil-rights movement. I believe Kennedy was also going to veer toward the civil-rights movement—just as Johnson did. But I don't think you get both—civil rights and the end of Vietnam. That mixture would have brought the Democrats down at the voting booth.

Is there any way the Vietnam War may have been avoided? Asking anyone to do the right thing back then was difficult. Had Franklin Roosevelt lived, maybe things could have been avoided. He had a guy on his team who was a communist, namely Stalin, and Roosevelt was not a fan of European colonialism. So he may have sided with Ho Chi Minh's desire to have an independent Vietnam, free from French rule. Had he lived longer, with all of his clout, I think that is the

best chance we would have had to avoid starting a war out there.

Vietnam is now awash with KFC restaurants, Coca-Cola, multiplexes, and other examples of American pop culture. So who really won the war? Well, that is the thing—they are now America's staunch allies. It shows that, first of all, as Sun Tzu said, the best tool to win a war is not always the military. It was American culture that eventually prevailed.

If you look at things like *Rambo* and all these other Hollywood movies that attempted to justify the conflict, it is obvious how much impact it had on the US. But it was just a blip on the radar to the Vietnamese. It cost them many more lives, but it was all part of a bigger struggle for independence.

Today, Vietnam has a huge young generation and this is all ancient history to them. They have moved on, but ironically it is the face of the US they now buy into.

● **Gulf of Tomkin Fabrication**
North Vietnamese ships are reported to have fired on a US patroller, the Maddox, in the South China Sea. President Johnson uses the event to justify going to war. Declassified documents later confirmed that no attack happened. **August 2, 1964**

● **The My Lai Massacre**
At My Lai, families are raped, tortured, and killed by US soldiers. Lieutenant William Calley, who instigated the horror, walks free, but world opinion becomes opposed to "America's war." **March 16, 1968**

● **Paris Peace Accords**
Nixon's government agrees to a cease-fire, with US ground troops and POWs returning home. The reunification of Vietnam is now a matter between the respective Saigon and Hanoi governments. **January 27, 1973**

● **Fall of Saigon**
The war ends with the North Vietnamese taking Saigon by force and celebrating a reunified country. Ho Chi Minh, who died in 1969, remains a national icon. Saigon is now known as Ho Chi Minh City. **April 30, 1975**

● **Tet Offensive**
On Vietnamese New Year, the North surprises the South with a sudden offensive. The city of Hue witnesses extensive fighting. South Vietnam and its allies suffer drastic losses. **January 30–March 3, 1968**

● **Ho Chi Minh at the UN**
Ho Chi Minh gives a rousing speech at the UN, but with the new Korea becoming an international trading partner, Western nations side with the US on Vietnamese reunification. **December 1956**

● **Gulf of Tomkin Fabrication**
Johnson, respecting Kennedy's opposition to communism in Asia and Latin America, fabricates the Gulf of Tonkin incident to justify entering the war in Vietnam. **August 2, 1964**

● **Failed Tet Offensive**
The North Vietnamese conduct a failed attempt to take Saigon, Hue, and other cities in South Vietnam. Forewarned about the attack, the US Army quickly repels their enemies. **January 30–February 14, 1968**

● **Free Elections**
Pressured into elections, US fears come true and Ho Chi Minh becomes president of Vietnam. However, believing this would expose the South Vietnamese to communist rule, the Eisenhower government argues the elections were fixed. **January 1956**

● **Fixed Elections?**
President Eisenhower releases a statement claiming that, "After an extensive CIA investigation we can reveal the elections in Vietnam were rigged." South Vietnam is to continue with a 'democratic' regime headed by an interim coalition of allied countries. **March 1956**

● **Kennedy's Speech**
Concluding with how close the world came to nuclear war during the Cuban Missile Crisis, President Kennedy affirms that all communist countries must be treated as rogue states. Military involvement is increased heavily in Vietnam. **October 1962**

● **Cambodia's Involvement**
The White House offers to supply Cambodia's Communist Party of Kampuchea guerrilla fighters in aid and arms if they can offer the US details of the Ho Chi Minh trail supply route. The deal is only revealed decades later. **August 1967**

● **Fall of Hanoi**
On Ho Chi Minh's birthday, the North Vietnam capital collapses under the military might of the US army. The war is over. China becomes so concerned that Mao immediately agrees to a trade pact with Coca-Cola. **May 19, 1968**

What if…
The Cuban Missile Crisis escalated?

THE CUBAN MISSILE CRISIS, 1962

NOTABLE NAMES:
- President John F. Kennedy
- Fidel Castro
- Nikita Khrushchev
- Major Richard Heyser
- Major Rudolf Anderson

IMPORTANT DATES:
October 14, 1962
October 28, 1962

What Really Happened…

An intense two-week standoff between the United States and the Soviet Union, the Cuban Missile Crisis began on October 14, 1962, and ended on October 28th. Fidel Castro had become allies with Nikita Khrushchev and the Soviet Union in 1959 and depended on them for economic and military aid. While making a pass over Cuba on October 14th, an American pilot, Major Richard Heyser, photographed a Soviet-made ballistic missile being assembled just 90 miles South of Florida. President John F. Kennedy and his executive committee determined this was unacceptable and for two weeks wrestled with how to approach the nuclear threat.

On October 22nd, the president notified Americans about the missiles and announced his plan to enact a blockade. Americans were terrified and many people began to stock up on food and gas. Two days later, Soviet ships heading towards Cuba approached the U.S. blockade, but stopped short. Had they not, they would have been met with a military confrontation. After enormous tension and the sole U.S. casualty of Major Rudolf Anderson, negotiations between Khrushchev and Kennedy were successful on October 28, 1962.

What would have happened if the Cuban Missile Crisis had escalated into nuclear war? I think that if the US had chosen to bomb and invade Cuba, it would not have worked out how they expected because there were tactical nukes on the island that they weren't aware of. It looks like, historically, the Soviet commander [on Cuba] had launch authority, and he probably would have used those missiles and that would have shocked the Americans. It could have easily escalated into an exchange of weapons.

The only thing that could have stopped this is if the Soviets realized how small their strategic forces were— [in terms of the] weapons they could hit the US with. America had an enormous arsenal of munitions that could be used.

Hopefully sanity would have prevailed, but often people get caught up in the situation and I think they could easily have gone on to a general war. In a general war the Soviet Union would have been obliterated. I mean, strategic forces on the side of the US were so strong, so I think the US would have survived the war. Now I'm only talking about 1962; if this war had happened several years later then the US would not have survived as a viable entity, because one of the major knock-on effects of the Cuban Missile Crisis was that the Soviets enormously increased their strategic forces and, within a decade, were on parity with the US.

What was the major turning point in the crisis?
From the revelations after the fall of the Soviet Union with historians being able to look at Soviet military records it's now apparent that, as soon as Kennedy announced the quarantine [a naval blockade on Cuba], Nikita Khrushchev immediately started taking steps to back down.

He stopped the ships that were carrying the missiles towards Cuba, so they did not push on and go "eyeball to eyeball." However, the Americans didn't realize that at the time because they weren't getting good intelligence on where exactly the ships were at sea. So Khrushchev really started to back down, but it could easily have still stumbled into war because they didn't have a good mechanism for communicating; the hotline [installed between the two leaders' offices after the crisis] didn't exist at this point.

If the crisis had escalated into all-out war, what would have happened first in your opinion? I think they would have been stumbling into war in gradual escalation. In this scenario, the US not only bombs Cuba but it invades. That's exactly what the military leadership in the US wanted to do. And if they had invaded, [a US city] would almost certainly have been hit by a nuke from the Soviets, killing tens of thousands of Americans.

At that point the invasion [of Cuba] is defeated, the Americans are stunned, and that would have required a response from the US. There would also have been a substantial amount of uncertainty and fear about what the Soviets already had on the island, and I think that the US would have felt justified in using both tactical

If the crisis had not been resolved it's likely several major US cities would have been targeted by nuclear weapons

Not a real photo.

"A US city would almost certainly have been hit by a nuke from the Soviets, killing tens of thousands of Americans"

and strategic nuclear weapons and we can be fairly sure that they would have unfortunately obliterated Cuba.

How would the war have played out? Soviet forces had about 100 tactical nukes, and I think that once [Cuba had been destroyed] the Soviet Union—in order [to save face] and maintain its international prestige—would have wanted to retaliate. They could have done this by taking Berlin with conventional forces, or they could have prepared to attack Europe or other places where there was tension. And this tit for tat—this unwillingness to be seen as compromising or backing down and trying to force the submission of the foe—would have been even more reckless.

People's emotions quickly get caught up in these things; they don't always make rational choices, and they don't always back down even if that's in their own best interests. [One such scenario could have been] that one of the Soviet light bombers dropped a bomb on New Orleans in Louisiana, where there was an infantry division embarking for the invasion of Cuba. With an American city destroyed at that point the world would sort of teeter [on the brink of war] and the Soviets would recognize very well that they were completely outgunned. Their number of strategic weapons was dramatically short compared to the Americans and they would feel the need to go for it [all guns blazing], because otherwise they're not going to get in any blows if they don't attack immediately.

How much of an advantage did the Americans have? The Soviets had 26 ICBMs [intercontinental ballistic missiles]—rockets that can be launched from the Soviet Union and hit the US—and they had none of their submarine-launched ballistic missiles at sea because all their submarines were in port; they were being worked on because they had problems with their nuclear reactors. And they had about 100 bombers that could reach the US. The US had 204 ICBMs, submarine-launched missiles at sea, almost 1,500 strategic

**INTERVIEW WITH...
DR. ERIC SWEDIN**

Dr. Eric Swedin is an associate professor in the History department at Weber State University in Utah, US. He is the author of numerous books including *When Angels Wept: A What-If History of the Cuban Missile Crisis*, which won the 2010 Sidewise Award in Alternate History, and *Survive the Bomb: The Radioactive Citizen's Guide to Nuclear Survival*. He also teaches courses on both modern and historical civilization.

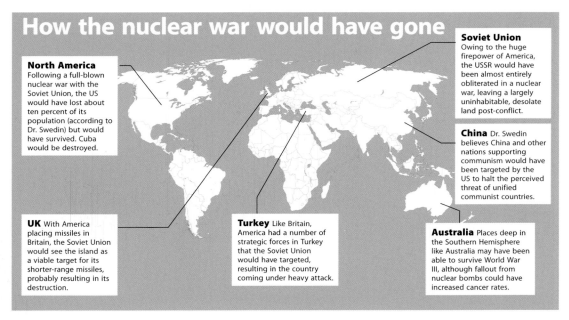

How the nuclear war would have gone

North America Following a full-blown nuclear war with the Soviet Union, the US would have lost about ten percent of its population (according to Dr. Swedin) but would have survived. Cuba would be destroyed.

Soviet Union Owing to the huge firepower of America, the USSR would have been almost entirely obliterated in a nuclear war, leaving a largely uninhabitable, desolate land post-conflict.

China Dr. Swedin believes China and other nations supporting communism would have been targeted by the US to halt the perceived threat of unified communist countries.

UK With America placing missiles in Britain, the Soviet Union would see the island as a viable target for its shorter-range missiles, probably resulting in its destruction.

Turkey Like Britain, America had a number of strategic forces in Turkey that the Soviet Union would have targeted, resulting in the country coming under heavy attack.

Australia Places deep in the Southern Hemisphere like Australia may have been able to survive World War III, although fallout from nuclear bombs could have increased cancer rates.

bombers, and they had enormous other forces. We're not even talking about something close to parity—we're talking about overwhelming power at that point because the Americans had been building up all through the 1950s driven by bad intelligence on how the Soviets had built up. Khrushchev before the Cuban Missile Crisis had wanted to spend money on the civilian economy, so he had been cutting the military budget. The Soviets reversed course after the Cuban Missile Crisis, though, spending a tremendous amount on strategic forces.

Do you think it would have been a case of mutually assured destruction (MAD)? It sounds horrible, but certainly the Soviet Union would have been destroyed. And Europe would have been largely destroyed because the Soviets had a substantial number of ever-shorter range weapons that could have been used on Europe; it's just they didn't have a lot of weapons that could hit the US.

I think the US could have been hit with enough weapons to kill maybe about ten percent of the population, but I think it would have been survivable. This was before [the time] people started putting their ICBMs into deep silos, so most of the explosions would have been airbursts as opposed to ground-bursts. That would have dramatically reduced the amount of fallout.

I think there were still substantial ecological consequences besides all the immediate destruction, but I don't think it would have been nuclear winter. Five years later, yes, it would have been because when you were trying to destroy the other country's missiles in the ground—when they're in deep silos—you're going to do ground-bursts to try and destroy them, not airbursts which the silos were designed to withstand.

People don't realize that there's a big difference between exploding a nuke in the atmosphere above a target and exploding it by letting it hit the ground. If you detonate it in the air, like over Hiroshima and Nagasaki [during World War II], you maximize your immediate blast effects, but you minimise your fallout. On the other hand, when you aim them at the ground you actually don't get as many blast effects except in the immediate area, but you maximize your fallout. And when I'm talking about minimise and maximize, we're talking about orders of thousands of percentage in magnitude between the two types [of explosion].

Would Europe have got involved in the conflict, and would it have led to World War III? I think it

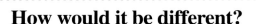

How would it be different?

● **The US Discovers Weapons in Cuba**
After a U-2 spy plane flying over western Cuba finds missile sites, the US begins considering both diplomatic and military actions. **October 14, 1962**

● **Naval Blockade of Cuba**
Following consideration of an invasion, President Kennedy instead opts to 'quarantine' Cuba with a naval blockade to prevent any more Soviet ships from reaching the island. **October 21, 1962**

● **Cuba Armed with Nuclear Weapons**
The Soviet Union—partially in response to the US placing missiles in Turkey—begins building missile facilities in Cuba capable of launching nuclear weapons at the US. **August 1962**

Real timeline

Real timeline

1959

Alternate timeline

● **Castro Comes to Power in Cuba**
Fidel Castro is sworn in as the prime minister of Cuba following the Cuban revolution and breaks ties with the US in favor of the Soviet Union. **February 16, 1959**

● **Bay of Pigs Invasion**
A counterrevolutionary military trained by the CIA to overthrow Castro fails in three days. In February 1962 the US announces an embargo on Cuba, which drives the communist nation to strengthen ties with the USSR. **April 17, 1961**

At the time, the Soviets didn't have many weapons that could have hit the US, but destruction of the USSR would have been assured

would have been World War III. We don't know exactly what the Soviet operating plan was, but we do know the US plan because parts of it have been declassified. The SIOP [Single Integrated Operational Plan] was [an outline] of what targets to hit during a general nuclear war.

The US would have attacked China because at that time they saw communism—even though it was changing—as a monolithic whole. Eastern Europe and other communist countries would have been hit for this reason too.

And the plan did not allow for a lot of modifications; it was designed to maximize the efficiency and the use of the weapons, and assuming the Soviets had a similar plan they would have also tried to destroy American forces and US allies. One of the causes of the factors of the crisis was that there were shorter-range US Jupiter and Thor missiles in Turkey and Britain. So at the very least those would have been considered completely legitimate targets. In a general nuclear war Europe would not have been able to avoid being embroiled—officially as targets rather than acting participants striking back. It was just the nature of the time period.

What state would the world be in today? I think you would have had substantial damage to the ozone layer and the Northern Hemisphere. You would have seen the complete collapse of the countries, societies, and economies of all of Europe and the Soviet Union. I think the US would have survived, but I think they probably would have drawn inwards since their foes were gone. You may have seen the Southern Hemisphere flourish because there would have been a lot less fallout and effects down there.

One thing we almost certainly would never have seen was a man walk on the Moon, as that was very much driven by Cold War rivalry. With no such war the US would not have been spending its money on the Apollo project—it would have been spending money on trying to rebuild its country. The enormous loss of the population would have been dramatic too. Continuing effects from radiation would have caused higher cancer rates in the north and probably the south too.

Could this situation ever happen again? We always hope that things like this won't happen. Since the end of the Cold War both the Soviets [now the Russians] and the Americans have dramatically built down their strategic forces. They're no longer on trigger alert towards each other like they were during the Cold War.

I think the most likely scenario that we'd see today is the use of a dirty bomb, or a rogue nuke, or a smaller nuke, and I think it would be similar to 9/11 except on a dramatically vaster scale. That being said, I can also see India descending into war, and I can easily see Pakistan losing some of its weapons and those falling into the hands of non-state actors and being used. I personally expect in my lifetime to see another nuclear weapon used, and it's going to be a terrorist group or non-state actor setting it off.

The US Goes to DEFCON 2
All Soviet ships en route to Cuba either slow down or reverse. The following day the US raises its military alertness to DEFCON 2, the highest level in American history. **October 24, 1962**

Khrushchev's Proposal
Soviet Chairman Khrushchev sends a letter to President Kennedy proposing that Soviet missiles will be removed from Cuba if the US agrees never to invade the island. **October 26, 1962**

The Crisis Ends
Khrushchev convinces Kennedy that the U-2 shooting was not under his authority. Kennedy accepts and a deal is reached to withdraw Soviet weapons from Cuba, while the US agrees not to invade and withdraws its missiles from Turkey. **October 28, 1962**

Invasion of Cuba
The US decides on a militaristic approach. On this day they attempt another invasion of Cuba in order to seize the weapons on the island. The US military alertness is raised to DEFCON 1. **October 25, 1962**

U-2 Shot Down
An American U-2 plane is shot down over Cuba, under the lone authority of a Soviet commander on the island, and its pilot Major Rudolf Anderson is killed. Tensions between the US and Soviet Union strain and nuclear war seems inevitable. **October 27, 1962**

Aftermath
90 percent of the US survives the nuclear war, but much of the rest of the Northern Hemisphere lies in ruins. Places deep in the Southern Hemisphere survive. Eventually, nuclear winter takes hold of large parts of the world, leaving parts uninhabitable. **1963**

Diplomatic Negotiations Cease
As the world teeters on the brink of a third World War, any hopes of a diplomatic resolution between the US and Soviet Union are quashed. **October 24, 1962**

First Nuclear Missile Launched
The Soviet commander in Cuba, under his own authority, launches a tactical nuke against the US. America is stunned and immediately begins preparations for a nuclear war. **October 26, 1962**

World War III Begins
The Soviet Union invades Berlin and fires upon targets in both the US and Europe, but the overwhelming firepower of the Americans makes the outcome of the war almost inevitable. **November 1962**

Obliteration
The US strikes Cuba, the Soviet Union, and other communist states with its full might. Ultimately, Cuba and the Soviet Union are obliterated, along with much of Europe as the USSR retaliates. **December 1962**

Fate & Circumstance

See how people's decisions and actions could have completely changed the world as we know it

134

130

140

144

What if...
Rome never fell?

EUROPE, 117-PRESENT

NOTABLE NAMES:
• King Alaric
• Odoacer

IMPORTANT DATES:
476

What Really Happened...

From a small town to one of the history's most powerful empires, there are several reasons why Rome eventually fell in 476. They experienced many military losses and setbacks, including a Germanic uprising, a sack of the city in 410 by King Alaric, a raid by the Vandals, and a revolt in 476 led by Germanic leader Odoacer, which deposed Roman Emperor Romulus Augustulus.

While they were also under attack, Rome was falling apart economically from a financial crisis. Between constant wars, overspending, oppressive taxation, inflation, a labor deficit, trade disruption, and more, Rome's economy and production was crumbling. Additional factors that led to the fall of Rome were the rise of the Eastern Roman Empire, overexpansion, military overspending, corruption, political instability, migration of the Barbarian tribes, the spread of Christianity, and the weakening of Roman legions.

INTERVIEW WITH... JERRY GLOVER

After completing his degree at Manchester University, Jerry Glover became a scriptwriter and television producer before turning to independent historical research with a particular interest in ancient societies in Europe, the Near East, and India. He has written dozens of articles for numerous publications, and in June to August 2013 he curated an exhibition in St. Albans dedicated to Medieval graffiti, based on his own photographs and research, the first such exhibition held anywhere. He has also published a book tracing intersections between art, crafts, and cultures across a multi-millennial timespan.

Can we pinpoint a time when the Roman Empire fell? We're speaking of the Western Empire, which after a long decline symbolically fell in Ravenna in 476. But an enhanced Senate continued to exist for more than a century afterward. The Roman concept of state was continued for almost a millennia, as the Holy Roman Empire and the Western Roman Empire continued to exist 'on paper', but only as a legal formality. Let's also not forget that the Eastern Empire continued until the 15th century. Given all that, it'd be a phenomenal situation if Rome never fell. 'Never' is the key idea here. For a Western Roman Empire still in existence today would have to be so different from the reality of what made it the Roman Empire that we could hardly call it that at all! A surviving Western Empire might well hold vastly disproportionate influence over human affairs everywhere. It would encompass, and indeed define, most if not the whole of Europe, as well as other parts of the world.

How possible is it for Rome not to have fallen; what would have to be different? From the end of the 2nd century, levels of trade and prosperity fell, never again achieving the levels of the early Principate. By the mid-3rd century, when the empire split into three competing empires and widespread civil unrest massively disrupted the trade network, the degeneration of imperial finances escalated. The state's inability to pay its troops increased too.

Essential items such as weapons, clothing, and food became part of soldiers' pay, and much trade took place without currency. One response was to debase the currency. In the second half of the 3rd century, the silver content of the antonianus collapsed, causing hyperinflation, which had to be dealt with by Aurelian in 271 and 274 by raising taxes and eradicating the bad coinage in Rome and Italy, but not the provinces. To prevent continual currency devaluing, Rome would have needed to grow its silver and gold reserves. Mines in Italy were not large or reliable enough, so instead Rome could stem the amount of silver it exported to India in return for spices, curtailing its taste for luxuries. Difficult! Preferably, they could discover new sources that exist in Central Europe or sub-Saharan Africa, or by voyaging to Mesoamerica where silver and gold is plentiful and fairly easy to reach.

Excellent cartography and astronomy borrowed from Persia is key to making this possible. In the Mesoamerican scenario, the Romans come up against the Maya, sparking conflicts the Romans would be hard-pressed to win in harsh jungles, and greatly outnumbered. Instead, they muster their advantage in technology and international connections to cajole the Mayans into a trade alliance to develop their civilization—exchange steel, machinery, and urban planning for Mayan gold and hardwood. With diplomatic outposts established in Mayan cities, Roman legions, consisting of Mayan warriors as well, march to the gold regions of Peru and California, returning to Rome with spoils that make the treasure of the Temple of Jerusalem look like a prize at a village fete lucky dip.

How would Rome's government be different?
To keep the empire stable, a balance would have to be struck between tight, autocratic rule by an elite oligarchy, intelligent decision making, and the machinations of prestigious, well-connected individuals. The expensive civil wars that contributed to the collapse could be averted if Rome had reformed the system by which the emperor was selected after the 3rd century, when the senatorial class was marginalized and any connection with the imperial family was sufficient to

A surviving Roman Empire might have resulted in an accelerated development of technology

make a claim. Almost all emperors after that time were army officers or imperial officials, and that stratocracy led to rivals and bloody conflicts. From the mid-3rd century, emperors also wasted time with matters that previously were dealt with by an imperial legate. If he was unwilling to trust anyone else to deal with a distant problem it would be neglected, and the trend toward smaller provinces made it even harder to get things done than ever before.

Diocletian's Tetrarchic system from 293 quartered the empire, each part ruled by a sovereign emperor. But each group selfishly favored its own aims over the empire. So the system crumbled from near-constant civil wars. With much more radical reform it might have worked if the Tetrarchy reformed into a Supreme Imperial Office comprising more regional co-emperors, who were chosen only from the Senate. And if reform included the chance to become a senator—or any official—on personal merits, not just for being one of the landed classes.

Intelligence and capability also have to carry real political influence, basically an oligarchy of technocrats. Each office is decided by a small closed election, a bit like the way the Pope is chosen from a group of cardinals. But the periods of service are fixed, like the president of the United States, so no office gets too much influence over the rest. Only soldiers are allowed to keep their jobs as long as they are performing well, but no general can become emperor. That's very important, as is keeping the army properly paid. It's a system where anyone can become an official, or even emperor. Yet still oligarchal and Roman enough to preserve the ideals that work so well in the empire's favor—conquest, assimilation, expansion. That's the basic theory, anyway.

How might Rome have progressed beyond the 5th century and onward? In the 7th century the new religion of Islam galloped out of Arabia, and Muslim armies began a war against both the Romans and the Sassanians, already fighting since the 3rd century. Many factors would have to go into Rome winning the war against this fresh expansion. For one, Rome would need the resources to defend the Middle East, which supposing they still have western Europe and north Africa, and are investing deeply into gaining a foothold in Mesoamerica as I envisage, it is still questionable unless they can make up with the Sassanians. It's a logical step for them to build strong diplomatic relations with other empires; the Hunnic, Sasanian, Rashidun, Umayyad, Mongol, and subsequent empires.

Despite all the negative connotations of being an empire, a surviving, generally non-belligerent Western Roman Empire would in some sense be the model of a well-governed, prosperous, cosmopolitan society, having evolved beyond the strife and economic problems that dogged its early history, exacerbating its actual demise. On the other hand, the cost of this may well be an even more hierarchical and brutal society, with slavery still rooted, and a very harsh law code.

Would the world as a whole be more or less technologically advanced? In certain areas I suggest it would be a lot more advanced, provided there's no stagnation of scientific inquiry that happened in Europe across Late Antiquity. Instead of the intelligentsia putting so much effort into Christian religious doctrine and hoarding ancient knowledge in closed monasteries, there is a freer circulation of information that allows engineering to innovate much faster. Steel was known to the Romans, and sooner or later they must have realized that making tools from it instead of just weapons, would increase agricultural productivity, and architecture would develop faster for its use in tools, cranes, and

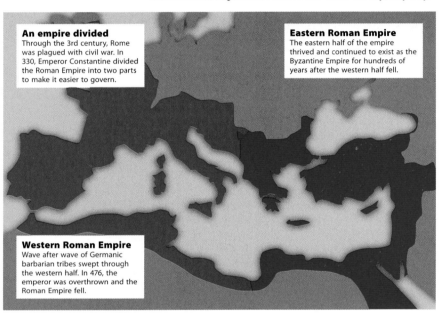

An empire divided
Through the 3rd century, Rome was plagued with civil war. In 330, Emperor Constantine divided the Roman Empire into two parts to make it easier to govern.

Eastern Roman Empire
The eastern half of the empire thrived and continued to exist as the Byzantine Empire for hundreds of years after the western half fell.

Western Roman Empire
Wave after wave of Germanic barbarian tribes swept through the western half. In 476, the emperor was overthrown and the Roman Empire fell.

How would it be different?

Loss of Britain
Following the removal of troops in northern and western Britain, Constantine's officials are finally expelled by rebellious British chieftains, ending direct Roman rule. In 410 they appeal to Emperor Honorius who urges them to "fend for themselves." **407-408**

Diarchy and Tetrarchy
Diocletian appoints officer Maximian as a second emperor with equal power. In 293 two more army officers are appointed junior Caesars with supreme authority, creating the Tetrarchy. Diocletian reforms taxation and coinage systems, but cannot enforce prices. **286-313**

Waves of Invasion
The Tervingi, a tribe of Goths under pressure from Hun tribes, are allowed into Roman territory. After their leader is killed, they rebel, invade Italy, and sack Rome before securing lands in Aquitaine and Gaul. They found a kingdom in former Roman Iberia (Portugal and Spain). **376**

Real timeline

Real timeline

117

Rome's Greatest Glory
With victorious campaigns in Mesopotamia and Dacia, Trajan achieves the greatest extent of the Roman Empire's territory. The Empire's population is around 70 million. **117**

Crisis of the 3rd Century
Upon Emperor Severus's murder by his own troops a string of short-term 'barracks emperors' fight, allowing frequent raids from foreign tribes. By 258 the empire splits into three states: Roman, Gallic, and Palmyreme. **235-284**

Foundation of the Eastern Empire
The city of Byzantium becomes the new imperial seat of the Eastern Empire, with Constantine naming it Constantinople. The empire maintains control of the eastern provinces, regaining territory in Italy, Sicily, southern Spain, and North Africa in the 6th century. **330**

Battle of Adrianople
Emperor Valens heeds the advice of the cautious Western general Richomer not to attack, instead of the hawkish Eastern general Sebastian who urges the order. Valens negotiates, stalling while reinforcements arrive, and wins the battle. **August 9, 378**

Alternate timeline

The Vandals sack a panic-stricken Rome

A depiction of Pilate's Forum

girders. The principle of steam power was already known to the Ancient Greeks.

If the Romans had cottoned onto the possibilities of that, combined with iron and steel, it's feasible they could have invented the steam engine, hence locomotives, revolutionizing long-distance transport, a rail network spanning the empire. The Industrial Revolution could have started a thousand years earlier, marking the beginning of the end for the slave system.

This isn't necessarily for everyone's benefit. More powerful engines of war, including firearms, might well have encouraged emperors to expand the empire's boundaries, bigger wars and extra pressure on state finances and reductions in the overall standard of living. But if the empire is not to fall, ambitions of conquest must be held in check, maintaining the delicate balance of international relations.

Are there any key events that could have stemmed Rome's fall if they went differently? One that stands out is the Battle of Adrianople in 378 when Roman forces of the Eastern Empire lost some 10,000 lives to the Visigoths under Fritigern. This gave the Goths free rein in Thrace and Dacia, a major instigator of the process that led to the fall of the Western Empire. The blame for this calamity rests with Emperor Valens (364 to 378). During negotiations, premature attack broke out from the Roman side, and Valens allowed this to force his hand, ordering an attack that spiralled into a disaster, including his own death. If Valens had kept his head, who knows? Instead of being the 'Last True Roman' as he's been called, he might have been the greatest of them all.

Accelerating the Decline
The deaths of four strong military leaders, Theodosius in 395, Stilicho in 408, Constantius III in 421, and Aetius in 451, are crucial in greatly accelerating the collapse of the Western Empire. **395-451**

First Sack of Rome
In their third attempt, Visigoths under Alaric ransack the city, killing and torturing citizens to reveal their hidden valuables. The Goths continue to ravage southern Italy. Roman refugees flee to North Africa. **August 410**

A Crucial Blow
The Vandals move on from Spain into North Africa, securing Carthage, then Sicily. This further weakens the state's revenue and ability to field an army, encouraging further Goth attacks that regain most areas of the Western Empire. **439-441**

Fall of the Western Empire
King Odoacer deposes Emperor Romulus Augustus and sends the imperial regalia to the emperor of the Eastern Empire at Constantinople. **September 4, 476**

Vandals Repelled
Majoran uses an enhanced fleet of 65 ships (not 40) to win against the Vandals at the Battle of Cartagena. He retakes Sicily and gradually reverses the Vandal usurpation of North Africa. Rome expands into sub-Saharan Africa. **461-475**

Black Death Averted
Grain ships carrying bubonic plague from Egypt sink in a storm before reaching Constantinople. The averted Plague of Justinian allows the Eastern Empire to populate faster by a factor of two. **541-542**

Invention and Expansion
The first outing of Minerva's Arrow, a steam engine that runs on rails, is a centerpiece of a yearlong festival of art and technology in Rome. The rail network gradually expands to all frontiers. **681-962**

Return of the Black Death
From one trade caravan on the Silk Road plague reaches Europe and then a ship bound for Mesoamerica. Half the empire's population and those of its neighbors, around 290 million, perish. **1346-1373**

No More War?
The Goths are assimilated, preventing their plunder in Thrace. With British territory stabilized, Rome trains on Scandinavia and the Ukraine, forming a frontier across the Baltic states. The ensuing massive cost entails harsh taxes, provoking empire-wide rioting. **378-415**

The Second Pax Romana
After three years of deliberation by the new Supreme Consilium, reforms are announced to forever eradicate corruption. Finances rebalanced, imperial wealth starts to surge. **475-635**

Holy Land Wars
A Roman-Axumite alliance prevents Islamic expansion into North Africa, but loses Mesopotamia to the caliphate powers. Rome loses control of Jerusalem. **635-700s**

New World Alliances
After exploration and conflict in Mesoamerica, Rome establishes relations with the Mayans, helping prevent their civilization's collapse. In Peru they extract tribute from the Chavin culture. In California they enslave Native American societies. **650-1251**

The HyperRenaissance
With a thousand years of super-accelerated progress in all fields of human knowledge at his disposal, Leonardo da Vinci is born in a suburb of the Florentia-Roma mega-city, the largest on Earth . . . **April 15, 1452**

What if...
The Vikings colonized North America?

NEWFOUNDLAND, 1000 CE

IMPORTANT DATES:
800
1066

What Really Happened...

The Vikings were a group of seafaring warriors that sought their fortunes away from their homeland. Some also say they left because of overpopulation. From 800 to the 11th century, the Vikings (or Norsemen) would be known as pirates, raiders, traders, and settlers throughout Europe, as well as parts of what is now known as Newfoundland, Greenland, Iceland, and Russia. What differentiated them most from the other Europeans they clashed with was that they weren't Christians.

By the mid-9th century, the Vikings targeted Ireland, Scotland, and England. Only one English kingdom—Wessex—successfully resisted Viking attack. They also colonized Iceland, where no one had yet settled. By the late 10th century, they moved west to Greenland, with some saying they were the first Europeans to discover and explore North America.

The end of the Viking Age came in 1066.

INTERVIEW WITH... PHILIP PARKER

Author and historian Philip Parker studied History at Cambridge University, UK, and provides historical and editorial consultancy services to a number of publishers. He has written widely on the Middle Ages and the ancient world. His 2014 book was the critically acclaimed, *Sunday Times* bestseller *The Northmen's Fury: A History of the Viking World*, which traces 500 years of exploration and culture of the legendary Norse tribes, who ranged from Scandinavia to the Russian Steppes in the east and as far as Newfoundland in the west.

What if the Vikings had colonized North America? If the Viking colony in North America had survived and prospered, it's hard to believe it could have been kept a complete secret for several centuries. Columbus's expedition of 1492 made landfall much further south, in the Caribbean, but those sent out by the English and French in the late-15th and early-16th century—such as that of John Cabot in 1497—went further north. In the early stages of European colonization, the French and English largely settled in different areas, but later on, North America saw clashes between them, which aggravated the rivalry between the two countries. It is quite possible a similar situation might occur regarding thriving Scandinavian colonies; eventually competition with other European settlements would have grown intense, which might have led to war.

Is there any reason to think Viking camps could not have thrived in the New World? The Viking Sagas tell us that the Norsemen made landfall in North America in regions populated by Native Americans (whom they called 'skraelings'). The large numbers of natives compared to the relatively small numbers of Vikings caused them to withdraw. However, the one undoubted Viking settlement we do know about, at L'Anse aux Meadows in Newfoundland, was occupied at a time when there is no archaeological trace of Native American settlement in the vicinity. A large number of Vikings might potentially, therefore, have been able to establish camps and farms that prospered in areas where the Native American population was sparse.

To do so, they would have required a larger influx of population than the small Viking settlement on Greenland (of no more than 4,000-5,000 people) could provide, but if word had spread back further east to Iceland and Scandinavia itself about a land offering rich new possibilities for settlement, it might have been possible to attract a suitable number of migrants [to settle and flourish].

There is some evidence of Viking contact—peaceful and otherwise—with the indigenous peoples. If Leifur Eiriksson had stuck around and the settlement of Vinland had grown, how do you think their relationship would have evolved? In many regions where the Vikings raided and settled, they were faced with more or less organized states (such as Alba in Scotland and Northumbria, Mercia, and Wessex in England), which already had urban communities and some kind of appointed royal officials. This enabled them to take over existing administrative structures and to rule over wide areas. In North America this would not have been the case, but a situation like that in Russia and Ukraine—where the Vikings established urban trading settlements that collected tribute from surrounding Slav tribes—might have developed.

What effect would the Norse have had on their culture? In Russia, the Scandinavian and Slav cultures ultimately merged to create the medieval Russian principalities. In North America, the cultural differences between Native Americans and Vikings

"There might have been a kind of 'United States,' but Norwegian- or Swedish-speaking"

The Vikings may well have ultimately integrated with Native Americans had they stayed in America

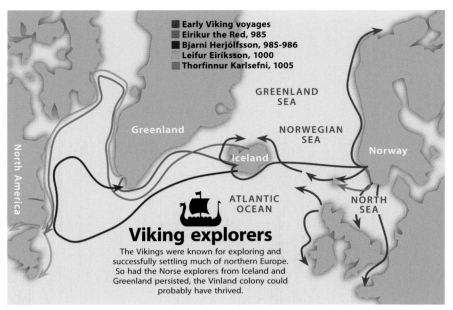

Early Viking voyages
Eirikur the Red, 985
Bjarni Herjólfsson, 985-986
Leifur Eiríksson, 1000
Thorfinnur Karlsefni, 1005

GREENLAND SEA

Greenland

NORWEGIAN SEA

Iceland

Norway

North America

ATLANTIC OCEAN

NORTH SEA

Viking explorers

The Vikings were known for exploring and successfully settling much of northern Europe. So had the Norse explorers from Iceland and Greenland persisted, the Vinland colony could probably have thrived.

An artistic depiction of the Vikings discovering America

"If word had spread back to Iceland and Scandinavia, it might have been possible to attract a suitable number of migrants"

would probably have been too deep to allow this to happen easily. The Vikings remained at a distance from non-Norse peoples, such as Inuit in Greenland and from the Saamior Lapps in northern Scandinavia, so they would probably have done the same in North America. Once the Vikings became Christian, this might have had an impact on Native American culture, with some groups accepting the new religion. As in many situations where groups face threatening outsiders, there might have been a consolidation of tribal groups into larger confederacies—as happened during the 17th and 18th centuries after the European colonization of the eastern seaboard.

How would a separate colony in the New World have affected Old World Norse culture? The Vikings were a fairly conservative lot culturally. In Greenland, they continued to try to farm much as they had done in Scandinavia, even though the climate and land was less suitable. In North America, they might have learned some new agricultural techniques from the Native Americans, such as the cultivation of maize. If the colony had thrived and grown in number, this would have changed the political balance with Scandinavia, allowing the other North Atlantic colonies, such as Iceland and Greenland, to grow further and become more independent. Both of those lacked wood for building houses and ships, and North America would have been able to provide them it in abundance.

How do you think the introduction and regular trade of certain goods, crops, wood, animal pelts, and so on, have changed the Old World economy? The

How would it be different?

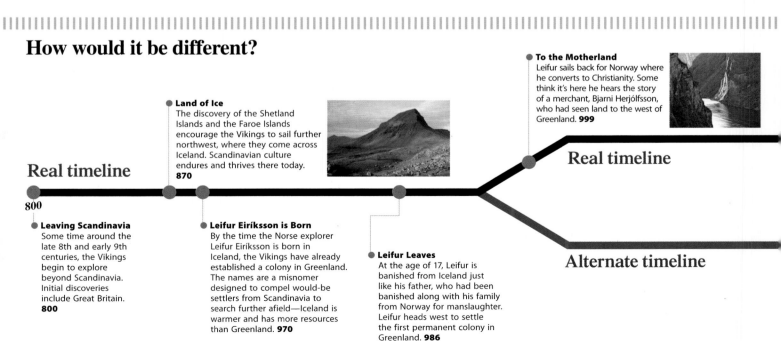

To the Motherland
Leifur sails back for Norway where he converts to Christianity. Some think it's here he hears the story of a merchant, Bjarni Herjólfsson, who had seen land to the west of Greenland. **999**

Land of Ice
The discovery of the Shetland Islands and the Faroe Islands encourage the Vikings to sail further northwest, where they come across Iceland. Scandinavian culture endures and thrives there today. **870**

Real timeline

Real timeline

800

Leaving Scandinavia
Some time around the late 8th and early 9th centuries, the Vikings begin to explore beyond Scandinavia. Initial discoveries include Great Britain. **800**

Leifur Eiríksson is Born
By the time the Norse explorer Leifur Eiríksson is born in Iceland, the Vikings have already established a colony in Greenland. The names are a misnomer designed to compel would-be settlers from Scandinavia to search further afield—Iceland is warmer and has more resources than Greenland. **970**

Leifur Leaves
At the age of 17, Leifur is banished from Iceland just like his father, who had been banished along with his family from Norway for manslaughter. Leifur heads west to settle the first permanent colony in Greenland. **986**

Alternate timeline

quantities of any given trade good that could be traded across the Atlantic could never have been particularly great, and not enough to make a significant difference to the Old World economy. Some pelts might have acquired 'exotic' status and become prized trade items among the rich. If the Vikings had somehow spread far enough to come into contact with the civilizations of Mesoamerica, this might have changed as some items – the potato in particular—ultimately made a huge impact on the nutritional intake of the poor in Europe.

Was the Norse discovery of the New World inevitable? Would other Norsemen have made it to the New World if it wasn't for Leifur? The discovery by Leifur Eiríksson—or Bjarni Herjólfsson, who is credited with it in some sources—seems to have been an accident, but the chances of being blown off course from Greenland, where there was an established Viking settlement, to the North American coast around Newfoundland or Labrador is actually fairly high, and in the 450-year life span of the Greenland colony, this is likely to have occurred sooner or later.

What was the legacy of Leifur's journey and the Vinland colony? If the Norsemen had stayed, could you say what impact that would have had on American culture in the far future, say around the time of US independence? Perhaps the US wouldn't even exist? The United States came into being because a growing and increasingly prosperous colonial population sought more say in the way they were governed. The physical distance between them and the European mother countries made this practical to achieve. The distance between Iceland and Norway enabled the Viking colony there to remain independent from Scandinavia for over two centuries, and the much greater travel time to North America could well have fostered a similarly independent colony.

The fierce individuality of the Icelandic Vikings, who dispensed with the rule of kings and established the world's first parliamentary assembly, might even have

Leifur Eiríksson first ended up in America by accident after having been blown off course

been mirrored in North America, where the colonists could have been just as antipathetic to royal rule as the American Revolutionaries in the 1770s. Who knows, there might have been a kind of 'United States,' but a Norwegian- or Swedish-speaking one.

By populating America 500 years earlier, do you think we would be seeing a much more populous American country today? The population growth of medieval Europe was comparatively slow before the Industrial Revolution, and suffered huge periodic set-backs such as the Black Death in the 14th century, which killed around a third of the continent's people. When you add this to the impact of the actual European settlement in the Americas in the 15th and 16th centuries, when a large proportion of the Native American population fell victim to diseases (such as influenza) against which they had no natural immunity, then a Viking colony in America that survived would probably not have led to a population of North America that was greatly different to the level we see today.

Fate Intervenes
On his way back to Greenland, Leifur and his crew are blown off course and discover the new land to the west. He returns to Greenland to mount an expedition. **999**

Columbus's Voyage
Nearly 500 years pass before the known voyage to the New World, when Christopher Columbus makes his first landfall far to the south of Vinland, in the Bahamas. **1492**

American Revolution
The Declaration of Independence is signed by the second continental congress in July 1776 and in the same year, it forces the British out of Boston. By 1783, the United States have fully separated from Great Britain. **1776**

Exploring the New World
Amply supplied and with a crew of 35, Leifur returns to Newfoundland, where he discovers and names several new places. They find fertile land with wheat fields and grape vines, which Leifur calls Vinland. The party eventually returns home to Greenland. **1001**

British Dominance
By the mid-18th century, the British have laid claim to most of Canada and eastern parts of what is now the United States, but that is to change with one significant event. **1750**

Canadian Independence
Canada's road to independence is longer and more diplomatic than the US's: the three colonies gain autonomy in 1867 and less than a century later, Britain grants them full independence. **1931**

Vinland Settled
Pleased with the new, fertile, and bountiful land he has discovered, Leifur Eiríksson brings his winter camp down to the new land to establish a permanent colony. **1001**

Viking Missionaries
The Newfoundland colonies have grown and prospered, but the indigenous peoples and the Vikings have given each other a wide berth until now. Christian missionaries move among the tribes, spreading their new faith. **1200**

Tribal Outrage
The threat to native culture from these Norse settlers is becoming more apparent, so some of the 'skraelings' consolidate to protect themselves and their way of life. **1400**

Complicated States
By the time the British have entrenched themselves in the New World, the Norse settlers have already staked their claim on large swathes of the land. War is brewing in America. **1750**

Colonial War
The Norse colonists refuse to relinquish their grasp on their long-held territory. The British are too arrogant and powerful to recognize the independence of the Norwegians. A bitter territorial war ensues. **1800**

What if...
China discovered America first?

AMERICA, 1408

What Really Happened...

While it's widely taught that Italian explorer Christopher Columbus discovered America on October 12, 1492, that's only partially true. Millions of people already lived there, so technically, he introduced the Americas to Western Europe and paved the way for them to form new nations.

But long before Columbus, a land bridge, called the Bering land bridge, connected what is now Alaska and Siberia. Ocean levels were much lower 15,000 years ago and the land between continents was hundreds of miles wide, allowing people from Asia the ability to walk across. There's also proof that the Vikings, led by Leif Erikson, briefly settled in Canada 500 years before Columbus.

The Americas have always been a land of immigrants, so while it's far from clear exactly who discovered America first, millions of American Indians and their ancestors were here long before Europeans.

Zheng He, born in 1371, is known as a great explorer during the Ming dynasty, undertaking seven voyages to distant lands. But who was he really? He was a close advisor and a person in the inner circle of the second emperor of the Ming dynasty. He was officially a eunuch, meaning he was not a legitimate officer or official, and he later became an admiral of the Chinese Imperial Navy in his late 20s and early 30s. He ascended from very humble beginnings. Being the personal advisor of the emperor, he was in fact involved in a coup d'état, which was successfully plotted by his master, who then became the new emperor. His life is full of incidents, conspiracies, and plots.

How did Zheng He rise to his position of admiral and what was happening in China at the time? The first emperor of the Ming Dynasty [Zhu Yuanzhang, 1328-98] was a very capable and ambitious man and had climbed up from a leader of several armies against the Mongols. Eventually he not only defeated the Mongols but also united China.

But once he became emperor, he had to find his successor among his sons and he wasn't happy with the choice. So he chose his grandson and jumped one generation [but there was a plot against him by one of his sons, Zhu Di, in 1402]. In that plot, Zheng He was one of the key advisors — that says a lot about him.

Zheng He is known to have travelled far and wide, but what were the purposes of his expeditions? This is very controversial. The official line is that he did it for China to show off the country's soft and hard power.

The former being diplomacy skills and traditions while the latter is showing off the navy by sailing record distances and visiting a record number of foreign destinations. But that was just what those in power put out there.

The unofficial line from my research is quite different. Why would the emperor send his key advisor overseas? My hunch is that Zheng He knew too much about the plot [against the Ming emperor], so Zhu Yuanzhang exiled him with dignity overseas. He continuously made seven voyages so that he would spend the rest of his adult life at sea, not coming back to China. He eventually died at sea, possibly on the way to Malacca [in Malaysia].

There are few records left on the exploits of Zheng He — what do we know about his expeditions from the limited information available? He basically covered all possible or known destinations in the Indian Ocean. That was the only record. His logs were systematically destroyed by the Ming court, but so far as we know he went to several ports in India, the Persian Gulf, and East Africa. He had several detachments so he actually sent his men away from his main forces to explore other possibilities.

He would have two detachments plus his own main force, so there would be three routes taken by his men at the same time. His fleet once had something like 200 vessels but if they all landed in any harbor they would fight for resources like fresh water and meat. It's better to have detachments so that the pressure on your land-based resources isn't that great. He would often control his own

"They would have had enough resources and know-how to take refuge in places like California"

Zheng He could have supplanted Columbus, 35 years before the Italian was born

fleet with a dozen or so large ships and the rest of his men would take different routes to the rest of Asia.

During one of his voyages, is it possible he could have gone to America by accident or otherwise? Yes, technically it is a possibility. By sheer accident, they could have got lost and some of them maybe would have landed. It would probably take a long time, being forced by storms or currents, but they would have had enough resources and know-how to take refuge in places like California.

If Zheng He had discovered America, would it have changed his standing among people in China? Probably not. He was not a real officer but a servant of the inner chamber of a Ming emperor. Moreover, he was not ethnically Chinese, he was Muslim, and he wasn't a member of the elite. People wouldn't listen to him.

How might Zheng He have reached America? I would say not on purpose. By accident, anything can happen. It's possible he could have unintentionally gone to America on the furthest points of his voyages.

INTERVIEW WITH... DR. KENT DENG

Dr. Kent Deng is a professor of economic history at the London School of Economics. He is an expert in Chinese maritime history and has written numerous publications on the voyages and expeditions of Zheng He, including his impact on Chinese history and the nature of his travels.

What if... China discovered America first? **121**

Their longest leg of a single journey was close to 4,000 or 5,000 kilometers [2,000 or 3,000 miles] so with that kind of a capacity, they can probably manage to cross the Pacific Ocean. However, the problem for them is that the ocean currents don't move across the Pacific, but from China to the seas of Japan, then from Japan to Alaska, from Alaska to Seattle, and from Seattle all the way to Mexico. If you want to ride from Mexico to China it's easy, but they would have a huge task to sail against the ocean current. If they tried to go to the Americas, the chances are they would probably wreck in Japan or Alaska.

If he didn't go to the West Coast, is there another way Zheng He could have reached America? It took the Spaniards 60 years to learn how to return to Mexico from the Philippines. They had to travel through Malacca, all the way across the Atlantic Ocean. They had to circumnavigate the whole globe to go back to Mexico, so I wonder whether Zheng He and his men could have had that kind of knowledge.

There's a possibility for them to get completely lost after the Cape of Good Hope [in South Africa] and then enter the Atlantic, and then surely the ocean current would bring them to Central America. Then they would have had a good chance to return home from the other end [by traveling across the Pacific on the ocean currents].

What might have happened had he landed in America? The Chinese sailors would do everything to return home — China offered individual and private land ownership so you can actually live very comfortably once you make money. You could buy land, become a landlord, plus you had family ties, and so they would have been really reluctant to establish another China or a colony outside of the empire. Most Chinese, 99 percent, would have gone back to where they really belonged, with one exception — criminals.

I don't think that once the Chinese landed they would immediately start a new kingdom like the Europeans did. By the time of Zheng He, China had more than a

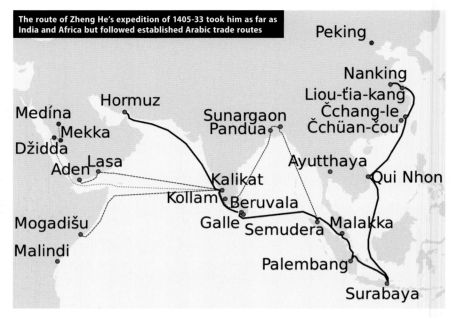

Peking
Nanking
Liou-ťia-kang
Čchang-le
Čchüan-čou
Hormuz
Medína
Mekka
Sunargaon
Pandua
Džidda
Lasa
Ayutthaya
Aden
Qui Nhon
Kalikat
Kollam
Beruvala
Mogadišu
Galle
Semudera
Malakka
Malindi
Palembang
Surabaya

"The Chinese sailors would do everything to return home"

1,000-year-long history of private family-based property rights so people would always have returned.

How might the elite in China have reacted to the discovery of America? We can only speculate about how news of the New World would have been greeted in China. Zheng He's fleet went to East Africa and brought a giraffe back to the Imperial Court — this was the closest to a new world that Zheng He got and ordinary Chinese did not seem to care too much about his adventures. But although they would be unlikely to start a colony there, they might have been interested in meeting and trading with Native Americans.

Would a Chinese discovery of America change its history at all? No, simply because the Chinese

How would it be different?

Exile at Sea
Possibly as he knew too much about the coup, Zheng He is appointed admiral and is sent on a grand voyage away from China. **1405**

● **Further Exploration**
Zheng He returns home but is sent out again on more voyages to India, the Arabian Peninsula, and East Africa. **1407**

● **Ocean Burial**
On his seventh and final voyage to Arabia and East Africa, Zheng He dies from disease and is buried at sea. **1433**

Real timeline

Real timeline

Alternate timeline

● **Overthrowing the Emperor**
Zhu Di leads a rebellion against his nephew and becomes the Yongle Emperor. Zheng He helps. **1402**

● **Arrives in India**
With a fleet of 200 ships and about 27,000 men, Zheng He arrives in Calicut, India. **1406**

● **Lost at Sea**
A freak storm sends Zheng He and his entire fleet off course, ultimately causing them to sail across the Atlantic Ocean. **1407**

● **Age of Discovery**
Zheng He and his crew make landfall in America, reaching the New World long before Europe would. **1408**

wouldn't have stayed. They would have probably got sweet potatoes and chilies and started a new business in China by growing and selling them. But a great empire — they just wouldn't have that incentive.

Would China have shared the news from this expedition with the rest of the world? That I don't know. Zheng He was not popular in his time — he spent a lot of money from the Chinese treasury and brought back nothing to the empire to show for it. There was also a conservative school of very powerful people against him, so much so that once people in Beijing heard that he had died in his last voyage, they quickly decided this must be the end of all voyages. They burned all of Zheng He's logs, all of the records, and even went so far as to destroy their vessels and close the shipyards.

Inside China, his journeys were considered extravagant and very economically unreasonable, so for this reason there's no official record left of any of it. His two lieutenants wrote and published a personal account of their travels each and these were circulated among the Chinese elite. They were full of strange stories — for example, they say that on one island people only had one eye and it was on their forehead. I think the lieutenants were trying to make sailing for profit very attractive but no one really had the drive or ambition to go and find a new land themselves.

If the news of his discovery had been shared, would it have made the Europeans go earlier? Yes, I would think so. We do have some surviving evidence showing that Zheng He probably passed some of his maps to the Arabs, and in turn the Arabs passed them onto the Europeans. There was huge money changing hands because it was very, very valuable information.

Would America have been colonized before Columbus even began his first voyage in 1492? I think the Europeans would have jumped at the first opportunity to conquer America, as history has told us, so maybe Zheng He would have been hired by the Spaniards in the place of Columbus. It is worth mentioning that

Zheng He was a hired gun, a mercenary, and would have done whatever he was told as long as he was paid. He was certainly willing to go where the money was.

He decided to offer himself as a eunuch, which is really very unusual. Most Chinese wouldn't do it as it meant you wouldn't have a family any more. But being a non-Chinese Muslim, this is a price to pay. So he probably would have been hired by the Portuguese or Spain or England. He would have spearheaded this colony outside China in the Americas and he would have probably become someone like Columbus, a governor of some sort. He's a very open-minded, flexible man — I admire him in that sense — but I doubt he would have had a Chinese following.

Would Zheng He be as famous today as Columbus if he had discovered America? It's hard to say. He and his men left tablets and statues in southeastern and south Asia but very few Chinese knew about them. His fame really began after 1949 as a means to promote Chinese nationalism, although Zheng He was not Chinese, Confucian, or Buddhist.

Zheng He was an interesting man, but the bottom line is that he was a marginal and unconventional figure. He managed to maneuver very smartly from a remote province of China at the edge of the empire to being in the heart of the country and becoming a personal servant of the emperor, involved in a conspiracy and a coup d'état. Then he got into trouble and he was exiled at sea for the rest of his life. That is really an extraordinary story.

An early 17th-century woodcut of Zheng He's fleet of treasure ships

The New World
Italian explorer Christopher Columbus 'discovers' America, ushering in an age of colonization. **1492**

All Hands on Deck
John Cabot arrives on mainland North America in the name of Great Britain. France and Portugal soon follow. **1497**

Colonization The Europeans begin to colonize the Americas in earnest, claiming various lands as their own. **16th century**

Columbus Day On the 300th anniversary of his discovery, the US declares that October 12 be known as Columbus Day. **1792**

Home Sweet Home
Zheng He is heralded as a hero for discovering a new world — but China shows no interest in colonization. **1410**

Early Colonization
England, France, and Portugal rush to follow suit, claiming land in the Americas as they see fit. **1420**

Declaration of Independence The United States of America becomes the first nation to declare independence from Europe, seceding from Great Britain. **1776**

European Colonization
The Europeans colonize the Americas, but the new nations ultimately declare independence from their founding countries. **15th century**

The Voyage Home
After trading goods and sharing information with the natives, Zheng He and his fleet set sail for their home country. **1409**

Zheng He for Hire
Hearing of his voyage, Spain pays a high price for Zheng He to return to America at the head of a Spanish fleet. **1412**

Christopher Who?
Zheng He leads a successful expedition to colonize the Americas, 35 years before Columbus is even born. **1416**

Chinese Isolation
Despite the exploits of the Europeans, China remains isolated and does not venture to the Americas. **1450**

Zheng He Day
On the 300th anniversary of his discovery, the US declares that October 12 be known as Zheng He Day. **1716**

What if...
The Gunpowder Plot succeeded?

HOUSES OF PARLIAMENT, ENGLAND, 1605

NOTABLE NAMES:
• King James I
• Robert Catesby
• Guy Fawkes
• Lord Monteagle

IMPORTANT DATES:
October 26, 1605
November 5, 1605

What Really Happened...

The Gunpowder Plot was a plan orchestrated by a group of English Catholics to blow up Parliament and King James I on November 5, 1605. Organized by Robert Catesby, it was a failed effort to end the persecution of Catholics by the country's Protestant government. Catesby, Guy Fawkes, and other conspirators rented a cellar below the House of Lords building in London where they planted gunpowder.

On October 26, 1605, Lord Monteagle received an anonymous tip to avoid Parliament on November 5. Monteagle reported this to the government, which resulted in an investigation. Around midnight on November 5, Guy Fawkes was discovered in the cellar with a fuse, a box of matches, and over 35 barrels of gunpowder.

He was taken into custody and tortured, confessing to the conspiracy and revealing the names of his co-plotters. Over the next few weeks, authorities captured or killed them all, and the surviving conspirators were held in custody and sentenced to be hanged. On January 31, 1606, as Guy Fawkes was about to be executed, he jumped off the ladder that led up to the gallows, broke his neck, and died.

**INTERVIEW WITH...
SINEAD FITZGIBBON**

Sinead Fitzgibbon is an Irish author and writer whose published history books include *A Short History of London,* *The Queen,* and *The Gunpowder Plot: History in an Hour.* She graduated from university with a degree in economics, working in investment banking in Sydney, Australia for six years before returning to the UK to pursue a career as a writer in 2007. She has a particular interest in art, literature, and of course, history.

What if the Gunpowder Plot had been successful?
Had the plot been successful the country's first major colonization of the New World—the establishment of Jamestown in Virginia in 1607—may never have happened. Perhaps the French or Spanish would have gotten there first. And had England failed to settle America, would we have then been in a position to colonize the West Indies? Without the profits generated from this colony, Britain might not have had the financial means to expand its horizons in the 19th century.

Had the British not settled America in the 17th century, would English be the global language it is today? Probably not. Perhaps we would now live in a world where French is the language of Hollywood and we in Britain would be the ones straining to read the subtitles on the big screen.

How close were Catesby and his co-conspirators to succeeding? Given the fact that Guy Fawkes, along with his hoard of gunpowder, was discovered by the King's men just a few hours before the fuse was due to be lit, some might say that the plot came very close to succeeding. Further investigation, however, reveals a very different story. Before its dramatic conclusion in the early hours of November 5, 1605, the Gunpowder Plot had been in the planning stages for over 18 months. During this unusually long gestation period, the original five conspirators found it increasingly difficult to deflect suspicion and keep their scheme under wraps. As time went on, necessity forced them to reveal their plans to various friends and family members. On October 26, 1605, an anonymous letter was sent to one Lord Monteagle warning him not to attend the upcoming opening of Parliament as "they shall receive a terrible blow this Parliament and yet they shall not see who hurts them." Monteagle raised the alarm and the King was informed. The Gunpowder Plot was, thanks to this letter, discovered a full nine days previously.

What would blowing up the Houses of Parliament have done to the political landscape of the day? Had the powder combusted properly and wiped out prominent members of the royal family and the country's political elite as planned, I doubt the country's political landscape would have greatly changed in the long term. Indeed, the fact that Catesby believed otherwise was naïve in the extreme. Common sense dictates that the powerful Protestant ruling families would surely have hunted down the perpetrators, while Protestant vigilantes, galvanized by the act of terror inflicted on their fellow men in Westminster, would have sought revenge against ordinary Catholic civilians. If anything, a successful Gunpowder Plot would have made life worse for English Catholics, not better.

How do you think British Catholics would have reacted to the untimely death of the Protestant James I? The majority of 17th-century Catholics would have viewed Catesby's actions in the same way

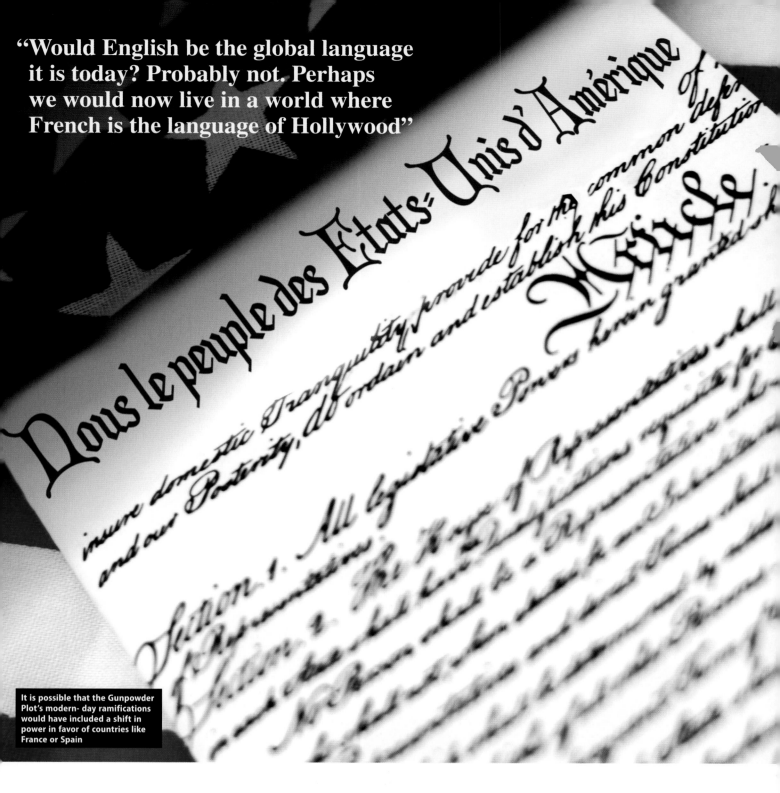

"Would English be the global language it is today? Probably not. Perhaps we would now live in a world where French is the language of Hollywood"

It is possible that the Gunpowder Plot's modern-day ramifications would have included a shift in power in favor of countries like France or Spain

Northern Irish Catholics reacted to the murderous campaigns of the IRA during the Troubles—that is, with abhorrence. Also, it's worth pointing out that James was not uniformly despised by the Catholic community; many still held out hope that he would be persuaded to lessen the restrictions placed on the Roman religion by his predecessors. After all, his mother was the Catholic martyr, Mary Queen of Scots. Protestants would have been outraged by the regicide, and I believe many would have taken the law into their own hands in an attempt to exact revenge. It's not difficult to envisage an eruption of anti-Catholic riots throughout the country.

How do you think the assassination of James I would have affected Britain's relationship with other countries? By the 17th century, relations between Protestant Britain and Catholic Spain had been strained for decades. Tensions had begun to escalate during the initial stages of the Reformation when Henry VIII divorced Catherine of Aragon [daughter of Spain's Ferdinand and Isabella], and had peaked with the failed invasion by the Spanish Armada in 1588. Even after 1588, some English Catholics continued to hope that the Spanish would one day succeed in overthrowing the country's Protestant rulers. This intervention never

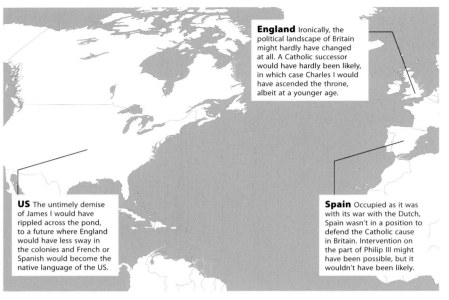

England Ironically, the political landscape of Britain might hardly have changed at all. A Catholic successor would have hardly been likely, in which case Charles I would have ascended the throne, albeit at a younger age.

US The untimely demise of James I would have rippled across the pond, to a future where England would have less sway in the colonies and French or Spanish would become the native language of the US.

Spain Occupied as it was with its war with the Dutch, Spain wasn't in a position to defend the Catholic cause in Britain. Intervention on the part of Philip III might have been possible, but it wouldn't have been likely.

materialized, thanks in large part to the strain imposed on Spain's military resources by the Dutch wars.

It's difficult to say how Spain would have reacted had Catesby's scheme borne fruit. Perhaps it would have tipped the balance in favor of the longed-for Spanish intervention. Maybe Philip III would have sought to capitalize on the plotters' triumph by attempting to install himself or a member of his family on the English throne—after all, his sister, Isabella, had once been touted by some prominent English Catholics as a possible successor to Elizabeth I. But while this scenario was possible, I don't believe it was very probable. By this point in the proceedings, Spain had largely abandoned English Catholics to their fate—indeed, the court of Philip III had previously declined to offer Catesby any assistance in his quest to mount a rebellion.

More broadly, I think the Gunpowder Plot would have had a significant impact on Britain's relations with the wider world, in that Catesby's scheme may well have put paid to the country's early colonial ambitions.

James I was a Scottish King—if the assassination had succeeded how would Scotland have reacted? This is an interesting point to consider. James had been Scotland's monarch for 35 years before succeeding Elizabeth I to the throne in 1603. And given that Scottish Calvinists had gone to great lengths to install James as king in the first place, I doubt they would have taken his assassination lightly. A Scottish invasion of England may well have been the result.

Who would have been the most likely successor to James I if a Catholic monarch was placed on the throne? In a bid to add legitimacy to his coup, it was Catesby's intention to install James and Anne's nine-year-old daughter, Princess Elizabeth, on the throne as a puppet monarch. Catholic guardians would have been appointed to oversee her re-education in the Roman faith, while a regent would look after affairs of state until she came of age. She would then have been married off to a Catholic prince from one of Europe's royal dynasties, re-establishing a Catholic line of succession. Again, this was a very ill-conceived plan, as it was unlikely Elizabeth would have been as pliable and cooperative as Catesby hoped.

What if James I had died but the Protestants retained control—who would have been crowned then? James's eldest son, Henry, was due to attend the opening of Parliament along with his parents on the fateful day. Assuming he too had been killed, the next in line to the throne was the youngest son, Charles [Elizabeth would have been precluded from the line of succession thanks to the laws of male primogeniture]. Just as Catesby had planned with Elizabeth, the Protestant establishment would have looked after the boy's, and indeed the country's interests until he reached the age where he could rule in his own right.

What effect would either outcome have had on the future lineage of Britain? In the case of Charles, there would have been no impact on the future line of succession, as he was destined to take the throne

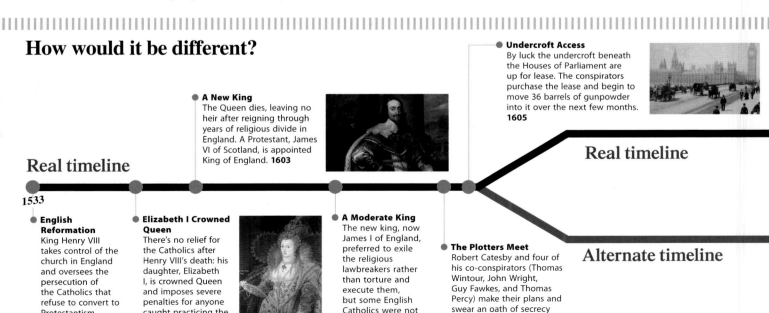

How would it be different?

Real timeline

1533

English Reformation
King Henry VIII takes control of the church in England and oversees the persecution of the Catholics that refuse to convert to Protestantism. **1533-1540**

Elizabeth I Crowned Queen
There's no relief for the Catholics after Henry VIII's death: his daughter, Elizabeth I, is crowned Queen and imposes severe penalties for anyone caught practicing the Catholic faith. **1558**

A New King
The Queen dies, leaving no heir after reigning through years of religious divide in England. A Protestant, James VI of Scotland, is appointed King of England. **1603**

A Moderate King
The new king, now James I of England, preferred to exile the religious lawbreakers rather than torture and execute them, but some English Catholics were not to be mollified so easily. **1603-1605**

The Plotters Meet
Robert Catesby and four of his co-conspirators (Thomas Wintour, John Wright, Guy Fawkes, and Thomas Percy) make their plans and swear an oath of secrecy in the Duck and Drake Inn, London. **May 20, 1604**

Undercroft Access
By luck the undercroft beneath the Houses of Parliament are up for lease. The conspirators purchase the lease and begin to move 36 barrels of gunpowder into it over the next few months. **1605**

Real timeline

Alternate timeline

Macbeth was thought to have been inspired by the Gunpowder Plot and so may never have seen the light of day had it been a success

anyway. In 1612, he became heir apparent when his older brother, Prince Henry, died of suspected typhoid fever [Charles eventually succeeded his father to the throne on the latter's death in 1625].

It is less clear what would have happened to the line of succession had Catesby succeeded in his plan to install Princess Elizabeth as monarch. Would Charles have tried to oust his sister once he came of age? Possibly. Perhaps Elizabeth would have willingly abdicated in favor of her brother, given he was the rightful heir. We shall never know. Elizabeth was, however, to leave her mark on England's royal lineage. When the House of Stuart eventually gave way to the House of Hanover [childlessness having done what a revolution, a beheading, and an abdication had failed to do], it was Anne's grandson, George I, who became the first Hanoverian king. There's a pleasing synchronicity in that, wouldn't you say?

Besides James I, there were some notable historic figures present in the house on the day. What would the knock-on effect of these collateral deaths have had on the history books? Had the architects of the Gunpowder Plot achieved their aims, the untimely death of Francis Bacon would have been a significant loss to posterity. A polymath who wrote prolifically, his works

greatly influenced the development of philosophical, scientific, and legal thinking. The biggest loser, however, would have been our English language. Both James VI and Bishop Bancroft had a part to play in the compilation of the King James Version of the Bible (KJV), which was destined to form part of the bedrock on which our modern language is built. Although work had started on the KJV in 1604, it wasn't finished until 1611, and you could argue that the project might never have reached completion had these two men perished in November 1605. The other great contributor to our language was, of course, William Shakespeare. It is sobering to consider that, without the patronage of King James [who funded Shakespeare's acting company, The King's Men], some of the greatest works of dramatic tragedy may never have been written. Certainly *Macbeth*, written in 1606 and widely thought to have been inspired by the Gunpowder Plot, may never have seen the light of day—because, as the contemporary writer Sir John Harington famously said, "Treason doth never prosper. What's the reason? Why, if it prosper, none dare call it treason."

What would Britain have been like today, politically and religiously? When all is said and done, I don't believe Protestantism would have been supplanted had the Houses of Parliament gone up in flames on that November day in 1605. I think the country's Protestant majority would have scuppered Catesby's plans, and Charles would have succeeded his father to the English and Scottish thrones. Puritanism may have flourished as a reaction to the atrocity, and perhaps Oliver Cromwell would never have had his day in the sun. From a global perspective, the picture may well have been very different. Had the political upheaval resulting from a successful Gunpowder Plot diverted attentions away from colonial expansion, the British Empire may never have got off the ground. It is entirely feasible to suggest that country might never have become a major player on the world stage; instead it may have been destined to play second fiddle in a French- or Spanish-speaking world. In short, Great Britain might never have achieved the requisite degree of greatness to justify its lofty name.

Timeline

Anonymous Tip-Off
Lord Monteagle receives an anonymous letter begging him not to go to the opening of Parliament on that fateful day. It proves to be key evidence in revealing the plot to the King. **October 26, 1605**

The Discovery
With knowledge of the plot, the undercroft is searched the evening before Parliament's opening. Guy Fawkes is discovered hiding there with 36 barrels of gunpowder, ready to light the fuse. **November 4, 1605**

Capture and Arrest
Over the next few days, the plotters are rounded up, arrested, and interrogated. Following trial, they're hung, drawn, and quartered—a particularly horrific form of execution reserved for traitors. **November 8, 1605**

Declaration of Independence
Britain's hold on the American colonies reaches a breaking point as an agreement is signed and a union is formed under one proposed nation: the United States of America. **1776**

Jamestown Settled
The Virginia company of London reaches the east coast of America, where a permanent settlement is established—Jamestown—that lasts as the colony's capital for nearly a century. **May 14, 1607**

US
After a century of war, the fledgling nation expands and prospers to the world power it is today. Britain's own fortunes wane as its empire diminishes, but English is an international language. **1776-present day**

Anonymous Tip-Off
Lord Monteagle receives an anonymous letter, but decides to keep its contents to himself. He makes his excuses to avoid Parliament on its fateful opening day. **October 26, 1605**

Parliament Destroyed
Amid the opening of the Houses of Parliament, there is a huge explosion from the undercroft beneath it. King James I, as well as a host of dignitaries, are killed. **November 5, 1605**

English Uprising
Inspired by the plotters, Catholics in many quarters rebel against the Protestants and, despite Charles I taking the throne, Britain is caught up in religious conflict. **1605-1606**

America Colonized
The first major colonies of America are established by the French and Spanish. The War for Independence is fought between the colonists and the old-world countries. **1607-1766**

The World Stage
Britain never becomes a superpower as it isn't involved in the land-grab of the 17th, 18th, and 19th centuries. French and Spanish are the dominant languages of the modern-day US. **1766-Present day**

© ALAMY

What if . . .
The Great Fire of London didn't happened?

LONDON, ENGLAND 1666

NOTABLE NAMES:
• Thomas Farriner

IMPORTANT DATES:
September 1, 1966
September 2, 1966
September 6, 1666

What Really Happened...

London circa 1666 was a city built from oak timber. Some houses had tar-covered walls, streets were narrow, houses were too close to each other, and firefighting methods were primitive. It was a disaster just waiting to happen...

On the night of September 1, 1666, a baker named Thomas Farriner was cleaning his shop on Pudding Lane. Around midnight, smoldering embers he had accidentally left behind ignited and soon, his house was in flames. Sparks spread from Farriner's bakery across the street. From there, the fire spread to Thames Street, where there were highly flammable warehouses filled with combustible materials. The fire spiraled out of control and the strong, dry wind carried it further.

Ultimately 13,000 houses, 90 churches, and tons of buildings were engulfed in flames. The Great Fire could be seen 30 miles away and wasn't extinguished until days later on September 6, 1666. Many historical landmarks were destroyed and 100,000 people were left homeless. Sixteen people were known to have died from the fire, one of whom was Thomas Farriner's bakery assistant.

The Great Fire of London began as an ember on Pudding Lane and, between September 2 and 5, 1666, grew into an inferno that ravaged the metropolis. Some claim that it ended the spread of the plague and, though that is debatable, it certainly changed the face of the city forever. If the fire had been quelled before it spread, the history of science, not to mention the look of London, would be very different indeed.

If only, working late in his bakery, Thomas Farriner had spotted a smoldering ember among the extinguished coals in his bakehouse, stamped it out, and had gone up to bed, the Great Fire of London could have been avoided.

How would it be different?

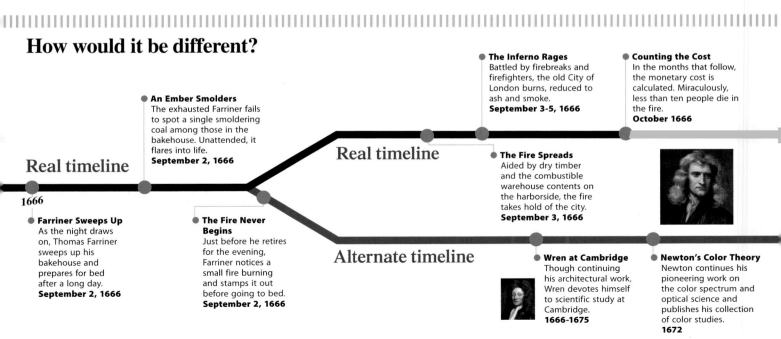

An Ember Smolders
The exhausted Farriner fails to spot a single smoldering coal among those in the bakehouse. Unattended, it flares into life.
September 2, 1666

The Inferno Rages
Battled by firebreaks and firefighters, the old City of London burns, reduced to ash and smoke.
September 3-5, 1666

Counting the Cost
In the months that follow, the monetary cost is calculated. Miraculously, less than ten people die in the fire.
October 1666

Real timeline

Real timeline

1666

Farriner Sweeps Up
As the night draws on, Thomas Farriner sweeps up his bakehouse and prepares for bed after a long day.
September 2, 1666

The Fire Never Begins
Just before he retires for the evening, Farriner notices a small fire burning and stamps it out before going to bed.
September 2, 1666

The Fire Spreads
Aided by dry timber and the combustible warehouse contents on the harborside, the fire takes hold of the city.
September 3, 1666

Alternate timeline

Wren at Cambridge
Though continuing his architectural work, Wren devotes himself to scientific study at Cambridge.
1666-1675

Newton's Color Theory
Newton continues his pioneering work on the color spectrum and optical science and publishes his collection of color studies.
1672

Of course, in 1666, the Great Plague had already ripped through London. So, without the fire to kill the rats, ridden with plague-carrying fleas, might that terrible illness have consumed the densely-packed city, leading to a death count that might have approached apocalyptic proportions?

Not so, says Adrian Tinniswood. "The old story that the Fire put an end to the plague is hard to sustain. Mortality rates were already falling." True, the plague was far from over. Playhouses remained closed; the annual Bartholomew Fair at Smithfield was canceled "for fear of a renewal of the contagion." And all through that August, reports of the epidemic poured in from around the country. "In Northamptonshire the sickness rages extremely, especially in Peterborough, Oundle, and Newport Pagnell, in which last, though a market town, only 700 or 800 people are left. At Cambridge it is so sore that the harvest can hardly be gathered in."

On the Kent coast, the situation in Cinque Ports was desperate. By the end of the month, three-quarters of those who stayed in Deal and risked infection were reported dead; Dover and Sandwich were affected, and the plague had moved inland to Canterbury and Maidstone.

"Surely the very fact that the plague wasn't confined to London demonstrates that the Great Fire could not be responsible for eradicating it? Put at its simplest, the capital wasn't the only source."

So, if Farriner's quick thinking in stamping out that ember wouldn't have lead to the spread of the plague, it could have changed the face of London forever.

Christopher Wren, toiling over his scientific experiments at Cambridge, would have never received the summons to the capital, nor the commission for over 50 churches, including the mighty dome of St. Paul's Cathedral. Instead, he would have continued at the university, uncovering the secrets of gravity. Years before Newton was fated to make the discovery,

If the first embers of the Great Fire had been extinguished, London would look completely different

Not a real photo.

it would have been Wren who announced that he had unlocked the mysteries of Earth's gravitational pull.

In a city so tightly packed and industrial as London, it was inevitable that a fire would break out one day and, years later, an inferno could have swallowed the port warehouses, packed as they were with combustibles. This time it wouldn't be Wren who rebuilt the city's churches, but the fashionable John Vanbrugh. From the fire-ravaged wastes, he would create a glittering city in which men such as Wren are honored amid a dramatic, Baroque landscape.

For Newton, the chance to achieve the status of legend would have slipped past without him ever knowing. His career would still have been remarkable, but he would remain an icon of the scientific community, rather than a name that persists through the centuries.

ADRIAN TINNISWOOD OBE

Adrian Tinniswood is senior research fellow in history at the University of Buckingham and author of By Permission of Heaven: The Story of the Great Fire of London (Pimlico, 2004).

CATHERINE CURZON

Catherine Curzon is a royal historian specializing in the 18th century. Her work has featured in numerous publications and she has spoken at venues including the Royal Pavilion, Brighton. She is the author of Life in the Georgian Court and Kings of Georgian Britain.

Plague Ebbs
In the wake of the fire the spread of the plague ebbs. Many wrongly attribute this to the flames.
Late 1666

Philosophiæ Naturalis Principia Mathematica
Isaac Newton's legendary Principia is the culmination of his work. In this masterwork, he unveils his law of gravity.
1687

Rebuilding London
Appointed by King Charles II, the City Commissioners and Christopher Wren begin work on plans for a rebuilt city.
October 1666

Erecting St. Paul's
Christopher Wren is commissioned to design St. Paul's Cathedral. Its construction takes over 50 years.
July 30, 1669

Newton the Icon
Lauded as a legend of the scientific community, Isaac Newton's reputation persists to this day.
1687–Today

Wren's Principia
Wren's legendary Principia is the culmination of his work and includes his celebrated laws of gravity. **1675**

A Warehouse Fire
On the London docks, a warehouse catches fire, thanks to a spark thrown from a nearby bonfire.
December 1700

The Inferno Rages
The fire burns through the tightly packed city, causing devastation. Much of London is reduced to rubble and ash.
December 1701

Vanbrugh Rebuilds London
Commissioned by the king, John Vanbrugh draws up plans for a Baroque rebuilding of London with the assistance of Nicholas Hawksmoor. **1700**

The New London
From the ashes of the city, a new London rises. In this glittering new metropolis, the Age of Enlightenment is honored.
1700-1750

Wren Lauded
In the newly rebuilt city Wren is honored in a statue created by John Michael Rysbrack. It stands to this day.
1730

© IAN HINLEY

What if...
Prohibition stayed in place?

PROHIBITION, US, 1933

IMPORTANT DATES:
January 16, 1919
January 17, 1920
December 5, 1933

What Really Happened...

On January 16, 1919, the 18th Amendment was ratified and was effectively enforced one year later on January 17, 1920. The National Prohibition Act, also known as the Volstead Act, was also passed in order to implement the 18th Amendment, which banned the manufacture, transportation, and sale of alcohol.

As a result of this legislation, bootlegging, speakeasies, gang violence, and organized crime increased. In the first six months alone, there were over 7,000 cases for violations. In the first year, there were over 29,000! And that number continued to drastically rise over the course of the next 13 years.

By the end of the 1920s, Prohibition had little support due to all the repercussions from its enforcement. On December 5, 1933, the 21st Amendment was ratified to repeal the 18th Amendment, officially ending Prohibition.

What would have happened if Prohibition hadn't been repealed in 1933?

Jack Blocker: It's hard to imagine enforcement of national Prohibition improving and it's easy to imagine it deteriorating if Prohibition had remained in place. The problem was the division of authority between the states and the federal government that was mandated by the 18th Amendment. That caused problems during the Twenties because some states devoted few resources to enforcement, leaving the whole burden on the federal government, which itself was not adequately funded to do the job of enforcement. As a result, enforcement against Prohibition was never carried out to the level necessary to provide full compliance with the Volstead Act. It's extremely unlikely that things would have gotten any better in the Thirties because both the states and the federal government were hard-pressed for revenues [due to the Great Depression of 1929]. So it's quite likely that enforcement would have been cut back.

Would rates of organized crime have increased?

Deborah Toner: In that kind of scenario it's very difficult to imagine how organized crime could have been reined in. This is where most people dwell on one of the key problems of Prohibition, this explosion in organized crime growing out of networks that had existed for at least 40 to 50 years before Prohibition came into effect. They really expanded rapidly because of the huge new economic opportunities that Prohibition created. And so one might have seen a escalation of organized crime and associated violent crime with gang warfare that we now see between the drug-dealing organizations in the US and elsewhere. It's quite possible that if the hardline approach [by the authorities] to Prohibition had remained, there could have been a massive escalation in organized crime. The continuation would have supported the development of super-organized crime gangs, the kind of cartels that we see in the drug business, across these two illegal industries [drugs and alcohol].

Is it likely the law would not have survived this increase in crime?

JB: Anybody transporting, selling, manufacturing, or importing liquor was by definition a criminal, but they might not have been part of a criminal organization. In other words, the deterioration of enforcement might have opened up a lot of space for ordinary citizens to make their own booze and pass it back and forth among friends. The decline in enforcement might also have reduced one of the real problems in public perception of Prohibition, in that when enforcement did take place it was often perceived as unfair when gun battles broke out in the streets between Prohibition agents and bootleggers. If enforcement was cut back that could have declined, which would have meant that one of the more visible problems as far as the public saw them would have been reduced. US citizens might have said: "Why not leave the law in the books because it's not having much effect, we're able to obtain liquor and the gun battles in the streets aren't taking place." So the law might have survived, in spite of or perhaps because of deterioration of enforcement.

If Prohibition had not been repealed it could have led to riots and running battles in the streets

Not a real photo, has been altered.

AEA
ALCOHOL ENFORCEMENT AGENCY

"It's quite possible that if the hardline approach to Prohibition had remained, there could have been a massive escalation in organized crime"

INTERVIEWS WITH...
DR. JACK BLOCKER

Jack Blocker is professor of History Emeritus at Huron University College, an affiliated college of the University of Western Ontario, Canada. He has authored and edited six books on the history of alcohol use and temperance reform, most notably on *Alcohol and Temperance in Modern History: An International Encyclopedia (2003)*. In 2020 he published *A Little More Freedom*, which examines African-American life in urban Midwest.

DR. DEBORAH TONER

Dr. Deborah Toner is a lecturer in Modern History at the University of Leicester, UK. Her research and teaching interests focus on the social and cultural history of alcohol in Mexico and the United States. She also convenes the Warwick Drinking Studies Network, a scholarly forum for the exploration of historical and contemporary debates surrounding alcohol and its place in society.

Could Prohibition have been modified in some form?

DT: My view is that the only way Prohibition could have survived, so that it could have avoided being repealed, was if the Prohibition camp, or the 'dry' lobby as they're often referred, accepted some modifications to the way Prohibition was being enforced through the Volstead Act. If that had happened and Prohibition had remained in a more revised format then actually a lot of the aims of Prohibition would have been achieved. For instance, with that change a lot more resources would have been diverted towards cracking down on the higher-level organized crime led by mobsters like Al Capone and so on.

JB: One of the proposals made consistently through the Twenties was to modify Prohibition to allow consumption of beer and light wines. If that change had been made Prohibition may well have lasted quite a long time because, as you know, beer and wine now make up the largest contributor of per capita alcohol consumption. It is possible to imagine an amended Prohibition continuing long after 1933.

Would that have been more successful?

DT: If there had been a more moderate approach towards scaling back Prohibition, making it less of a burden to the average American and concentrating resources on cracking down on the highest levels of organized crime, then we might have seen a more effective management of that process. If things like beer and light wine had been legalized during the course of Prohibition, even if spirits and other high-percentage alcohol drinks had remained illegal, that really would have reduced the market that organized crime had to sell to. I strongly think that had those changes towards the legalization, particularly of beer and wine, been taken in the Twenties, Prohibition would have continued for a very long time.

Was there a turning point where Prohibition might not have been repealed?

JB: The turning point probably came in the late Twenties after Herbert Hoover's election [as US president] in 1928. He created a commission to look at Prohibition, the Wickersham Commission, and if that had recommended modifying Prohibition that could well have been a turning point. But by that point the main Prohibitionist organization, the Anti-Saloon League, was in extreme disarray, although there were a lot of people who continued to support national Prohibition, so there could have been a political firestorm had they recommended modifying it.

DT: In the mid-to-late Twenties there were continued attempts to try to persuade the government to introduce changes to the Volstead Act so that things like beer and wine could be legalized. But members of the 'dry' lobby, particularly led by the Anti-Saloon League, completely refused to countenance any changes whatsoever, either to the Volstead Act or to the 18th Amendment. It's really that intransigence and unwillingness to compromise in any way that pushes the two camps, pro-Prohibition and pro-repeal, into completely opposite positions.

Al Capone (center) was one of the US Government's biggest enemies during the Prohibition era

How would the economy have fared if Prohibition had remained unchanged?

DT: It's possible that there may have been a very entrenched period of depression in the Thirties that Prohibition contributed to. From the Fifties onwards there might have been a positive effect in terms of greater worker productivity, higher levels of personal savings, and so on. Those were major goals for the Prohibition campaigners before it was brought into force, but that simulating effect on the economy didn't manifest itself in the Twenties to any great degree because of the knock-on effect of people going out of work, there being lower tax revenues coming in and so on. With the dire situation of the US economy

How would it be different?

Decision on Prohbition
The Wickersham Commission must make its decision on whether Prohibition should be modified or tackled with more enforcement to combat crime. **January 6, 1931**

Enforcement of Prohibition Begins
Over 1,500 federal Prohibition agents are tasked with enforcing the strict laws of the Volstead Act. **January 17, 1920**

Wickersham Commission
Hoover establishes the Wickersham Commission to study the effects of Prohibition and suggest changes to lower crime levels. **May 20, 1929**

Real timeline

Real timeline

1919

18th Amendment
The 18th Amendment to the Constitution of the United States is ratified, prohibiting the production, transport, and sale of alcohol. The country will go dry later that year. **January 16, 1919**

Prohibition Struggles
With resources stretched, the government struggles to successfully police Prohibition laws, allowing criminal alcohol gangs to grow in wealth and power. **1921-1928**

The Great Depression
The Wall Street crash of October 1929 sends the US economy plummeting into a downturn. **October 1929**

Alternate timeline

in the midst of the Great Depression, if anything, continued Prohibition would have helped to cement that depression. What we have to think about is the temptation for more and more ordinary people to take a criminal path. If we are imagining an even further expansion of organized crime, then with that comes a greater need for the government to tackle organized crime. With the government having less and less resources in the midst of the Great Depression and having to spend ever-more on enforcement, it doesn't spell a happy picture for the economy.

Would a lack of repeal have encouraged attempts by other countries to bring in prohibition?

JB: A number of other countries and territories adopted forms of Prohibition during the early 20th century. There were various international Prohibitionist organizations at work, such as the World League Against Alcoholism, and I suspect the repeal of US Prohibition represented a real body blow to efforts to internationalize that reform. Without repeal, there may well have been an instance where Prohibition became more widespread around the world.

Would continued prohibition have affected the US's involvement in World War II?

DT: The only thing that might have prevented that was an economic situation if Prohibition had continued and affected the economy very badly. But it's widely believed that with World War II came an economic recovery because of all the additional opportunities for exporting and manufacturing goods and weaponry, and that probably still would've had that effect in the context of continued Prohibition. If anything, a continued commitment to Prohibition might have enhanced the sense of the US being able to export a kind of morale-idealized society to other parts of the world, that kind of evangelizing undertone to US foreign policy might have actually been heightened by continued Prohibition.

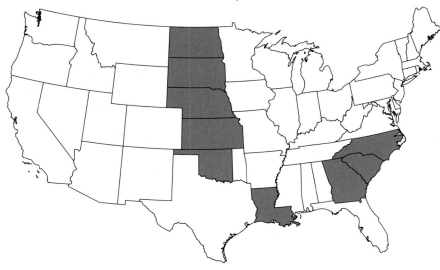

States that voted to keep Prohibition, 1933

How long might Prohibition have lasted if it was not repealed in 1933?

DT: If a more modified form of Prohibition had been introduced, it might have been gradually lifted according to provincial interests and be replaced by regulatory systems, in effect lifting Prohibition once its job had been done. An altered form of it could have lasted for decades, and in several states even now Prohibition is still effectively in force. But I think the Sixties or Seventies would probably have been the maximum life span for Prohibition in that modified form. If Prohibition had remained unchanged in its radical original version, it's difficult to see how that would have survived for long. The mounting economic pressures, expansion of organized crime, and generally being out of sync with the rest of the world on this issue would probably have brought itself to bear by the time of World War II. In terms of the economic demands of the US in the post-World War II era, it's difficult to see how that kind of radical Prohibition could have survived.

Level of Enforcement Increased
The Wickersham Commission recommends more extensive law enforcement to ensure compliance with Prohibition laws across the US, but it is not successful.
January 7, 1931

Prohibition Repealed
The 21st Amendment to the US Constitution repeals the 18th Amendment, re-legalizing the distribution and consumption of alcohol.
December 5, 1933

World War II
With a now-prosperous economy, US enters World War II, swinging the war in the Allies' favor. **1942**

Minor Prohibition Continues
Several states in the US continue to keep some form of Prohibition laws, allowing the distribution of certain types of alcohol. **1960**

New Deal
President Roosevelt's 'New Deal' economic recovery plan allows the US to emerge from the mire of the Great Depression. **1936**

Super Gangs Super-organized crime gangs emerge, taking complete control of both alcohol and drug traffic in the country. **1938**

Prohibition is Modified
The Wickersham Commission recommends modifying Prohibition laws to allow for lower percentage drinks like beer and light wine.
January 7, 1931

Prohibition Continues
Even though Prohibition laws are relaxed to allow weaker drinks, a lack of repeal makes it increasingly difficult to tackle organized gangs peddling stronger alcohol.
December 5, 1933

Economy Worsens
Despite Roosevelt's best efforts with his New Deal economy plan, the continued attempts to police Prohibition sees the economy get even worse.
1936

World War II
The US enters World War II, which provides a much-needed economic boost to the ailing country and also strengthens the cause of the Prohibition camp.
1942

Prohibition Repealed
Eventually Prohibition is repealed, perhaps as it has fulfilled its goals or because it cannot be maintained, although some states keep their anti-alcohol laws.
1960

© ALAMY, CORBIS

What if...

The Nazis never gained power?

GERMANY, 1933

What Really Happened...

In the year 1932, Adolf Hitler rose to prominence as a result of the German people's frustration with a poor economy, the harsh peace terms of the Versailles treaty, and their defeat in the Great War. Charismatic and convincing, he gained support for his emerging Nazi party, and in a July 1932 election, the Nazis won 230 governmental seats.

President Paul von Hindenburg was intimidated by Hitler and his supporters, so he refused to make him chancellor. However, he was eventually swayed through a series of negotiations and agreed to appoint Hitler as chancellor, as long as other non-Nazis remained in positions of power to contain Hitler's temper and brutality.

On January 30, 1933, Hitler became chancellor of Germany, and his radical plans were officially underway. After President Hindenburg died from lung cancer, Hitler was elected president of Germany through a plebiscite vote—based on fear and intimidation—on August 19, 1934. After that, there was little anyone could do to stop Hitler, his cruel dictatorship, and the Nazis.

How was Germany run after Wilhelm II abdicated?
In the last weeks of [World War I], a popular revolution began with sailors in the port of Kiel and it spread to industrial cities, then throughout the country. Throughout the winter of 1918 a revolution unfolds in Germany and like all revolutions it was very contested. On the radical end were workers, who established workers councils—soviets—in the factories and this spread even to artistic realms, in theaters, and all through the country. They were demanding a kind of radical democracy. Not really Bolshevik communism, but some kind of system in which workers would at least have influence over the economy. But the more moderate socialists, who were deathly afraid of 'Bolshevik chaos' as they called it, moved quickly to establish a parliamentary democracy.

The Social Democratic Party—the same party that we have today in Germany—in alliance with the liberal [German Democratic Party] and the Catholic Center Party formed the Weimar Coalition. Their coalition prevailed at the election of January 1919 and then they empanelled a constitutional convention, which appointed a committee, that met in Weimar because of the civil war raging in Berlin. They drafted a constitution in summer 1919 and on that basis the Weimar Republic was created. This lasted until January 30, 1933, when Hitler was named chancellor.

What was life like in 1920s Berlin? There was most definitely a lot going on. It was tumultuous and crisis ridden, but at the same time, it was one of the most creative eras of the 20th century. Perhaps there is a relationship between the two—we can never prove it—but the fragility of the political order, I think, contributed to the kind of artistic ferment that is still with us today. Particularly in the cities—Berlin of course was the center—there was vital artistic experimentation going on. Here we have the creation of artistic modernism; expressionism in painting and theater; very creative film, the new popular medium of the 1920s; radio, also. Martin Heidegger's *Being and Time*, Thomas Mann's *Magic Mountain*, Bertolt Brecht and Kurt Weill's *The Threepenny Opera*—all of these incredibly innovative and creative works emerged in the [Weimar Republic].

In the wake of the 1918-19 German Revolution, political factions vied for power

INTERVIEW WITH...
ERIC WEITZ

Once a distinguished professor of History at The City College of New York, Eric Weitz was also the author of *Weimar Germany: Promise and Tragedy*, as well as *Creating German Communism, 1890-1990: From Popular Protests to Socialist State*.

"Jewish life also flourished— another sign of openness"

There was a lively cabaret scene again in the cities, a very lively public life with people out in the streets. They were having very open discussions about sexuality.

I sometimes laugh to myself when people in the United States say discussing sexuality is so new, when Germans were having them in the 1920s.

So it was very socially progressive? Quite vibrantly so! There were discussions about homosexuality and pressures to reform Germany's highly restrictive abortion law. They also set up public health clinics that offered counselling about sex. The Weimar constitution was probably the most democratic constitution anywhere in the world in the 1920s. Proportional representation, which ultimately contributed to the paralysis of the political system, was far more democratic than the American system of winner-takes-all. The security services sometimes responded brutally to public demonstrations, but in general there was a lively free press and freedom of assembly.

Jewish life also flourished—another sign of openness. There was still prejudice and areas like the Officer Corps were closed off to Jews. But it was possible for Jews to get university professorships.

How did right-wing groups gain ground? In the early 1920s, you have literally hundreds of extreme right-wing organizations. Many of them were very small and local, but troublesome. These right-wing groups were by and large demobilized soldiers, let go under the armistice conditions and the final Versailles Peace Treaty.

These demobilized soldiers were aghast at the prevalence of socialists and communists in public spaces and leading government—as well as Jews in high-level positions. In 1919 the Jewish social democratic chancellor of Bavaria, Kurt Eisner, was assassinated. In 1922 the Jewish banker and intellectual, foreign minister Walter Rathenau was killed. So there was a lot of right-wing terrorism going on, carried out by these small groups. The Nazis eventually unified these groups under the Nazi Party—that was one of their first accomplishments. In 1923, when hyperinflation completely disrupted economic and social life, these right-wing groups grew in size and the Nazis made their first attempt to seize power [in the failed Munich Beer Hall Putsch].

Was the Nazi Party's rise inevitable? Actually, between 1924-29, the so-called 'golden years' of the Weimar Republic, there was a move back to the political center. You see it in the elections of 1928 when both the extreme right and extreme left lose significant support. The Nazis in 1928 are a small party, they're a police problem, but they're not really a political threat. Hitler has been banned from speaking in many of the German states. They're really nowhere until 1929 when the Great Depression hits and that then gives wind—I mean a thunderstorm, a hurricane force of wind—to the Nazi sails. But even in

The Weimar Republic's vibrant nightlife inspired the movie *Cabaret*

How would it be different?

Real timeline

Real timeline

Alternate timeline

● **Kaiser Wilhelm II Abdicates**
Following the Kiel Mutiny, a revolution spreads through Germany. Kaiser Wilhelm II is forced to abdicate and the Weimar Republic emerges.
November 9, 1918

● **The Great Depression**
Reliant on American loans under the Dawes Plan, the Wall Street Crash has a devastating effect on Germany. Politicians struggle to find a meaningful solution.
October 29, 1929

● **Political Chaos**
Three governments collapse in Germany in 1932, with Chancellor Brüning resigning, Franz von Papen failing to win votes, and Schleicher's regime lasting two months.
1932

● **Hitler Appointed Chancellor**
On the advice of Franz von Papen and several colleagues, President Hindenburg abandons his opposition to Adolf Hitler and appoints him as the new Chancellor of Germany.
January 30, 1933

● **Hitler Given New Powers**
The German parliament—controlled by a Nazi coalition with other right-wing parties—votes to make itself redundant passing the Enabling Act, allowing Hitler to rule by decree alone.
March 23, 1933

● **The Nazi Party Collapses**
Though the Nazis were the largest party in the fractured parliament, they still only had 33 percent of the vote. Dissatisfied with Hitler's leadership, an attempted coup leads to a schism and ultimately the dissolution of the party.
1933

● **Chancellor Papen Returns**
With Hitler no longer a tenable option for chancellor and limited alternatives, President Hindenburg appoints his old friend Franz von Papen to the post once again.
January 30, 1933

the 1930 elections, the Nazis got slaughtered with only 18 percent of the vote. It was a shock. The highest vote they would get in popular election was 37.4 percent in July 1932. Now that's a large chunk to be sure, but it's not a majority and that's significant because they never had a majority. You know, before the Third Reich, they never had a majority of popular support.

If the Nazis were polling so badly, how did Hitler become Chancellor of Germany in 1933? There is a popular understanding that the German people let Hitler into power, but that's absolutely wrong. So all through 1932 while the economy keeps falling, the political system has completely fragmented. There are three major elections in the course of 1932, two parliamentary elections and one presidential election. The biggest electoral turnout the Nazi Party gets is 37.4 percent. In November 1932 they lose again and this time are down to 32 percent. There is discontent within the Nazi Party about Hitler's leadership, and I think it is possible to imagine the dissolution of the party.

However, in the end, in January 1933 a group of alpha men, bankers, army officers, high public servants—including Franz Von Papen, Kurt Von Schleicher, and the president's own son, Oskar von Hindenburg—prevail upon Hindenburg to name Hitler chancellor. So in the very end it's a small group of powerful men around the president who are responsible for the Nazis coming to power.

Why did these figures want to help Hitler? Their motives were to destroy the republic and replace it with some kind of conservative authoritarian system and to overthrow the Versailles Peace Treaty so that Germany could become a great power again. Basically, you have a coalition of interests between older, more traditional conservatives and the Nazis. Each side is using the other, but the conservatives find that they cannot actually contain the Nazis. Not at all.

If the Nazis had dissolved or Hindenburg had maintained his opposition to Hitler, could the Weimar Republic have survived? The assessment would be that the Weimar coalition parties would gradually win more support, people would come back to the center, and you would have a viable social democratic parliamentary government, as we were getting in Sweden in the same period in the 1930s. But when the Great Depression comes, it hits Germany so fast and it affects them more than any other place. At the same time, the Social Democrats were exhausted and the political system fragments and becomes unworkable. Even before the Nazis seize power, the president signed emergency orders one after the other to issue budgets, to pursue his deflationary policy that worsened the economy.

Without Hitler, was World War II inevitable? I think World War II was inevitable when the Nazis came to power, but I don't think it would have been with a conservative group in power. It would have still been a nasty military dictatorship probably, but they would have been far more cautious. We know that because the conservatives thought Hitler was too radical with his moves into the Rhineland in 1936, and Czechoslovakia in 1938—they're much more cautious and don't support those measures.

Money became worthless during Germany's 1923 hyperinflation crisis

© DANIEL SINOCA, GETTY IMAGES

Hitler united Germany's various far-right groups under a single banner

Night of the Long Knives
In a bloody purge of the SA leadership and Hitler's political rivals, Papen narrowly escapes with his life.
June 30, 1934

Nuremburg Laws
Hitler announces new measures that establish apartheid in Germany, with Jews losing their civil rights and becoming second-class citizens.
September 15, 1935

Reoccupying the Rhineland
Hitler marchs 20,000 German troops into the Rhineland, directly contravening the Treaty of Versailles.
March 7, 1936

Buchenwald Opens
SS authorities open the Buchenwald concentration camp. The following year, almost 10,000 Jews were sent here.
July 16, 1937

Kristallnacht Pogrom
Joseph Goebbels leads an attack against German and Austrian Jews, which is called the 'Night of the Broken Glass' after the devastation it causes, including piles of smashed shop windows.
November 9, 1938

World War II Declared
Following the invasion of Poland two days before and Hitler's refusal to withdraw, Britain and France declare war on Nazi Germany.
September 3, 1939

Reichstag Fire
When Van der Lubbe is charged with burning down the Reichstag building Papen seizes on this opportunity, arresting communist leaders.
February 27, 1933

Election Victory
With widespread anti-communist feeling and votes from former Nazi supporters, Papen's Center Party wins at a general election.
March 5, 1933

Authoritarian Democracy
With a mandate to govern, Papen passes ultra-conservative laws and perhaps even seeks to reform the constitution.
1934

Military Dictatorship
Advocating the seizure of power as early as November 1932, Papen exploits Hindenburg's death to combine the chancellorship and presidency.
August 2, 1934

Renegotiate Versailles
While Papen would not risk starting a war, he would strengthen the military to force Britain and France back to the negotiating table.
1936

Peace for our Time?
War-weary Britain and France allow Germany to annex Czechoslovakia in return for Papen de-escalating his military build up.
1938

What if…

The Beatles never formed?

LIVERPOOL, ENGLAND 1960

NOTABLE NAMES:
- John Lennon
- Paul McCartney
- George Harrison
- Ringo Starr
- Brian Epstein

IMPORTANT DATES:
July 6, 1957
December 10, 1962
August 18, 1962

What Really Happened…

On July 6, 1957, 16-year-old John Lennon was playing guitar and singing in his band, the Quarrymen, at a church garden party in Woolton, Liverpool. In the crowd was 15-year-old Paul McCartney, who just so happened to be watching the band, impressed. After the set, the two met and McCartney even played a song for Lennon, who then asked McCartney if he wanted to join the band. He accepted.

Soon, George Harrison (also 15) joined the Quarrymen, and they went on to perform several gigs around England. Between 1958 and 1959, the band's name was in a state of flux, but eventually, they landed on the Beatles. While they struggled to keep a regular drummer, they hit their stride and were discovered by Brian Epstein. On December 10, 1962, Epstein finally approached the band about becoming their manager and by January 1962, the Beatles signed their first music contract. Later, Epstein fired their drummer and replaced him with 21-year-old Ringo Starr two days later on August 18, 1962. From there, the Beatles as we know them were officially formed and music was never the same again.

The runaway success of American stars like Frank Sinatra, Johnny Ray, and Elvis Presley ensured that by 1957, Britain's teenage market for short, catchy songs delivered by handsome men was firmly established and clamoring for homegrown talent.

But if a 16-year-old tearaway from Liverpool called John Lennon had decided not to enlist the services of one James Paul McCartney into his skiffle group, The Quarryman, they might never have become The Beatles, and whatever happened next, it certainly would not have occupied us as it has for the last 65 years.

A self-confessed know-all, Lennon could easily have dismissed the younger McCartney out of hand, no matter how impressed he was that the kid could play *Twenty Flight Rock* and knew all the words. But early the following year, George Harrison joined at McCartney's suggestion and the die was cast. Fame and fortune would soon follow.

Had Lennon ploughed on without them, it's likely The Quarrymen would have remained a mystery to the world, although after enrolling in Liverpool College of Art in 1958, their leader could well have pursued a more solitary creative path.

McCartney had the chops and the charm to follow his own star and may well have done well in showbiz—a TV presenter, perhaps. Harrison too had the talent, looks, and ambition to make it—maybe as a guitar prodigy; a Clapton of the North. At that time, Ringo Starr was making his name as a drummer-for-hire and would certainly have done very nicely out of that before a later career in acting beckoned, or maybe as a booking agent, or even a life as a promoter.

By 1962, as The Beatles scored their first hit, *Love Me Do*, Britain's growing pop music industry was hitting its stride. Tommy Steele, Adam Faith, Helen Shapiro, and, most significantly, Cliff Richard—Britain's answer to

How would it be different?   Alternate timeline

1957

Paul Meets John
John Lennon's skiffle group, The Quarrymen, play a church garden party witnessed by Paul McCartney, who is subsequently introduced to Lennon. **July 6, 1957**

George Meets John
Haunted by his dismissal of "that chubby kid McCartney," Lennon invites 14-year-old guitarist George Harrison to join The Quarrymen. **February 6, 1958**

Stones Begin to Roll
Mick Jagger, Brian Jones, and Keith Richards play their first gig as The Rollin' Stones at the Marquee Club in London. **July 12, 1962**

Ringo Approached
The Quarrymen invite drummer Ringo Starr to leave his safe gig in Rory Storm and the Hurricanes and join them. He declines. **August 18, 1962**

Stones on their Way
Having produced hits for the likes of Jimmy Young and Dickie Valentine, Dick Rowe signs The Rollin' Stones to Decca. **May 1963**

Dylan Stays True
The album *Another Side of Bob Dylan* is released and its creator is lauded for resisting the urge to go electric and copy the Stones. **August 8, 1964**

Cliff Richard and The Shadows are the biggest rock band in Britain in a world where the Beatles never formed

Not a real photo, has been altered.

Elvis—were big stars, but they were safe, sanitized, and as likely to be as popular with parents as they were with the kids. They did as they were told, sang the songs they were given, and towed the line.

That was never enough for The Beatles, who from the outset challenged the status quo by writing their own material, then turned their backs on touring and demanded unlimited studio time with complete creative freedom. As long as they remained bankable the industry was in no position to refuse them. But without them to lead the charge, what would have become of their immediate musical contemporaries?

The Rolling Stones would still have formed, but without Lennon and McCartney to gift them their first top 20 hit—*I Wanna Be Your Man*—they would either have continued to imitate American rhythm & blues or given in to Mick Jagger's attraction to fame and fortune and churned out a series of Tin Pan Alley hits.

Similarly, the members of The Kinks and The Who would have found one another through London's R&B and jazz scene, but if they'd never heard The Beatles' early originals, would Ray Davies have co-opted music hall to create a new musical vernacular, or Pete Townshend have found the courage to cook up a rock opera?

In America, Brian Wilson herded The Beach Boys into a maelstrom of creativity as a direct result of The Beatles' *Rubber Soul* album, but without that catalyst, perhaps his demons would have consumed his talent even more completely, making it easier for the group to simply follow the money.

Dylan would still have happened, but The Byrds would never have married his vision of folk music to a Beatle beat and sounded the West Coast psychedelic sirens, leaving only the dystopian distortions of New Yorkers like The Velvet Underground or Mid Western agitproppers the MC5 to drive the creative imperative.

In a world without The Beatles, something else would have filled the commercial vacuum as technology drove a new kind of teen audience through transistor radios, portable record players, and the television, but it would have looked and sounded very different indeed.

NICK CHURCHILL

Nick Churchill is a writer, journalist, and critic who has been immersed in pop music ever since he taped a hairbrush to the Eubank and sang along to I Feel Fine. His book Yeah Yeah Yeah: The Beatles & Bournemouth did more for one than the other.

Jesus Stalls Stones
Reacting to their stranglehold on the pop charts, Cliff Richard reminds fans that Jesus is bigger than The Rollin' Stones. **August 5, 1966**

Stones Ground Down
The Rollin' Stones career is effectively ended when Jagger and Richards are arrested at the latter's mansion on drugs charges.
February 12, 1967

The Devil in Iggy
As The Stooges release their debut album, Iggy Pop says the devil has all the best tunes because he gave them to them.
August 5, 1969

Reagan Assassinated
Pop music fan Mark David Chapman, 25, shoots US President-elect Ronald Reagan in Washington in a seemingly motiveless attack.
December 8, 1980

Lennon-McCartney, Finally
Local artist John Lennon and vicar George Harrison reform The Quarrymen in Liverpool for their 60th anniversary and invite game show host Paul McCartney to join them.
July 8, 2017

© DANIEL SINOCA

What if...

The Soviets won the space race?

SOVIET UNION VS THE US, 1957-1969

What Really Happened...

During the Cold War, space became another stage for the competition between the world's two greatest powers: the democratic and capitalist United States and the communist Soviet Union. Each side was determined to prove the superiority of its technology, military power, and political-economic system.

On October 4, 1957, the Soviet Union successfully launched Sputnik, the world's first man-made satellite, into Earth's orbit. On February 1, 1958, the U.S. launched Explorer I and on July 29, 1958, NASA was officially created. Over the next decade, the space race continued with each country volleying accomplishments, as well as failures, in space exploration. Eventually, on July 16, 1969, American astronauts Neil Armstrong, Edwin "Buzz" Aldrin, and Michael Collins set off for the moon on Apollo 11. They landed successfully on July 20 and Armstrong officially became the first man to walk on the moon, winning the space race.

What if the Soviets had won the space race? I think they would have perhaps established some kind of permanent lunar base in the way they colonized Earth orbit [in the Seventies and Eighties]. It might have been that they continued to run with a presence on the Moon instead of just sort of going there for a few days and coming back and then never returning, as essentially what has happened now. However, you've got to imprint upon the effect that the break up of the Soviet Union had on the space program. That really caused a massive underinvestment, which might have ultimately led to any lunar base being abandoned—and we'd be back where we are today.

Did the successful launch of the Soviet Union's Sputnik 1 in 1957, the first man-made satellite in space, inspire America to reach for the Moon? Oh yes, undoubtedly. The 'Sputnik effect,' as it's called, was a significant player in ensuring that Apollo succeeded. President Eisenhower commissioned the Saturn V rocket and he boosted brainpower by investing in universities. I think Apollo made America smarter for that period— and the legacy of that was, of course, not just to win the Moon race but the spin-offs that happened. Not least the micro-computing processing revolution and ultimately the Internet, of which the early DARPA [Defense Advanced Research Projects Agency] structures were the forerunner, as they were all wrapped up in the Cold War investments the government had made. We've got our modern society to be thankful for because of that initiative, that 'Sputnik effect.' We're still living off that. It was profound, what Eisenhower did.

When was the moment that the United States took the lead in the space race? The Zonds [Soviet spacecraft] were racing around the Moon unmanned in 1968, so I think you have to point to Apollo 8 [in December 1968], which was this very audacious and perhaps even somewhat reckless mission to pull off. Apollo 8 was previously just an Earth orbit mission, but they instead went straight [around] the Moon on the first Saturn V launch, which was a very, very brave thing to do. Ultimately that bravery, that gamble that they somehow managed to pull off, was the turning point without a doubt.

Was there any other major turning point that happened during the space race? The N1 disaster [the Soviet Moon rocket that failed five times] was obviously a colossal setback. But it wasn't just about booster technology; the Russians easily matched the Saturn V, they were ahead in booster lift for many years. But the clincher was the computing power, that is where the Russians were really falling short.

How far behind were the Russians in terms of their computing power? While the Russians might have been able to orbit the Moon, it was a far cry from landing on it. The thing that really clinched the success of Apollo, in no uncertain terms, was their computing power. The fact that NASA had invested significant amounts of money in the manufacturing of integrated circuits in order to create the micro-computers that were light and small enough to be able to fly on these [Apollo] spacecraft, and make these precise landings

With better computer power the Soviets could have won the space race and put a man on the Moon

Not a real photo, has been altered.

on the Moon. The Russians, as far as I'm aware, didn't really have that sort of micro-processing capability in those days. Their systems probably wouldn't have allowed them to really make a successful landing. It wasn't impossible, but it was quite unlikely.

Did the Soviets realize this? I think they were just sort of gambling on the judgement of their pilots and hoping they could pull it off without this computing power. The Russian approach to spaceflight in the Sixties, both robotic and human, was a little bit of fingers firmly crossed behind your back as they launched. Everybody needed an element of luck; luck goes hand in hand with skill and engineering when it comes to spaceflight, of course. But the Russians relied on luck a bit more, and the reason I say that is because they essentially ran for

all these very quick firsts in human spaceflight in the Sixties. For example, they were the first to put three people in a capsule, and they only did that by depriving them of their pressure suits so they could squeeze them into a two-man capsule. Things like that were clearly a bit reckless with the way they went forward. While they probably were aware that their computing power was inferior to the Americans, I think they just thought they'd wing it and their pilots would hopefully be able to pull [a lunar landing] off just manually.

If they had landed first, how would it have changed the Soviet Union as a whole? Well, you've got to look at how they reacted to Gagarin returning [in April 1961], and Valentina Tereshkova [the first woman in space in June 1963], and the other heroes of spaceflight

**INTERVIEW WITH...
DR. CHRISTOPHER RILEY**

Dr. Riley is a writer and filmmaker who specializes in science, space, engineering, and history. He has worked on numerous documentaries including *In the Shadow of the Moon, First Orbit*, and *Neil Armstrong—First Man on the Moon*. You can follow him on Twitter @alifeofriley.

Soviet success in the space race could have spurred America into further space exploration and led to man walking on Mars

Russian history and how their society changed in the Eighties and Nineties, I don't know. It would have been great when it happened in the Sixties, but perhaps it wouldn't have made a big difference in the grand scheme of things.

Which Soviet cosmonaut do you think might have taken the first steps on the Moon? Alexei Leonov's name often comes up as the first Moon walker, having done the first spacewalk [in March 1965] and contended with those difficulties and survived the mission. I think he likes to think he would have been as well from his writings and interviews since—and I dare say he's right.

Would they still have proclaimed the Moon 'for all mankind' as the Americans did? If you listen to Khrushchev's speeches at the time, they were all about how Gagarin's flight was for everybody. The whole point was it was a gift to the world and it was Russia's great gift to human history, so they would have, I'm sure, done the same thing [on the Moon]. Whether they'd have taken a UN flag, which was proposed initially for the Americans to fly rather than the stars and stripes, or whether they'd have planted their own hammer and sickle I don't know. I suspect they would have planted their own flag, but their speeches and plaques that they unveiled I'm sure would have had the same sentiments [as Gagarin's flight].

that placed Russia so high on the world stage. I think a successful returning lunar cosmonaut would have been celebrated and lauded around the world in exactly the same way. If you look at the 'Giant Step' tour that the crew of Apollo 11 went on in the summer of 1969 when they got back, 40 countries in 30 days or something like that, touring the world with millions of people coming out on the street and giving these ticker tape parades wherever they went, you can imagine that absolutely would have happened to the Russians as well. Whether it would have had a material change on the course of

What might their first words on the Moon have been? Well, [Neil] Armstrong was given complete freedom, as were all of the previous crews of Apollo 8. They decided what they would read or speak, and no one intervened. In fact, while Armstrong had obviously given it a lot of thought, he had a number of options from what his mother told me last year and he made his final decision as to what was going to be said when he was going down the ladder. I think with the

How would it be different?

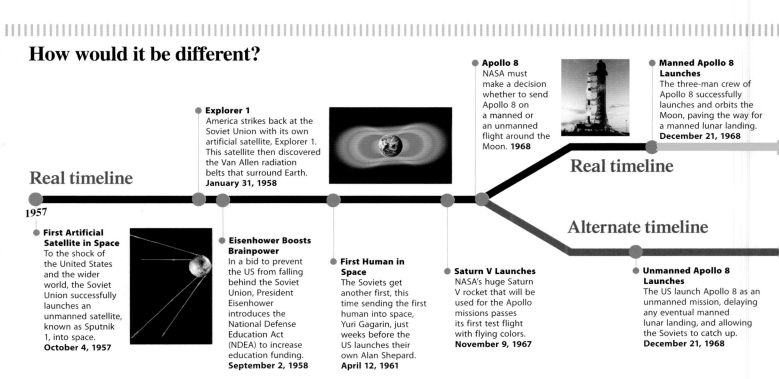

Real timeline

Real timeline

Alternate timeline

1957

First Artificial Satellite in Space
To the shock of the United States and the wider world, the Soviet Union successfully launches an unmanned satellite, known as Sputnik 1, into space.
October 4, 1957

Explorer 1
America strikes back at the Soviet Union with its own artificial satellite, Explorer 1. This satellite then discovered the Van Allen radiation belts that surround Earth.
January 31, 1958

Eisenhower Boosts Brainpower
In a bid to prevent the US from falling behind the Soviet Union, President Eisenhower introduces the National Defense Education Act (NDEA) to increase education funding.
September 2, 1958

First Human in Space
The Soviets get another first, this time sending the first human into space, Yuri Gagarin, just weeks before the US launches their own Alan Shepard.
April 12, 1961

Saturn V Launches
NASA's huge Saturn V rocket that will be used for the Apollo missions passes its first test flight with flying colors.
November 9, 1967

Apollo 8
NASA must make a decision whether to send Apollo 8 on a manned or an unmanned flight around the Moon. **1968**

Manned Apollo 8 Launches
The three-man crew of Apollo 8 successfully launches and orbits the Moon, paving the way for a manned lunar landing.
December 21, 1968

Unmanned Apollo 8 Launches
The US launch Apollo 8 as an unmanned mission, delaying any eventual manned lunar landing, and allowing the Soviets to catch up.
December 21, 1968

Russians, knowing a bit about how their society worked at the time, it would have been very carefully written. There's a speech that Gagarin makes before he climbs in the rocket [on the first spaceflight in April 1961] and it's beautifully and poetically sculpted in terms of its message to the world, and it was completely written for him by the central government. I think it would have been a similar sort of speech that would have been written for the first lunar cosmonaut.

Do you think that a successful lunar landing, broadcast to the world, would have prevented the eventual collapse of the Soviet Union? No, I don't. If you look at what it did to America, they won this race and very quickly the country got sick of spending money, and within a few missions after Apollo 11 the program was canceled. The political direction afterwards, both in positive and negative terms, was not really influenced by the success of Apollo, perhaps sadly. So I suspect in Russia it would have been exactly the same. They would have had this time that they carried on running their bases, maybe on the Moon as we've talked about, certainly building a space station in Earth orbit, until effectively politics and perhaps society and the rest of the world overwhelmed them.

Would the US have tried to one-up the Soviet Union by attempting to go to Mars? It's nice to imagine that the race could have hurdled us down the Solar System to further away, and there's some sort of validity in that the Cold War had continued to saber-rattle its way into the Nineties. Would America have gone even further to prove a point? It's possible. Remember Spiro Agnew, the vice president at the time Apollo 11 left for the Moon, said they were going to be on Mars by 1980! So there were plenty of plans; [American rocket scientist] von Braun's bottom draw had loads of concepts in it for adapting and modifying Apollo configurations to send them further. It's a lovely thought to imagine that with

Apollo hardware, you could have actually had a human footprint on Mars by now.

Would they have succeeded? I don't know. I mean, it took four million human years to put those 12 Americans on the Moon—the work of 400,000 people for a decade. I think you could have multiplied that by 100, maybe 1,000, to land on Mars. It would have been very difficult to do, and it still remains so.

How would modern space exploration be different if the Soviets had been first on the Moon? If—and this is an enormous if, and not one I think likely—the Russians had got to the Moon first and the Americans had gone to Mars, I think we would have skipped the space station stage as it were. The [International Space Station] was largely conceived and built to justify the Space Shuttle, so we probably wouldn't have gone down that route. We would have just been pushing the frontier of human footprints across the Solar System, on and on. I think if we'd become as advanced as we are now, and then changed this mindset from racing to collaborating as a community, we'd again be looking at a sort of equivalent to the space station—a laboratory, but somewhere on the Moon or Mars instead, rather than in Earth orbit. It would have ultimately been a completely different picture from the years of shuttle flights and space stations that we've lived through instead.

"The International Space Station was largely conceived and built to justify the Space Shuttle, so we probably wouldn't have gone down that route"

The Soviets Fall Behind
The Soviet Union's answer to the Saturn V, the N1 rocket, explodes on its first launch and fails a further three times by 1972. **February 21, 1969**

International Space Station
The US, Russia, and other nations continue to collaborate and operate the International Space Station in Earth orbit, but no humans have ventured further since 1972. **2013**

A Giant Leap for Mankind
Neil Armstrong and Buzz Aldrin become the first humans to set foot on the Moon on the Apollo 11 mission, winning the space race for the US. Five more occur by 1972. **July 20, 1969**

Space Stations
By the Eighties, both the United States and Soviet Union (later Russia) have focused much of their efforts on space stations and missions to Earth orbit. **1980**

Soviets Aim for the Moon
Buoyed by the stagnation in the American lunar program, the Soviets ramp up their efforts to send humans to the Moon, culminating in a successful test of their N1 rocket. **1969**

Soviet Landing
While the US debates the future of Apollo, the Soviets stun the world again by sending a single cosmonaut, Alexei Leonov, on a daring mission to the lunar surface, from which he returns a hero. **July 1969**

America Shoots for Mars
Still reeling from the Soviet space race victory, America attempts to one-up the Soviets, announcing their intentions to land humans on Mars. They ultimately succeed in doing this in 1980. **1970**

Space Colonization
After four decades of exploration—and thanks to the collapse of the Soviet Union—the US, Russia, and other nations collaborate on human exploration endeavors throughout the Solar System. **2013**

© NASA, CORBIS

What if . . .
John Wayne joined George Wallace?

USA, 1968

What Really Happened...

In 1968, George Wallace, the former governor of Alabama, ran in the presidential election against Richard Nixon (Republican) and Hubert Humphrey (Democrat) as the American Independent Party candidate. While he didn't expect to win, his goal was to prevent the two parties from winning a majority in the Electoral College.

As his running mate, Wallace considered many candidates for vice president, including the famous Hollywood actor, John Wayne. When Wayne was approached regarding the opportunity, he quickly turned it down, throwing his support behind Richard Nixon. Even before Wallace's inquiry, he had been asked to run for national office, but Wayne remarked he didn't believe the public would seriously consider an actor in the White House.

Remembered as one of the silver screen's most iconic heroes, there was a time when John Wayne's accomplishments could have stretched even further, away from Hollywood and toward Washington. So what drove Wayne politically?

"Throughout Wayne's early years he voted Democrat and called himself a socialist," says Carolyn McGivern. "He was very liberal and concerned about Americans. Later, as he became disillusioned with the chaos he saw around him, he turned towards conservatism,

which represented his anti-government stance. His ideas were fresh and unusual and not always Republican. The only consistent thing about his politics was his love of America."

Come 1968, Governor George Wallace was considering an offer to Wayne to join his ticket for the presidential election. "Wallace became the American Independent Party candidate in the 1968 presidential election, and in the period of the Civil Rights Movement he famously stood for 'Segregation now, segregation tomorrow, segregation forever,' even standing

in front of the University of Alabama in an attempt to stop the enrolment of African American students in 1963," states McGivern. "Wayne told everyone that he supported Nixon for president, but if there was one thing that might've tempted him to join Wallace, it was his campaign slogan, 'Stand Up for America.'

"Wayne confided in his secretary that he didn't like the 1964 Civil Rights Act outlawing discrimination based on race, religion, color, and sex. He felt that people who owned their own property or business

---

How would it be different?

Wallace Targets States
Wallace wants to split the conservative vote and deny an Electoral College majority. He peaks at 21 percent in the polls. **September 1968**

LeMay Joins Wallace
Despite turning down two previous requests, Curtis LeMay finally agrees to become Wallace's vice presidential running mate. Wallace's polls slump. **October 1968**

Wallace's Democrat Nomination
Governor Wallace of Alabama unsuccessfully goes up against President Lyndon Johnson for the Democrat nomination following the assassination of JFK. **1964**

Real timeline

Real timeline

1963

Wallace Opposes Civil Rights
In a pivotal moment in America's civil rights struggle, George Wallace tries to stop two Black students from entering the main campus of the University of Alabama. **1963**

Alternate timeline

Wallace Calls Wayne
Scrambling for a running mate, Wallace picks up the phone to Wayne and rather than decline, the actor agrees. **September 1968**

Poll Ratings Soar
Wayne's personal sway and popularity helps Wallace build on his 21 percent poll share of September. The conservative vote is increasingly split. **October 1968**

CAROLYN McGIVERN

Carolyn McGivern is the author of the acclaimed biography John Wayne: A Giant Shadow, which has been updated and extended to coincide with the actor's 110th birthday. She has also written The Lost Films of John Wayne and studied at both York and Brunel University.

should have the right to refuse service. He and Wallace shared similar views toward communism, law and order, and patriotism."

So what could have happened if Wayne hadn't turned Wallace down? McGivern predicts that "the election would probably have been closer, with the Humphrey/Muskie ticket representing the left, Nixon/Agnew the center, and Wallace/Wayne the right. Wallace/ Wayne would have run a 'law and order' and a 'Stand Up for America' campaign, and election night would have been nail-biting."

With Wayne joining Wallace, there would have been an interesting dynamic. But how would Wayne influence Wallace, and the campaign itself?

"Wayne would have opposed Wallace's generous increases for beneficiaries of social security and Medicare," says McGivern. "Wallace also pledged to withdraw troops from Vietnam if the war was not winnable within 90 days of him taking office, but Wayne couldn't understand a 'pull out' attitude."

With a star like Wayne on the ticket, could it have helped Wallace win the election? McGivern doubts it. "It would have been impossible, mainly because of Wallace's lack of strength outside the Deep South. He carried five states in the South, but he wasn't able to challenge Nixon in the Border States. He came close in North Carolina and

Tennessee and could have taken those with Wayne as a running mate. It would only have taken those states and a shift in New Jersey or Ohio towards Hubert Humphrey and the election would've been thrown into the House of Representatives."

If Wayne had steered his career in a different direction, it could've had a bigger cultural impact. "Wayne wouldn't have made movies after 1968, robbing Americans of the roles that were part of their education in what it is to be American," McGivern explains. "America wouldn't have had a man who attempted to put it on the high road. Even now, he represents the idea of how Americans see themselves."

Wallace Loses Election
Wallace rallies against Big Government and wins over 13.5 percent of the electorate with 9.9 million votes. Richard Nixon wins.
November 5, 1968

Re-Elected as Governor
Now a Democrat again, Wallace is elected Governor of Alabama for a second term, running on a distinctly anti-Black agenda.
1970

Assassination Attempt
Having decided to contest the presidency as a Democrat, he is shot five times during campaigning in a Maryland shopping mall, leaving him a wheelchair.
May 15, 1972

Loses the Nomination
Although he does well in the south, Wallace fails to win the nomination, which goes to George McGovern. Nixon remains president.
November 7, 1972

Runs a Final Time
Wallace hopes to be nominated as the Democrat candidate in the 1976 election but withdraws during the primaries. He retires from political life in 1986. **1976**

Wallace has Power
Wallace falls far short of becoming president himself, but the conservative vote is indeed split and Hubert Humphrey enters the White House.
November 6, 1968

Wayne Makes Gaffes
Wayne speaks his mind and has little energy or time for diplomacy, which gets him into trouble. He promptly apologizes. **1970**

Wayne Becomes President
Some nine years before actor Ronald Reagan becomes president, John Wayne takes office as the 38th president of the United States.
November 7, 1972

Beats the Anti-Communist Drum
Fiercely anti-communist, John Wayne delights in the USSR's Era of Stagnation, the worst financial crisis in the Soviet Union. **1973**

Wallace Takes States
Wayne's influence helps Wallace takes the states of North Carolina, South Carolina, and Tennessee. Humphrey takes New Jersey and Ohio.
November 5, 1968

True Grit Released
True Grit is released in the cinema but Wayne's involvement with Wallace ensures it is his last movie. Clint Eastwood is cast in The Undefeated. **1969**

Wayne Makes Presidential Bid
Although he says he has never been interested in public office, Wayne decides to run for president and gains the Republican nomination. **1972**

No Watergate Scandal
With Richard Nixon having never become president, the USA's top office is not blighted by the scandal that was Watergate. **1972**

©DANIEL SINOCA

What if...
The Berlin Wall never fell?

GERMANY, 1949-2000

IMPORTANT DATES:
August 13, 1961
November 9, 1989
October 3, 1990

What Really Happened...

The Berlin Wall was a concrete border lined with barbed wire that the Communist government of the German Democratic Republic (GDR) of East Germany began to build on August 13, 1961. The purpose of the wall was to keep the West from entering and undermining the socialist government, but also to prevent people in the East from fleeing to the West.

As the Cold War began to thaw, on November 9, 1989, a spokesman for East Berlin's Communist Party announced that citizens would be free to cross the border. At midnight, more than 2 million East and West Berliners surrounded the wall to not only cross the checkpoint, but also knock down the wall itself with hammers and picks. As one journalist wrote, it was "the greatest street party in the history of the world" and today, the Berlin Wall is one of the most iconic symbols of the Cold War. East and West Germany was officially reunified on October 3, 1990.

What if the Berlin Wall had never collapsed?
Basically you would have had something not dissimilar to North Korea. The only way it would have worked is through massive repression. I think for the wall not to have fallen, it would have, first of all, meant that we would have experienced a different Eastern Bloc than the one we had in the 1980s. They would have had to stop the reforms, Gorbachev particularly, and if that had taken place it would mean that the Cold War would have continued.

Can you envision a scenario where the Berlin Wall is still standing and East Germany, much like North Korea, still exists as a separate country? It is very difficult to imagine this but, theoretically, I suppose they could have cracked down on dissent. There are a few reasons behind the fall of the Berlin Wall. The first, and most simple, is that the East German economy simply did not work. They had very few natural resources and terrible problems with inefficiency. Then, moving into the 1970s and 1980s, the Russians had stopped selling the East Germans cheap oil. This caused more economic problems. There are pictures of East German shops from the 1960s and 1970s, and then the 1980s; they tried to make it look as if everything was wonderful, but there was not much to buy except a few turnips. Another thing that needs to be established is that by the 1970s they were also being loaned a lot of money from the West Germans, which they became very dependent on. Then, of course, there is the Helsinki Accords, which the East cynically signed up to—but they could not really offer the freedoms that they had just promised. Nevertheless, they wanted the kudos of seeming forward thinking and freedom loving, albeit without paying any of the costs for that. Inevitably, though, over time, there were some brave people in East Germany who demanded the freedoms of the Helsinki Accords and, unless the authorities started to crack down on them, returning them to a Stalinist regime, it is difficult to see how the communists could have stayed in power.

So, let us imagine they did go down the route of announcing a state of emergency, offering the Stasi complete control over law and order and thousands of people were imprisoned or murdered. We are back to the idea of East Germany as a contemporary North Korea. How would the wall have evolved? Well it is interesting because the East Germans were actually quite good at basic electronics. They were skilled at putting together cheaper versions of Western electronics—and they had a plan to build a high-tech Berlin Wall. Moving into the 1990s and the millennium, it would have all kinds of alarms so that you wouldn't need armed guards. You would basically have an electronic surveillance system. However, while that was the goal, I don't think they had the financial or logistical ability to achieve that.

If this high-tech version of the Berlin Wall had come into practice, how much longer can you envision East Germany hanging on for? No more than a few years after 1989. The huge sums they would need to spend in order to keep their new high-tech wall going would, I think, lead to the end in about 1995.

How would West Germany have benefited, if at all, from the continuation of East Germany? In some ways it might have benefited West Germany to keep the East in business, because it would result in more cheap labor. East Germany, from the 1960s onwards, was a place where Western manufacturers had their

**INTERVIEW WITH...
FRED TAYLOR**

Fred Taylor was born in Aylesbury, Buckinghamshire, England. In 1967 he was awarded a history scholarship to Oxford University. After graduating, he pursued postgraduate studies at the University of Sussex, researching a thesis on the German far-right before 1918. He has since worked as a publisher, a translator of fiction and non-fiction, a novelist, and a scriptwriter. He edited and translated *The Goebbels Diaries 1939-1941* and his books include *The Berlin Wall: August 13, 1961—November 9, 1989* and *Exorcising Hitler*, about the destruction and resurgence of post-war Germany.

work done cheap. In West Germany, back when I lived there, you could get 24-hour film development done—straight from your camera—back in the days when you delivered it to a chemist. But they would actually ship it over the border to East Germany and ship it back again. That was true of textiles and other businesses.

So if I can imagine an East Germany, with this high-tech Berlin Wall still intact, I think it would be one that had basically become an economic colony of West Germany. It would have re-established a Stalinist regime to keep everybody quiet. The selling of political prisoners to the West was also an enormously profitable

trade for the East, so that would probably have continued. In fact, there were rumors that they were arresting people just so they could make some income from selling them back.

Let's say the Berlin Wall falls, as it did in 1989, but the majority of East Germans want to remain part of a separate state. Is this imaginable? A few idealists at the time did actually want to try a third way—a liberal socialist state of sorts. But, honestly, the only reason that East Germany could have, and perhaps should have, survived for a few more years was for the

At the Brandenburg Gate on June 12, 1987, President Ronald Reagan made his famous speech asking Mikhail Gorbachev to "tear down this wall"

"There was an Eastern Bloc joke—we pretend to work, they pretend to pay us"

economy. When unification did happen, it was a bit of an economic car crash. All of these totally uncompetitive East German businesses were faced with the full force of competition from the West, as well as these carpet-bagging yuppies that went straight into East Berlin, in particular, and looked for profit. So I think a few years of adjustment, with some economic advantages and privileges and a loose political confederation, before total reunification, would have been a softer landing for most people. It was pretty bad for a lot of East Germans when the wall came down. East Germany was horribly uncompetitive. But the West Germans were already bailing them out before the border fell, and I suppose when you are paying somebody else's bills you demand power over them. So reunification, in light of that, had to come from the most practical economic solution. But had there been some way to have a two-tier system, so that the East could adjust to the new economics, I think it would certainly have helped.

In East Germany there was no unemployment, free health and childcare, and a supportive welfare state—but no freedom of speech and a wealth of political prisoners. Now, in a reunified Germany, there is plenty of homelessness and poverty but, of course, you can take to the streets in protest. So what was really the best outcome for so-called 'freedom', in retrospect? That's the very question we are all asking ourselves, isn't it? What is freedom? What is democracy? And does one type of freedom potentially undermine and even destroy the freedom of a different kind of person? Unemployment was a criminal offence in East Germany, as it was in Russia at the time, but the problem is they built up this fake economy to keep people working. That economy was running up huge deficits and that is what caused the financial implosion of the Eastern Bloc in the 1980s. There was an Eastern Bloc joke—we pretend to work, they pretend to pay us. So, yes, everybody was working but productivity was

How would it be different?

The Warsaw Pact
The Cold War gets even chillier when eight Eastern Bloc countries, including East Germany, sign up to The Warsaw Pact—a pledge to defend any nation sympathetic to the Soviet cause from attack. **May 14, 1955**

Erection of the Berlin Wall
Perhaps the most famous event of the Cold War, The German Democratic Republic erects a barrier between East and West Berlin. The wall is designed to stop the mass emigration from East to West. **August 13, 1961**

West German Republic
In February 1948, the United States, Britain, and France meet in London, where they agree to unite each of the Western occupation zones into a greater German Republic. The Soviets, meanwhile, oversee a separate East German state. **February 1948**

Real timeline

Real timeline

1945

Yalta Conference
Shortly before the Red Army reaches Berlin, Winston Churchill, a critically ill Franklin D. Roosevelt, and Joseph Stalin agree that after World War II, Germany will split into four separate 'occupation zones' under America, Britain, France, and Russia. **February 4-11, 1945**

East German Constitution
The German Democratic Republic (better known as East Germany) is officially formed, complete with its own constitution. East Germany offers the right to emigrate and to trade union protection, however, inevitably, as with all Soviet-aligned nations, a heavy-handed one-party rule would soon surface. Amendments that will further limit personal freedoms of East Germans would emerge in a 1968 draft. **October 7, 1949**

Alternate timeline

East German Constitution
Rather than maintaining influence from the Weimer era of the country's politics, the first constitution of the German Democratic Republic explicitly maintains a totalitarian, Stalinist state in which Western influences are banned outright. **October 7, 1949**

Germans stand on top of the Berlin Wall in the days before it fell

Winston Churchill, Franklin D. Roosevelt, and Joseph Stalin at the Yalta Conference in February 1945

low. So this façade of full employment was stirring up trouble for itself. However, we have certainly gone too far the other way now. Being a sentimental old social democrat, I think the 1960s and 1970s were when we found a decent balance that we have since lost. If you don't, to some extent, curb the freedoms of the very wealthy few to help those who have less power and money, you have a society where different kinds of pressures build up.

We have touched a little on the North Korea analogy. Finally, then, can we look at the East-West divide in Germany and really make that comparison? In reality, I don't think so, because the balance between North and South Korea is different to the relationship that existed between East and West Germany while the wall was up. There was always, aside from during the

first few years of the wall being built, a cordial political relationship as well as travel going on between the two German states. Pensioners, for instance, could leave the East for the West if they wanted, and if they did not want to come back, it was not a big deal. They were just a burden on the state anyway. There was a lot of family visiting going on between the two states too and a functioning economic relationship.

The two Korean countries have none of that. If North Korea suddenly collapsed, then 25 million people, some of them starving, would flee to Seoul or to China and look for a job and a handout, which would cause economic devastation for those countries. That is why North Korea manages to hang on—China simply does not want that problem to develop. West Germany was different—reunification was actually the goal there and it was inevitable.

Killing of Peter Fechter
Perhaps the most notorious execution of anyone trying to flee from East to West shows the world the brutality of the German Democratic Republic. Fechter, just 18 years old, is shot in the pelvis and left to bleed to death. **August 17, 1962**

The Helsinki Accords
35 countries meet in Finland. An agreement between communist and democratic nations is signed that guarantees numerous human rights and freedoms, but such declarations are later seen as a sham. **July-August 1975**

Reagan's Speech at the Brandenburg Gate
President Reagan gives one of his most iconic speeches in West Berlin, urging Mikhail Gorbachev, leader of the Soviet Union, to "tear down this wall." **June 12, 1987**

The Wall Falls
The 'Peaceful Revolution' begins in East Germany during the summer of 1989. The climax comes on a winter's day in 1989 as East Germany, struggling to maintain order, declares the borders to be open for all. **November 9, 1989**

The End of East Germany
With no borders to separate the East from the West, the German Democratic Republic is dissolved and a country that has been split apart for 45 years is finally reunified. **October 3, 1990**

Suppression of the Peaceful Revolution
25,000 East Germans are sent to prison, and thousands more shot dead, in a Tiananmen Square-style suppression of political protest in the middle of East Berlin. **June 30, 1989**

A New High-Tech Berlin Wall
"The wall is here to stay," states Egon Krenz, the latest unapologetic leader of East Germany. He reveals plans for a new high-tech Berlin Wall that will have state-of-the-art security. **January 1, 1990**

Military First Program
Influenced by North Korea, parliament announces a Military First program to sustain the financially ailing state. State employment will be increased by mandatory military service for all under-35s. **October 1996**

The Last Man Standing
East Germany remains the lone wolf of Europe and a testament to the lasting effects of the Cold War. The annual visit from Kim Jong-un garners world attention, but little else. **Present day**

The Warsaw Pact
East Germany pressures the Soviets, who would give the Mongolian People's Republic 'observer status,' to widen the signatories to include nations in Africa, Latin America, and Asia. **May 14, 1955**

Erection of the Berlin Wall
East Berlin's notorious Stasi, the country's official state security, forewarn all members of East Germany that anyone found to even be plotting to escape will be imprisoned for a minimum of ten years. **August 13, 1961**

Long Live Leonid Brezhnev
The hard-line Soviet leader surprises many with his Castro-like ability to stay healthy. He makes it to the end of the 1980s in perfect health and celebrates his 83rd birthday. Gorbachev, who? **December 19, 1989**

The USSR Crumbles
A belated attempt to sustain the Eastern Bloc comes to nothing and the Soviet Empire is no more. But East Germany refuses to budge and proudly proclaims a new trade partnership with China. **November 9, 1994**

Wall for the Millennium
The Berlin Wall remains active on January 1, 2000 despite rumors it may be dissolved to celebrate the millennium. Armed guards return as, among power outages, the technology becomes too expensive to sustain. **January 1, 2000**

© IAN HINLEY

What if... The Berlin Wall never fell? **149**

What if…

Fiction's greatest alt-history timelines

What if the Nazis had conquered Britain? Could Rome have evaded the Dark Ages? We run down some of the best alternate history stories in fiction

"Truth is stranger than fiction, but it is because Fiction is obliged to stick to possibilities; Truth isn't." Mark Twain's words may have transcended into idiom, but they ring true throughout history. The timeline of our civilization is filled with flashpoints; moments where the fate of one kingdom, country, or empire was decided on a historical flip of a coin. We know what happened when the coins landed, but what if they'd fallen on a different side?

That's the joy of alternative fiction; exploring those fixed points in time as they play out with different victors, survivors, losers, and victims. By taking already-established events and figures, authors from across the centuries have been able to take the familiar and weave in the unknown by adjusting even the smallest of true events to create enthralling new stories that blur the line between the facts you know and the fiction you don't. Whether it be film, TV, or literature, the historical route less traveled remains an ever-intriguing one.

Over the next few pages, we've compiled some of the finest examples of alt-history in . . . well, history. We take a detour into a chivalrous tale of satire and adventure where one errant knight helps to stop the famous fall of Constantinople from the seemingly unstoppable might of the Ottoman Empire. We'll follow the recolonization of Europe by the peoples of the East following a Black Death pandemic in the 1300s that kills 99 percent of the population rather than only a third. We'll follow the Nazis as they win the war, crushing Britain and fighting to install an eternal Reich. And we'll ponder whether the survival of the French monarchy and the end of the Republic would mark an entirely new future for the French people.

Key

WAR
An epic battle is won by a different side than in real history.

ASSASSINATION
A historical figure is or is not assassinated.

MIRACULOUS RECOVERY
A historical figure recovers from an illness and/or lives longer than expected.

BUTTERFLY EFFECT
Some minor change—a boat arrives late, a fire is put out—changes the entire course of history.

EMPIRE
A historic empire lasts longer (possibly into the modern day) than it did in actuality.

TIME TRAVEL
The protagonist visits an alternate history via some form of time travel.

If It Had Happened Otherwise,
edited by J.C. Squire (1931)

Churchill also envisaged Confederate general Jeb Stuart preventing WWI

Many of the essays in this collection suggest major future events, such as WWI, would be drastically changed centuries prior

Perhaps one of the most famous literary works in the alt-history genre—most notably for the fact that it includes a contribution by none other than Sir Winston Churchill—*If It Had Happened Otherwise* collects together a set of fascinating essays covering many a key world event. Take the entry from Anglo-French poet and satirist Hilaire Belloc, who uses the essay "If Drouet's Cart Had Stuck" to explore the biggest turning point in French history—the attempted flight of King Louis XVI during the French Revolution.

In reality, the Flight of Varennes failed and the monarchy of France was put to the blade, ushering in a new era of republic. For Belloc, history would have been quite different had Louis and co. actually been successful in their escape. It could have started a counter-revolution away from the capital, and the Battle of Valmy (where the newly formed French government clashed with the Holy Roman Empire) could have ended with a decisive French defeat and the restoration of the monarchy. No longer a republic, France's economy continues to fester and when it eventually enters World War I two centuries later, its lack of strength leads to an Austro-Hungarian victory.

"History would've been different if Louis had escaped"

Then there's "If Napoleon Had Escaped to America" by English historian H.A.L. Fisher, which sees Napoleon avoiding a surrender to the British following his defeat at Waterloo and escaping on a ship to New York City. Arriving on American soil, the disgraced emperor instead begins to journey into South America. According to Fisher, Napoleon forms an alliance with the Venezuelan military leader, Simón Bolívar, thereby helping him liberate large portions of South and Central America from both Spanish and Portuguese control. The former emperor remains in exile, but he does so still gripping one last bid at power.

Then there's Sir Winston Churchill's contribution, a musing on the outcome of the American Civil War if Robert E. Lee and the Confederates had won and how the Americas and the rest of the world would have been shaped. For Churchill (who would later be awarded the Nobel Prize in Literature in 1953), the result of the Confederate Army's success does lead to independence, but not without its problems. With hostilities potentially ready to break out again, the British Empire steps in to mediate a peace agreement. In actuality, Britain orchestrates a deal whereby the empire forms a coalition with both the Union and the Confederate States of America known as the 'English Speaking Association.'

11/22/63 by Stephen King (2011)

Having dominated horror for so long, it seems fitting that the often-imitated talent of Stephen King should turn his attention to the ever- diverse alt-history genre. His novel 11/22/63 (and the TV series of the same name) follows the story of a divorced high school English teacher who happens upon a time portal hidden in the pantry of a diner. The portal is a gateway to the past—to September 9, 1958 at 11:58 a.m. to be exact—whereupon our protagonist plans to stop Lee Harvey Oswald and prevent JFK's assassination.

King's take on time travel imposes a set of stringent 'rules' that become a lynchpin of the story: a) However long our protagonist Jake Epping spends in the past, only two minutes would have elapsed in the present; b) Every trip back into the portal nullifies the actions of the previous journey; and c) Time will attempt to balance out any changes. Epping makes the journey multiple times before eventually spending years in the past fabricating a new identity and tracking the path of Oswald. He does eventually succeed in thwarting the assassination attempt on JFK, but it creates an alternative timeline that leaves his 2011 present in a far different state.

We learn that his trip and his actions have caused years of inexplicable earthquakes across the country, killing thousands of people. One such event causes Vermont Yankee Power Plant to have a catastrophic leak, which pumps radiation across New England and Southern Quebec. The disaster causes untold ecological and economical ramifications, forcing Epping to have to use the portal once more to unravel the timeline and restore the world he knew.

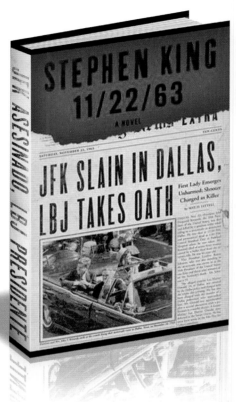

In 2016, an eight-part TV adaptation of the book was made starring James Franco as Jake Epping

Lest Darkness Fall by L. Sprague de Camp (1939)

Cited as a key influence by author Harry Turtledove (a novelist whose own alt-history work features in our list), L. Sprague de Camp's gripping tale of time travel and historical intrigue remains a timeless classic. A blueprint for the many stories that followed in its footsteps, *Lest Darkness Fall* sees an American archaeologist, Martin Padway, transported back in time to 535 AD following a thunderstorm at the Pantheon. When he comes to, he finds himself in a land far different from the one recorded in our own history books.

Italy is not ruled by the Eastern Roman Empire (one of the last vestiges of the Roman Empire before it completely waned during the Middle Ages), but is instead under the dominion of the Ostrogoths. The empire has been conquered, but the new master of the Romans offers a far more open society where religious practice is neither limited nor dictated. Padway soon makes a home for himself, using his knowledge to create everything from crude printing presses to telescopes. His popularity soon sees him involved in state politics, and before long he's embroiled in all manner of treacherous plots and betrayals.

What makes L. Sprague de Camp's novel so influential is how Padway's actions change the face of Europe forever. While his knowledge of tactics simply unheard of in that era enables him to create a stable and prosperous Italo-Gothic kingdom, it also helps that corner of the continent to avoid the cultural and academic stagnancy that we now know as the Dark Ages.

In the novel, Padway encounters and influences many real-life figures, including Theoderic the Great

The Difference Engine by William Gibson and Bruce Sterling (1990)

Another novel that represented a revival for alt-history fiction in the early 1990s, The *Difference Engine* remains one of the most intriguing novels in the genre (especially considering it takes its turning point from a scientific breakthrough rather than a matter of conflict). Gibson and Sterling (both authors who helped define and popularize both the cyberpunk and steampunk genres) craft a world where English polymath Charles Babbage lives to see his titular mechanical computer successfully work in 1824.

The device helps facilitate a radically faster Industrial Revolution, one that extends far beyond the concept of engineering and commerce. It also elevates Babbage to a powerful political position, eventually clashing with the Tory government led by the Duke of Wellington. His rise to power facilitates the rise of the Industrial Radical Party and British society is practically recoded as a result. Inherited peerage is discarded in favor of academic merit. Where the arts fall from favor, science becomes king.

It's a fascinating 'what-if' scenario that sees the rest of the world changed as a result. Timely relief aid helps Ireland avoid the dreadful Irish potato famine (effectively eradicating the Troubles of our own timeline), while America fragments into divided nations in the wake of Britain's technological innovation.

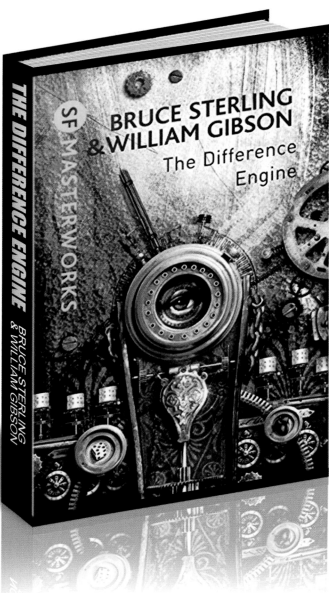

Hacking is one of many subjects in the novel, making it an intriguing analogue to today's online culture

"The device facilitates a radically faster Industrial Revolution"

Tirant lo Blanch by Joanot Martorell (1490)

Arguably the oldest example of alternative history in Western literature, the *Tirant Io Blanch* has proved to be one of the most divisive works to ever emerge from the city of Valencia in the 15th century. Part satire, part romantic chivalry, Joanot Martorell's story tells the tale of a Tirant, a knight from Brittany who travels the continent fighting wars and seeking adventure.

For Martorell, this loosely semi-autobiographical story takes a detour into alternate history when Tirant arrives in Constantinople. In real life, the jewel of the Byzantine Empire (and the site of modern day Istanbul) fell to an Ottoman siege in 1453, but in Martorell's story Tirant arrives as the final attack on the city commences and is tasked with defending it. Given the title of megaduke

(an actual position, and one that marked the highest honor one could receive in the Byzantine Empire), Tirant goes on to save the city and bolsters the Christian hold on Europe in the 15th century.

Constantinople's fall marked one of the greatest losses for Christianity in Europe's actual timeline

---

The Man in the High Castle by Philip K. Dick (1969)

One of the most well-known alt-history stories (due in part to its use of the popular 'What if the Nazis had won WWII' conceit and the excellent TV adaptation currently on Amazon Prime), *The Man in the High Castle* depicts a 1960s America where the nation has been carved in two by a victorious Germany and Japan. Dick's foray into alt-history fiction is as suitably bleak and dystopian as his strong bibliography in science fiction, offering a fascinating glimpse into how the US could have functioned under the Axis.

Much like Len Deighton's similarly angled *SS-GB*, *TMITHC* deals with the idea of a homegrown resistance and how it works to unseat the new masters of North America, as well as presenting an intriguing dichotomy of how relations between Germany and Japan begin to sour. We also get a glimpse into how this reality came to be, including the assassination of Franklin Roosevelt in 1933, the continuation of the Depression, the Nazis conquering Russia, Italy controlling Africa, China occupied by Japan, and mass genocide across Europe as Hitler reshapes the continent before jointly invading the US with Japan in 1947.

Dick's brilliance as a storyteller enables him to do something few others have ever tried—an alternative history within an alternative history. In the TV series, this is presented as a film that shows the defeat of the Axis in 1945. In the novel, a book called The Grasshopper Lies Heavy is used, which describes an even stranger timeline where WWII ends a few years later with the trial of Adolf Hitler. This alt-alt-history story describes a world where the Soviet Union collapses, Mao is defeated in China (wiping out socialism in the region), and the US and the UK enter a Cold War of their own.

In *TMITHC*'s reality, Hitler lives on into 1960s but is incapacitated by ill health, thus creating a power vacuum

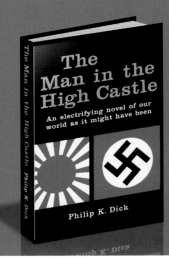

Pavane by Keith Roberts (1968)

By delaying the Armada by a few weeks, the assassination of Queen Elizabeth I changes English history forever

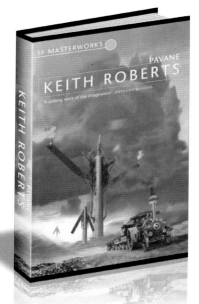

Collecting together a number of shorter stories published throughout this career, Keith Roberts' *Pavane* tells the fragmented story of a 20th- century England where the unopposed rise of Catholicism has drastically shaped the progress of the world. For Roberts, the key turning point comes in 1588 with the assassination of Queen Elizabeth I.

The death of the Virgin Queen—who had seemingly managed to achieve the impossible in 1558 by agreeing a Religious Settlement between Catholics and Protestants—sends England back into a state of turmoil as the Spanish Armada successfully invades the little isle. English soil is dyed red with Anglican blood as Spain effectively eradicates the New Faith in a bloody and ruthless religious purge. Roberts' fix-up story suggests a powerful resurgence of Roman Catholicism that sweeps through Europe following the capitulation of the English.

Without England as a resolute Anglican presence, the Protestant Netherlands fails to gain independence from Spain and Catholicism reasserts its grip upon the western world. Now the de facto ruler of the continent—and the New World by association—the Pope introduces doctrine where scientific innovation and artistic experimentation are suppressed. As a result, society descends into a second Dark Age where 20th-century England still operates on technology on a par with the 1800s.

Roberts' vision of an alternate timeline isn't just fascinating because it uses the proliferation of religion as the driving force of its historical distinctions, but for how he presents these stories throughout the novel. Rather than presenting a single narrative, the English author uses a 'fix-up' setup that collects together short stories from the same timeline and arranges them to show just how England would have fared under Vatican rule.

Resurrection Day by Brendan DuBois (1999)

"Everyone remembers exactly what they were doing the day President Kennedy tried to kill them," muses the protagonist of Brendan DeBois' thrilling alt-history tale, a Boston journalist chronicling the events that led to a global nuclear war between the United States and the Soviet Union. The turning point? The Cuban Missile Crisis—a political rattling of the saber that was narrowly avoided in our timeline but serves as a terrifying flashpoint for the alternate history of DuBois' take on the Cold War.

Set in 1972—a whole decade since the conflict—Washington, D.C., New York, Omaha, San Diego, Miami, and other major cities have either been destroyed or rendered uninhabitable by nuclear fallout and the US government now operates out of the new capital, Philadelphia. Martial law still exists and American society is attempting to recover from JFK's brutal conflict with the Soviets. Outside of the US, Cuba remains an irradiated ruin and Russia has completely collapsed following a barrage of deadly nuclear strikes.

As we explore the history that led to the war, we also see glimpses of DuBois' post-nuclear world. A cloud of fallout hangs over Asia, killing millions in the process, while in Europe a relatively unscathed continent is now led by France and a reunified Germany. NATO is long dead, another casualty of the war, but the use of nuclear warheads has prompted every country to disarm their own arsenals. The US alone retains such bombs, and its destruction of the USSR has irrevocably alienated it from the rest of the world.

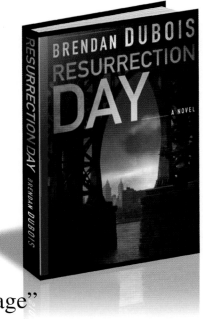

"Russia has collapsed following a nuclear barrage"

In DuBois' novel, the Cuban Missile Crisis served as the turning point for an irradiated alternative history

The Guns of the South by Harry Turtledove (1992)

Another very popular subject for the genre, especially for alt-history novelists based in the United States, is the American Civil War drawing to a close with the Confederates defeating the Union. For Harry Turtledove—a man considered one of the premier voices in alt-history fiction—a Southern victory doesn't come from a natural turning point following an alternative path but from time travellers returning to the past to arm the South with modern day weaponry.

Written in 1992, Turtledove imagines a 21st- century group of South African white nationalists (members of the real-life neo-Nazi organization, Afrikaner Weerstandsbeweging) traveling back in time to January 1864 to approach Robert E. Lee with an offer of support. They arm the Confederate soldiers with AK-47 rifles (based on chemical and mechanical engineering far beyond anything on the battlefield at that time), provide impeccable intelligence on Unionist movements, and even help treat Lee's failing heart with nitroglycerin pills.

Told mostly from the point of view of Lee and the Confederates, we see an alternative history that differs yet mirrors many of the period's actual events due to the constant intervention of the time-traveling neo-Nazis. The Afrikaners want to help shape a United States where slavery is never abolished, where relations between Black and White communities are never fostered. Rather than just giving us gratuitous violence, Turtledove explores the political fallout of Lee winning the war and how America would be shaped not just by his leadership but also by future technologies that would help the US become one of the most advanced countries in the 19th-century world.

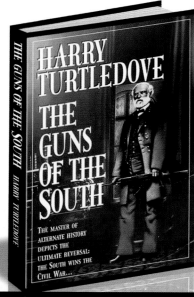

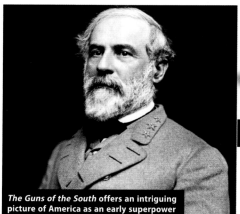

The Guns of the South offers an intriguing picture of America as an early superpower

SS-GB was adapted into a BBC series in 2017 by longtime Bond writers Neal Purvis and Robert Wade

SS-GB by Len Deighton (1978)

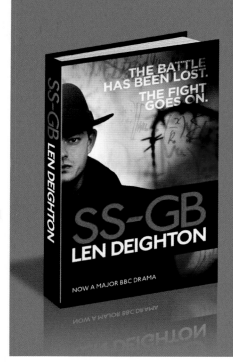

A vision of the world where the Third Reich won World War II has become one of the alt-history genre's most well-trodden destinations, but few attempt to encapsulate what life would have been like in Britain with new fascist overlords. Len Deighton's measured thriller, *SS-GB* (1978), tries just that, and conveys the complexities of a broken Britain in the wake of a Nazi invasion.

Through the lens of a murder mystery, we see a world where Operation Sea Lion (Hitler's real life plan to invade Britain during the Battle of Britain) has succeeded. One year on and King George VI remains imprisoned in the Tower of London, Churchill has been executed, and the SS patrol the streets of London. As the story's protagonist—Detective Superintendent Douglas Archer of London's Metropolitan Police—looks to solve the slaying of a wealthy man in Shepherds Market, we get a glimpse into a world where Britain has become a political battleground for Archer's superiors and the SS.

This is one of the reasons it works so well. Deighton never tries to undo or unravel his alt-history timeline by unseating the Nazis. Instead, we get to see how a British Resistance might function (and just how far it might go to drive out the fascists), as well as how a country so opposed to another regime would be reshaped by another. As bleak as its story becomes, it remains one of the best alt-history novels to be untouched by time travel or other narrative complications.

Lion's Blood by Steven Barnes (2002)

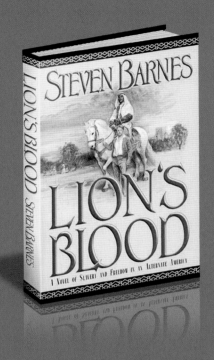

Perhaps one of the most unique entries in the alt-history genre, mainly due to the unique way it attempts to rewrite the timeline we know, *Lion's Blood* presents a vision of the world where Africa has become the most technologically advanced continent while Europe wallows in a primitive malaise. Through the eyes of two very different characters—Aidan O'Dere (an Irish slave captured and sold by Vikings) and Kai ibn Jallaleddin ibn Rashid (the son of a powerful African noble)—we see a world where slavery still exists in the 19th century, but it's white Europeans who are in chains.

The story dates back its flashpoint in time to Alexander the Great, who chooses to conquer the West rather than the East, setting the stage for the rise of two of the most powerful African civilizations: the Abyssinian and Egyptian kingdoms. As Europe stutters in its progress, the roving raiders of Scandinavia rise to power and build their legacy off the back of a vast trade in white slaves. The pharoahs of Egypt endure, while Islam becomes the most influential religion in the powerful continent of Africa.

North America—or Bilalistan as it's known—has also been found and is now a divided state carved in half by an Egyptian-Abyssinian coalition and the Vikings. Much like our own timeline, the New World has become a hub for the slave trade, and it too eventually becomes a subject that is both defended and protected passionately.

Lion's Blood alternates dates back to Alexander the Great's decision to conquer the West instead of the East

Fatherland by Robert Harris (1992)

This thrilling book was Robert Harris' first work of fiction. Centered around the classic alt-history conceit of the Nazis winning WWII, the English novelist deftly combines his famous flair for gripping storytelling with a meticulous attention to historical detail in this best-selling novel.

That detail—which fleshes out a detective thriller where a policeman investigating the murder of a high-ranking Nazi official uncovers a political plot within the German government—gives *Fatherland* an almost historical record quality, with Harris going as far as using a cast of real-life individuals to help the murder mystery feel more rooted in a partially believable reality.

That reality diverges from our own timeline in 1942, with Reinhard Heydrich (the high ranking member of the SS who played a key role in orchestrating the Holocaust) surviving an assassination attempt and leading a successful campaign against the Soviets on the Eastern Front. Harris' timeline also sees the Nazis discovering that the Enigma Machine code has been broken, which subsequently enables them to coordinate a ruthless U-Boat blockade that eventually starves an ailing Britain into submission.

After the war, the world of *Fatherland* sees the Nazis now in control of Europe in its entirety, carving the whole continent into separate Nazi states. Elsewhere, the United States defeats the Empire of Japan with atomic bombs, but by 1946 Germany has also cracked nuclear-based weaponry and explodes a non-nuclear missile over New York City to remind the US it can be struck at any moment.

Having been released in 1992, it only took two years for a film to be made of *Fatherland*

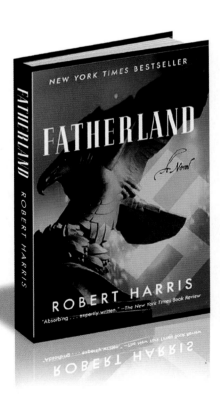

The Years of Rice and Salt
by Kim Stanley Robinson (2002)

Much like Steven Barnes' *Lion's Blood*, Kim Stanley Robinson's acclaimed 2002 novel presents a world where the Europe we know from our own history books never developed beyond the 1300s due to a Black Death outbreak that kills 99 percent of the native population. With a story that covers hundreds of years (ranging from the 14th century to the new millennium), Robinson's grand saga paints a picture of a Europe slowly repopulated by peoples of the East and how the rest of the world changes forever as a result.

By avoiding the 'Great Man theory' angle (where authors and writers use major battles or the death of a key historical figure to create a temporal jumping-off point), Robinson instead explores a socio-political dissection of how other civilizations would have responded to a continental landmass becoming practically uninhabited in the course of a few years. By breaking up his novel into ten separate mini-books, Robinson is also able to present us Europe's new history from 1405 to 2045, with each of the major characters reincarnated into new generations.

From the perspective of these characters we see a fascinating alt-history narrative unfold, with Europe's population all but wiped out by the Black Death pandemic (Robinson's story suggests the wave that took place in our own timeline occurred here, but was followed by another deadlier outbreak at the turn of the century) that brought the continent to its knees. From here we start to see history played out from the most influential powers of the east, including China, Japan, and a number of Islamic kingdoms.

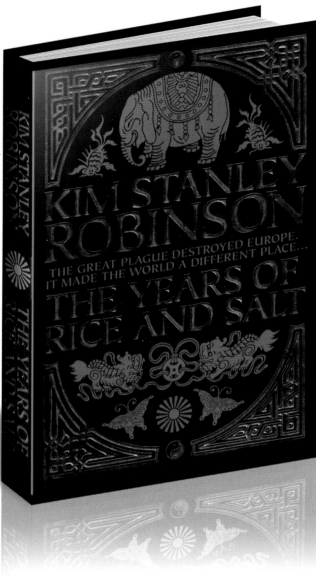

In real life the Black Death ravaged Europe, reducing its total population by a third

Both Europe and North America become new battlegrounds for both war and colonization as the great remaining powers in the world begin to expand while still attempting to one-up each other. The biggest conflict of the 700-year war sees the two most powerful nations of China (which expands to conquer Japan in 1722 and large parts of South America and Europe in the following years) and a collective of Muslim states embroiled in what Robinson describes as the 'Long War.'

We see scientific breakthroughs happening roughly around the same time that they occurred in Western civilization in our own timeline, although now these 17th-century developments are made in both China and Samarkand (what would be modern-day Uzbekistan). By the 20th century, the Long War now rages between three global states: the Chinese Empire and its colonies, the fractured Muslim world (Dar al-Islam), and the democratic Indian and Hodenosaunee Leagues. It's a bloody affair as the feudal nature of Robinson's world rages on around its band of generation-leaping characters.